Advance F
22 Accessible Road Trips

"Following Candy's advice and suggestions is like having her as your personal tour guide easing your way to and into the best our country has to offer. It's perfect for someone in a wheelchair, a slow walker, or someone who thinks that life's too short to be rushing everywhere."

—**Judy Colbert**, Author, *Insiders' Guide to Baltimore*

"Candy Harrington, self-professed 'road trip junky,' discovered that you don't have to go overseas to find colorful characters, lush scenery and exotic regional cuisine. It's all right here in the U.S. Veteran traveler Harrington lays out 22 terrific (and accessible) road loops across the U.S. Her itineraries offer wheelers and slow walkers lots of well-tested advice and counsel, but not so much as to dampen the spirit of adventure. This book is a great tool for planning a driving vacation but the fun part, of course, will be discovering for yourself the richness of the American landscape."

—**Sam Maddox**, Christopher Reeve Foundation

"With useful, detailed accessibility information about driving itineraries and destinations across the country, *22 Accessible Road Trips* is an indispensable resource for wheelchair and slow walking travelers. Candy Harrington has illustrated once again that a disability needn't preclude exciting and fulfilling travel experiences."

—**Paul Lasley** and **Elizabeth Harryman**, OnTravel.com.

"Beware—this book may make you a road trip junkie like author Candy Harrington. On display in these 22 accessible road trips is not just the beauty and unique heritage of each region of the U.S., but also the power of the Americans with Disabilities Act. Our country is out there for all of us to enjoy, and this wonderful book makes it so easy to hit the road with a minimum of planning, even for those using a wheelchair. As an added benefit, readers can check for access updates on the book's website. Now that's a great innovation!"

—**Laurel Van Horn**, Open Doors Organization

"Candy Harrington brings forward a valuable travel resource that will inspire a road trip adventure possible for all abilities. For those who thought their disability meant an end to fun and recreation, Candy Harrington will change your mind."

—**Ann Johnson**, National Multiple Sclerosis Society

"Candy Harrington's latest book will set your wheels in motion! She includes suggestions for unusual side trips, not forgetting America's general stores and classic diners. Harrington is hooked on travel. You will be, too, after reading her lively book. Her travel enthusiasm is contagious, her humor delightful. I'm ready to pack my bags for an adventure!"

—**Roberta Beach Jacobson**, Staff Writer for JustSayGo.com

"In Boy Scouts they told me to 'be prepared.' Now I know what they were trying to teach me. Read Candy's book, *22 Accessible Road Trips: Driving Vacations for Wheelers and Slow Walkers*. Then take off for the open highway with wheelchair, walker, cane, or just a comfy pair of shoes and discover America."

—**Scott Rains**, Rolling Rains Report

"Candy has meticulously mapped out 22 different vacations with accessibility foremost in mind. As our travel agent, she has designed road trips that feature points of interest, picturesque scenes, great places to eat, and best times to travel. She even highlights unique events and local festivals along the way.

Best of all, Candy tells us how to travel smart—her pre-trip check list includes contact info for wheelchair and accessible van malfunctions, and even plans for prescription needs should they arise during our trip. Candy's well-thought-out plans dissolve any travel fears and open up a new world of trips we can take without hesitation. She broadens our horizons and gives us the road map for a richer life."

—**Linda Dunnigan**, SCI Support Group Coordinator, Cincinnati, Ohio

22 Accessible Road Trips

DRIVING VACATIONS
FOR
WHEELERS
AND
SLOW WALKERS

22
Accessible
Road Trips

DRIVING VACATIONS
FOR
WHEELERS
AND
SLOW WALKERS

Candy B. Harrington

PHOTOGRAPHS BY
CHARLES PANNELL

demos
HEALTH

Visit our website at www.demoshealth.com

ISBN: 9781936303267
e-book ISBN: 9781617051029
Acquisitions Editor: Noreen Henson
Compositor: Diacritech

Medical information provided by Demos Health, in the absence of a visit with a health care professional, must be considered as an educational service only. This book is not designed to replace a physician's independent judgment about the appropriateness or risks of a procedure or therapy for a given patient. Our purpose is to provide you with information that will help you make your own health care decisions.

The information and opinions provided here are believed to be accurate and sound, based on the best judgment available to the authors, editors, and publisher, but readers who fail to consult appropriate health authorities assume the risk of injuries. The publisher is not responsible for errors or omissions. The editors and publisher welcome any reader to report to the publisher any discrepancies or inaccuracies noticed.

Library of Congress Cataloging-in-Publication Data
Harrington, Candy B.
  22 accessible road trips : driving vacations for wheelers and slow walkers / by Candy B. Harrington ; photographs by Charles Pannell.
    p. cm.
  ISBN 978-1-936303-26-7
  1. People with disabilities—Travel—United States—Guidebooks. 2. Automobile travel—United States—Guidebooks. 3. United States—Guidebooks. I. Title. II. Title: Twenty two accessible road trips.
  HV1568.6.H38 2012
  917.304′932087—dc23

                                                                  2012013699

Special discounts on bulk quantities of Demos Health books are available to corporations, professional associations, pharmaceutical companies, health care organizations, and other qualifying groups. For details, please contact:

Special Sales Department
Demos Medical Publishing, LLC
11 West 42nd Street, 15th Floor
New York, NY 10036
Phone: 800-532-8663 or 212-683-0072
Fax: 212-941-7842
E-mail: rsantana@demosmedpub.com

Printed in the United States of America by Bang Printing
12 13 14 15 / 5 4 3 2 1

TO
Charles

Acknowledgements

Although this certainly isn't my first book, it was my most difficult. First off, the research was mind-boggling; as it took many years and many, many miles to visit, inspect, photograph and catalogue all of the destinations that I included. Then of course there was the organization; deciding how to put all of the information into a readable and useful format was somewhat of a chore. And last but not least, there was the writing itself.

Although the first two steps took a good deal of time, I met my biggest challenge in the writing process itself. Not that it was difficult to write, but it was difficult to work around all the disasters and annoyances that seemed to pop during crunch time. From a death in the family, to breaking three computers; to unexpected power outages, coming down with a sinus infection which turned into an abscessed jaw, and even a tree falling on my mountain home, there were times when I truly thought I would never make my deadline.

But I did—although not without a little help from my friends. So although I'd like to offer up a huge thank you to everyone who helped me along the way, some folks deserve an extra special mention.

- To Kay Grant, who first encouraged me to do road trips, and who freely offered ever-so-many tips on how to survive them.

- To Lee Ann Clamurro, who introduced me to GPS many years ago. I'd literally be lost without Maynard (my GPS unit).

- To Erin, Claire, Linda and Grace, for holding down the home front when we were away on editorial research trips. My flock was very well cared for!

- To the American Automobile Association, for their excellent maps, with rest stops that had restroom clearly marked. They came in handy more than a few times.

ACKNOWLEDGEMENTS

■ To Brian and the Arbor-Tec crew, for removing the remnants of the 100-foot pine tree that fell on my place. And for working smarter, not harder.

■ To Chet, Dan and Levi, for repairing my roof and deck before the first snowfall. Chesterman Construction rocks!

■ To the wonderful Delta agent who made it possible for us to get back home after a family emergency, even though half of the flights were cancelled due to Hurricane Irene.

■ To SiriusXM radio, for making my road trips more enjoyable with a constant stream of music, comedy, news and other great shows.

■ To all of my Facebook friends, who offered encouragement through the long and arduous production process of this book.

■ To Noreen Henson, my boss at Demos and my friend in real life. She does each job equally well, and knows when to wear which hat.

■ To Charles, for all of his wonderful illustrations and photographs, for fixing the three computers I broke, and for being a wonderful companion on every single trip. As always, I couldn't have done it without you, Love.

Contents

Foreword

I have to admit that when Candy asked me to introduce her book, I thought she'd sent her invitation to the wrong person. I'm no expert on disability issues and travel, although I've written an article or two about it in the past (with Candy's generous help). Nor am I a disability rights activist in the traditional sense of the word.

But as I read her remarkable work, I began to understand. Candy's belief is that destinations should be accessible to everyone. It comes through in every word and every chapter. As a consumer advocate, it's a conviction I share. But on a more personal level, *22 Accessible Road Trips* transcends the traditional definition of accessibility and the traditional audience for such a book. And I'm all about challenging conventions.

Sure, you'll find important information about getting around if you're in a wheelchair or use a walker. As someone who travels with my retired parents and my 93-year-old grandmother with some regularity, I found that to be useful information. But as the father of three young kids, and with memories of packing a double stroller in the recent past,

I wish she'd written *22 Accessible Road Trips* a few years ago. It would have come in handy for us youngsters, too.

This book will probably resonate with you in another way. Because it's about driving vacations, which seem to be becoming increasingly popular. I'd rather avoid air travel these days. In fact, as I write this, I'm halfway through an ambitious one-year road trip around the country with my family.

Candy's spare but engaging writing style give away her background as a wire service reporter (one that we share). She doesn't waste your time. I like that. I think you will, too.

I think I've said enough. Why don't we get right to it?

Christopher Elliott
Editor-at-Large
National Geographic Traveler

Preface—Drive, She Said

O ver the past 10 years, I've made a concentrated effort to explore the good old USA. But that wasn't always my mindset. Truth be told, after 25 years of thinking that I hadn't really traveled unless I'd gotten my passport stamped, I came to the realization that the US has just as many off-the-beaten-path attractions, unique regional foods and colorful characters as just about any overseas destination.

Of course I didn't realize that until I actually took my first domestic first road trip. And although that first one was just a short fly-drive package, it took me out of the big city and landed me squarely in the heart of rural America. And I loved every minute of it. The pace was relaxing, the itinerary was flexible and boy howdy did I ever meet some interesting characters. And aside from the flight delays, crappy airline food, TSA gropings and outrageous rental car surcharges, Charles liked these fly-drive road trips as well. So we started taking more of them. And I wrote about them in *Emerging Horizons* and in my other outlets.

And then a funny thing happened. Readers starting writing me and telling me that they liked my road trip articles and they wanted to read more of them. Apparently I wasn't alone in my new found fondness for road trips. So I decided to take the next logical step, and remove the flights from our next fly-drive package; and make it a true road trip, from start to finish.

And now I'm totally hooked; in fact, I'm the total road trip junkie. Now don't get me wrong, it's not that I never fly these days; it's just that I do it grudgingly, and only when I absolutely have to. But deep in my heart, I'm happiest when I'm cruising down the open road.

Somewhere along the way we also learned how to plan longer road trips, so it's not unusual for us to be gone for a month or so at a time. As an added bonus, we don't have to deal with airline delays and rental car lines; so there's less time wasted time in our driving itineraries. Truth be told, it's a very efficient way to travel.

Road trips are also a particularly attractive option for wheelchair-users and slow walkers, for a number of reasons.

- You can pack along all the equipment you need.

- You can take a restroom break whenever you need it.

- You can alter your itinerary if you're having a bad day.

- You don't have to worry about the airlines damaging your wheelchair.

- You'll always have accessible transportation.

- You don't have to buy an extra air ticket for your attendant.

- You can take things at your own pace.

And at the risk of sounding like an ethnocentric alarmist, I also have to add that I just feel I have more control when I'm exploring my own country. After all, Charles and I were stuck in London for an additional two weeks after the World Trade Center disaster. Granted if we had to be stranded somewhere, London wasn't a bad pick; but it wasn't home either. Again, it's not that I'm giving up foreign travel; in fact

I'm looking forward to exploring New Zealand's South Island later this year. It's just that I'm really enjoying my domestic trips.

And I wrote this book so you can do the same. Not that it's a hard and fast guide, but it will give you the resources, information and tools to plan your own road trips. Each chapter contains a loop route, which can easily be driven in two or three weeks; in addition to the following information to help you customize your trip.

Along the Way

Major stops or highlights along the route, including accessible lodging suggestions.

Timing

When to go, and when to avoid each route; including information about winter road closures, traffic jams during peak season and other seasonal delays.

Great Eats

A unique accessible restaurant or two along the route. Not necessarily fine dining, but definitely memorable.

Don't Miss It

A special event or festival, quirky roadside attraction or just a certain day to visit a specific place.

Linger on in the Gateway

Things to do in the gateway city for an extended stay, before or after the road trip.

Fly-Drive Option

Gateway airport and accessible rental van information for folks who want to do the trip as a fly-drive option.

Alternate Entry Points

Alternate starting points along the loop.

Variation on a Theme

Ideas to customize the route, make it a longer trip, combine two routes together or even do day trips from the gateway city.

If You Go

CVBs, access guides and other resources to help you plan your trip.

And of course, like in all my other books, I've included meaningful access information, so you can make the best choices for your abilities. And last but not least, there's also a chapter with general tips, resources and road trip planning tools. All in all, it's a pretty comprehensive resource.

Additionally, since access changes over time, I've dedicated a portion of my book website to these changes. So surf on by www.22 AccessibleRoadTrips.com for access updates, before you hit the road.

The key thing about this book is that it allows for a maximum of flexibility. You *can* do it your way. So use this book as a guide and a resource, but don't be afraid to think outside the box and customize your trip to meet your individual tastes, time frame, access needs and budget. After all it's your road trip, not mine. And drop me a note and let me know how it all went. Hopefully you'll end up just like me— totally hooked on road trips.

Candy Harrington
PO Box 278
Ripon, CA 95366
horizons@EmergingHorizons.com
Facebook: Candy Harrington

Road Trip Tips and Resources

E ven though road trips are an excellent choice for wheelers and slow walkers, they still require a modest amount of planning. And just like any other kind of travel, you should also make a few what-if plans, so you will have a definite plan of action if disaster strikes.

For example, what if you lost your prescription or your wheelchair needed to be repaired along the way? What would you do? Having well thought out solutions to these scenarios helps things go smoother, when and if disaster strikes. In this case, good solutions would be to carry along the phone numbers of wheelchair repair places in the cities you plan to visit; and to get duplicate prescriptions from you doctor. Although you can't plan for every possible hiccup, having a what-if plan in place for major disasters also gives you a certain peace of mind.

Additionally, it's best to start our with a short trial road trip, before you jump into things head first and take off on a month-long adventure. That way you can sort out the kinks, and still be relatively close to home in case you need to return quickly.

And although you'll continually refine your pre-trip check list, here are a few things to consider before you hit the road.

CAR AND DRIVER

- Make sure you have emergency road service before you leave home; however remember that very few towing companies have wheelchair-accessible tow trucks. To avoid being stranded on the highway, check out specialty services such as ADA Nationwide Roadside Assistance (800-720-3132, www.americandriversalliance.com), which also provides lift-equipped transportation to the garage.

- Take along a can of Fix-A-Flat tire inflator. It's quick and easy to use and it beats waiting for the tow truck.

- If you have an adapted van, carry along the phone number of your van conversion place. That way if you any problems with the electronics or lift, they can direct you to the nearest repair facility.

- Always carry a cell phone with you, and don't forget the charger. Consider installing a CB for long trips, as you may encounter cellular dead zones and hefty roaming charges in some places.

- A GPS navigation system is a handy tool, but remember to also pack along maps and directions as a backup, especially in rural areas. The American Automobile Association has maps that show the locations of roadside rest areas. These maps are available free to members, and most of the rest areas have accessible restrooms.

- Take along plenty of bottled water, as you never know when you will encounter a delay.

- Keep your prescription medications in the car, rather than the trunk. The trunk heats up faster than the passenger compartment, and this excessive heat may cause some medications to spoil.

- To fight off boredom on long drives, get some books-on-tape to play along the way. They're free at your local library.

- Check traffic conditions and the weather on the internet, along your route before you set out each morning. Road closure information can be found at www.fhwa.dot.gov/trafficinfo, while weather information is available at www.weather.com.

ALONG THE WAY

- For the best accessible restrooms, look for newer fast food restaurants. Most fast food restaurants are consistent in their restroom design; so when you find a restroom that has the access features you need, stick with that fast food chain.

- Consider packing a portable ramp, such as the ones manufactured by Handi Ramp (847-680-7700, www.handi-ramp.com). They are compact and they come in handy for buildings that have one or two steps.

- Most Pilot – Flying J truck stops (www.pilotflyingj.com) have accessible shower rooms, complete with a roll-in shower, a roll-under sink and a toilet with grab bars. There is a charge for using the shower room, but it's a good emergency alternative if you can't use the shower at your hotel. They also have nice accessible restrooms, which are free.

- Get your America the Beautiful Access Pass (www.nps.gov/findapark/passes.htm), as it's good for free admission to national parks and monuments that you might want to visit along the way. This free lifetime pass is available at all national park entrances. Proof of disability is required.

- Check out Roadside America (www.roadsideamerica.com) for a large collection of fun, quirky and oddball attractions along your route. Stopping at interesting roadside attractions is a good way to break up the drive and get out of the car for a few minutes.

AT THE HOTEL

- Make advance reservations for hotels along your route, as it's almost impossible to find an accessible room on a walk-in basis.

- Look for Microtel (www.microtelinn.com) properties along the way, as they are constructed from the ground up with access in mind. They are conveniently located along interstate highways and they also offer very reasonable rates.

- There's no need to unload and load heavy suitcases at every roadside hotel. Just roll up an entire set of clothes for each day when you pack; then simply remove one set at each stop.

- Depending on the length of your trip, you may need to plan for a laundry day along the way. Try to find a hotel with a guest laundry, as it has a better chance of being accessible than the local laundromat.

- If you are staying at city center hotel, ask about parking charges when you book your room. Sometimes these fees can be as much as $20 per day. Properties outside the city usually have lower rates and free parking.

- Don't forget to take your parking placard with you, as it's valid throughout the US, except in New York City. Additionally, it's a good idea to consult the FIA World Parking Guide (www.fiadisabledtravellers.com/en/home) for disabled parking regulations in different states.

- If you plan on staying in a major city for a few days, check to see if a CityPASS (www.citypass.com) is available for it. These affordable ticket books provide admission to many top attractions, and even express entry at many sites.

Finally, don't forget to pack your sense of humor when you leave home. Be flexible and don't stress out if things don't go exactly the way you planned them. After all, travel is all about experiencing new things.

Pacific States

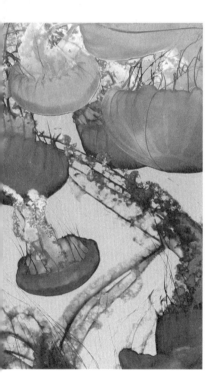

Left: Jellyfish at Monterey
Bay Aquarium.
Upper right: California, Frank's
Diner in Spokane, Washington.
Lower right: Visitor Center at
Lassen Volcanic National Park,
California.

California's Natural Treasures

Although it would take years to explore all of California's Natural Treasures, this route offers a good sampling of the highlights. From the majestic high Sierras to the vast Mojave Desert and the beautiful Central California coast, there's something for just about every taste and ability on this trip.

ROUTE

This route begins in San Francisco, travels east through California's Central Valley, then continues along Highway 120 to Yosemite Valley. Then it's over Tioga Pass to Highway 395, and south to Mammoth Lakes. From there, continue south on Highway 395 to Lone Pine, then go east on Highways 136 and 190 to Death Valley. Next, it's out the east park entrance, south to Baker, across the desert to Barstow and south on Interstate 15 to Victorville. To complete the loop, continue west to Ventura, then head north on Highways 101 and 1 through Cambria and Monterey, before arriving back in San Francisco.

ALONG THE WAY

Yosemite Valley

Yosemite Valley is certainly worth an extended visit. Getting around is easy, as free lift-equipped shuttle buses stop at most of the major attractions in the valley. And if you need a little help getting around, the bicycle rental stands (209-372-8319) at Yosemite Lodge and Curry Village also stock scooters and manual wheelchairs. Handcycles are also available at the same outlets.

Yosemite Falls, which plummets 320 feet to the valley floor, tops the must-see list in the park. A barrier-free trail leads from the bus stop to a

Upper Yosemite Falls in Yosemite National Park.

bridge near the base. This ¾-mile trail is paved and level, with plenty of spots to stop and rest along the way.

Just up the road, you'll also find an accessible trail at Happy Isles. This gently sloping trail is covered with decomposed granite and crosses the Merced River in several places. As an added bonus, it's also nicely devoid of the crowds that flock to Yosemite Falls. And although the nearby road to Mirror Lake is not accessible, visitors with a disabled placard can drive on this park road, which is closed to all other vehicle traffic. Unfortunately the trail around the lake is not accessible; however you can get a great view of Half Dome and Mirror Lake from the parking area.

And don't miss the drive up to Glacier Point for a panoramic view of the valley. There's a nice 300-yard paved trail out to the viewpoint, and accessible restrooms, a snack bar and a gift shop near the parking area. And for a spectacular view of Half Dome, as well as Nevada, Vernal and Illilouette Falls, make sure and stop at Washburn Point, just a half-mile below Glacier Point. It's less crowded than Glacier Point, with an accessible route out to the overlook.

View along the Eastern Sierra Scenic Byway near Mammoth, California.

Delaware North Companies (801-559-4884, www.yosemitepark.com) offers several accessible lodging choices in Yosemite Valley. The Ahwahnee, Yosemite Lodge and Curry Village all have wheelchair-accessible rooms with roll-in showers or tub/shower combinations. Delaware North Companies also operates accessible bus tours to Glacier Point, Tuolumne Meadows and Mariposa Grove. Call (209) 372-4386 to reserve a space.

Eastern Sierra Scenic Byway

The Eastern Sierra Scenic Byway, which runs along Highway 395, from Topaz Lake to Little Lake, also boasts a number of unique and accessible natural treasures. At the top of the list are the unusual tufa towers in and around Mono Lake. Formed when calcium-bearing underground water welled up through the salty lake, these spire-like towers were once all submerged. Today, now that the lake level has drastically dropped, they're visible in, and even around the lake.

For a good view of the tufa filled lake, head over to the David Gaines Boardwalk, located off Highway 395, just north of Lee Vining. This quarter-mile crushed gravel and boardwalk trail leads down to the shore; while a shorter crushed gravel spur heads up to higher ground, where you'll get a panoramic view of the lake.

For a closer look at the tufa towers, stop at the South Tufa Area. Just head south on Highway 395, turn east on Highway 120 and follow the signs. This loop trail begins with a pavement and boardwalk section down to the lake, followed by a sandy beach, with a hard-packed and rutted trail back to the start. And although only the first section of this loop is accessible, the massive tufa formations located along the way definitely make it a must-see.

Another worthwhile detour is the June Lake Driving Loop. This 15-mile drive begins just north of Highway 120 East, and travels on Highway 158 past June, Silver and Grant Lakes, before rejoining Highway 395. It's especially scenic in the fall, when the Aspens put on a very colorful show.

Located off of Highway 395 near Mammoth Lakes, Devils Postpile National Monument (760-934-2289, www.nps.gov/depo) is also worth a stop. During the peak season, visitors must use the park shuttle to access this site, but people with a disabled parking placard can drive in anytime. The .4-mile trail to the formation is doable for some folks. The first part of the trail is hard packed with some sand along the way; but a few steep sections make it difficult for manual wheelchair-users. Still, give it a try, as the columns of extruded lava that make up the postpile are truly a fascinating sight.

And don't forget to get your free Roadside Heritage audio files (www.roadsideheritage.org) for your journey down Highway 395. They are entertaining, informative and great to listen to along the way.

Death Valley

In stark contrast to the Sierras, Death Valley features great expanses of barren desert, an arid landscape and it's own unique ecosystem. For a good perspective of the vastness of it all, make sure and stop at the Salt Creek Boardwalk. Located at the bottom of Cottonball Basin, this half-mile loop boardwalk is wide, level and great for wheeling. It's also nicely devoid of railings, which allows wheelchair-users unobstructed views of the surrounding landscape. And if you happen to visit from February to May, you'll see

Pupfish—a species that only exists in Death Valley—swimming in the creek alongside the boardwalk.

Death Valley also boasts a number of scenic driving routes. At the top of the list is Artist's Drive, which is located south of Furnace Creek on the east side of Badwater Road. This nine-mile drive features a good view of the alluvial fans in the surrounding mountains, and it's especially stunning in the late afternoon.

And if you'd like to go a little off-the-beaten-path, then check out the drive through 20 Mule Team Canyon. This one-lane road features three miles of spectacular canyon scenery; and although there are some twists and turns along the way, it's still passable in a car.

For a good primer on Death Valley history, stop by the Borax Museum at Furnace Creek Ranch. There's ramp access to this free museum, which contains a pictorial history of early Death Valley. Outside, there's a nice assortment of antique stagecoaches, mining tools and even a vintage locomotive.

And don't miss Harmony Borax Works, located just north of Furnace Creek. This former Borax refinery includes a collection of 1880s Borax mining equipment. A paved half-mile trail winds through this open-air museum; however, manual wheelchair-users will probably need some assistance up the incline. Still it's an interesting stop, and you can also get a good view of the operation from the lower viewpoint.

If you'd like to overnight in the park, Furnace Creek Resort (760-786-2345, www.furnacecreekresort.com) offers accessible rooms with roll-in showers at The Ranch at Furnace Creek, and an accessible room with a tub/shower combination at the Inn at Furnace Creek. The accessible rooms at both properties include hand-held showerheads, toilet and shower grab bars, roll-under sinks and portable shower chairs.

Cambria

For a laid back coastal break, spend a few nights at the Cambria Pines Lodge (805-927-4200, www.moonstonehotels.com). Located in Cambria, this 126-room property borders an undeveloped natural area filled with native wildlife. Access is first-rate throughout the property, with level paths, accessible parking, plenty of room to navigate in a wheelchair or scooter and an accessible ground floor suite with a roll-in shower.

Harmony Borax Works in Death Valley National Park.

Just up the road, you'll find one of the top attractions in the area, Hearst Castle (866-712-2286, www.hearstcastle.com). This palatial estate of William Randolph Hearst features 165 rooms, 127 acres of gardens and a top-notch collection of European and Mediterranean art. The standard tours require a lot of walking and stair climbing, but the Accessibly Designed Tour features transportation in a lift-equipped vehicle to the hilltop mansion and a barrier-free route through the house. This popular tour must be reserved at least 10 days in advance, so plan ahead.

Located just 4.4 miles north of Hearst Castle, the Piedras Blancas Elephant Seal Rookery (www.elephantseal.org) is also worth as stop. A hard-packed dirt trail leads from the parking area to a wide level boardwalk, where you'll get a great view of the resident elephant seal colony. There are several viewing spots along this short boardwalk, and it's wide enough to accommodate pedestrian traffic and wheelers.

No visit to Cambria is complete without a swing by Nit Wit Ridge. Located at 881 Hillcrest Drive, this architectural marvel was constructed by local trash hauler Art Beal, from scrap metal, old tire rims, bottles and hundreds of beer cans. And although the structure itself isn't accessible, it's worth a stop, as you can get a good look at it from the dirt parking area across the street.

Monterey

Monterey is a required stop on any California coastal drive. Located just a few hours south of San Francisco, the coastline features dramatic scenery, abundant wildlife and attractions that showcase the natural beauty of the area.

The Monterey Bay Aquarium (831-648-4800, www.montereybay aquarium.org) tops the attractions list, with over 200 exhibits featuring more than 250,000 marine creatures. Visitors can pet a sting ray, enjoy the playful antics of the resident sea otters or check out the incredibly cute blackfooted penguins in the Splash Zone. There is barrier-free access throughout the aquarium, with limited accessible parking available on a first-come basis. Call (831) 648-4840 for accessible parking information.

Save some time to wander around Cannery Row, the namesake street from Steinbeck's classic tale. Pick up a free *Cannery Row Visitors Guide* (www. canneryrow.com), then check out the original sites that later became Steinbeck's Lee Chong's Market, the La Ida and Doc's Lab. Curb-cuts are ubiquitous throughout the area, with accessible public toilets located across from the aquarium will-call ticket window.

And for some spectacular coastal scenery, the Pebble Beach 17 Mile Drive is a must. Make sure and stop at Spanish Bay along the way for a breathtaking ocean view. Accessible picnic tables are also located there, and it's the perfect spot for a quiet lunch or a quick mid-afternoon break. Afterwards, follow the 1.8-mile boardwalk along the shore, over to Bird Rock for more majestic scenery.

And for a nice hike from Cannery Row to Fisherman's Wharf, check out the Monterey Recreational Trail. This 1.2-mile section of the trail is paved, level and wheelchair-accessible. Fisherman's Wharf houses a number of accessible shops and restaurants, with accessible restrooms at the end of the wharf.

You'll also find the Portola Hotel & Spa (831-649-4511, www.portola hotel.com) near the wharf. This 379-room luxury property features nine accessible guest rooms, four of which have roll-in showers. You just can't beat the location, the service and the ambiance.

TIMING

· ·

Tioga Pass is usually closed from November to May; however, it has opened as late as July 1 and closed as early as October 31. Yosemite Valley is a madhouse in the summer, and Death Valley temperatures can get into the 120s at that time; however, early fall is pleasant in both places. The optimal time to drive this route is in early September, just after Labor Day. That way, you'll dodge the crowds in Yosemite Valley, miss the peak heat in Death Valley and enjoy the fall colors in the High Sierras.

GREAT EATS

· ·

Located in Lee Vining, the Whoa Nellie Deli (760-647-1088, www.whoanelliedeli.com) is a cut above your average deli, with house specialties like cajun chicken jambalaya, lobster taquitos and fish tacos. Add in some great wheelchair-access, clean accessible restrooms and a beautiful view of Mono Lake, and you can see why this casual eatery is such a popular stop along Tioga Pass Road.

And if you happen to be in Yosemite Valley on a Sunday, make sure and hit The Ahwahnee (209-372-1489, www.yosemitepark.com) for brunch. Although this award winning restaurant shines any day of the week, they really outdo themselves on Sundays, with a buffet that is second to none. Food stations include hot and cold breakfast staples, a wide selection of sea-food, several kinds of pasta, meat and fish entrees, a carving station, a crepe station, freshly baked breads and a wide array of decadent deserts. And with level access to the ground floor dining room, it's ideal for slow walkers and wheelers.

DON'T MISS IT

Located halfway between Independence and Lone Pine on Highway 395, the Manzanar National Historic Site (760-878-2194 ext. 2710, www.nps.gov/manz) is a must-see for anyone interested in World War II history. Opened shortly after the attack on Pearl Harbor, this former relocation center housed over 10,000 Japanese American Citizens for the duration of the war.

Housed in the former auditorium, the Visitors Center has ramped access and features interpretive exhibits and an information desk. Be sure and pick up a map of the 3.2-mile camp driving tour. Although the buildings were dismantled shortly after the war ended, you can still see the sentry post, guard towers, historic orchards, rock gardens and even the cemetery.

The nearby Eastern California Museum (760-878-0364, www.inyocounty.us/ecmuseum) also boasts a substantial collection of historic photographs of Manzanar, as well as a replica of a typical barracks apartment and lots of personal artifacts. Best of all, admission is free at both sites.

LINGER ON IN THE GATEWAY

If you'd like to extend your stay in San Francisco after your road trip; rest assured, there's no shortage of accessible diversions in the City by the Bay.

■ Enjoy a city tour on the Historic F-line Trolley (415-956-1472, www.streetcar.org). These restored street cars run from Fisherman's Wharf to the Castro, and feature roll-on access via boarding platforms and wayside lifts.

- Take a tour of Alcatraz (415-981-7625, www.alcatrazcruises.com). There's accessible boat transportation over to the island, and a shuttle service up to the hilltop prison for wheelers and slow walkers.

- Visit the Hyde Street Pier (415-447-5000, www.nps.gov/safr), where you'll find a sampling of vessels from the early nineteenth century. There's level access around the pier, and ramped access to the Eureka Ferry, which features a collection of vintage automobiles on the car deck.

- Take a hike at Crissy Field (www.crissyfield.org, 415-561-3000). This former airfield now boasts a restored tidal marsh, miles of level hard-packed trails and a great bay view.

- Pick up an On the Level Walking Tour (415-921-1382, www.onthe levelsf.com) booklet, and strike out on your own. These self-guided walks are less than a mile long and travel along level pathways with curb-cuts and wide sidewalks.

- Visit the Asian Art Museum (415-581-3500, www.asianart.org), the Museum of Modern Art (415-357-4000, www.sfmoma.org) and the Contemporary Jewish Museum (415-655-7800, www.thecjm.org). They all feature level access and barrier-free pathways through their galleries.

- Explore Fisherman's Wharf (415-674-7503, www.fishermanswharf.org), then walk down the street to Pier 39 (415-705-5500, www.pier39.com). There's plenty of curb-cuts, accessible parking and level access throughout the wharf area.

- Take a cruise on the bay. Blue and Gold Fleet (415-705-8200, www. blueandgoldfleet.com) offers narrated bay cruises, most of which are wheelchair-accessible.

- Catch an accessible cab and hit the town. Yellow Cab (415-333-3333, www.yellowcabsf.com) is just one of several companies that offers ramped taxi vans with roll-on access.

FLY-DRIVE OPTION

To make this a fly-drive vacation, fly to San Francisco International Airport (800-453-9736, www.flysfo.com), Oakland International Airport (510-563-3300, www.flyoakland.com) or Mineta San Jose International Airport (408-392-3600, www.flysanjose.com); then rent an accessible van at Wheelchair Getaways (800-638-1912, www.wheelchairgetaways.com).

ALTERNATE ENTRY POINTS

- From the San Diego and Los Angeles areas, take Interstates 5 and 405 north, then follow Highway 101 north to Ventura.

- From Sacramento, take Highway 99 south, to Highway 120 and head east to Yosemite.

- From Reno, go west on Interstate 80, then follow Highway 89 around Lake Tahoe, to Highway 395 south to Mono Lake.

- From Las Vegas, take Highway 160 to Pahrump, then follow State Line Road to the east entrance of Death Valley.

VARIATION ON A THEME

For a shorter trip you can do Yosemite Valley as an overnight excursion from San Francisco. Likewise, you can add on a Death Valley side trip to a Las Vegas visit. And if you want to extend your road trip adventure even more, head east to Las Vegas, then explore some of Utah's national parks on the Utah's Big Five route.

- IF YOU GO
  - Yosemite National Park, (209) 372-0200, www.nps.gov/yose
  - Eastern Sierra Scenic Byway, www.drive395.org
  - Mono County Tourism, (800) 845-7922, www.monocounty.org
  - Death Valley, (760) 786-3200, www.nps.gov/deva
  - San Luis Obispo County Visitors & Conference Bureau, (805) 541-8000, www.sanluisobispocounty.com
  - Monterey County Convention & Visitors Bureau, (831) 657-6400, www.seemonterey.com
  - San Francisco Travel Association, (415) 391-2000, www.sanfrancisco.travel
  - Access Northern California, www.accessnca.org

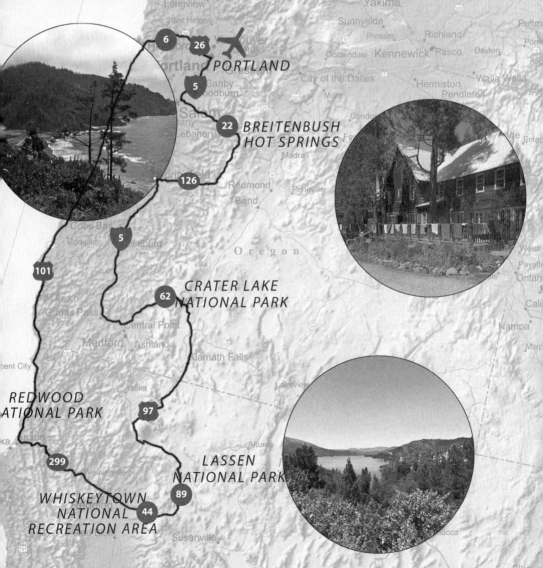

Mother Nature's Glory in the Pacific Northwest

PORTLAND

BREITENBUSH HOT SPRINGS

CRATER LAKE NATIONAL PARK

REDWOOD NATIONAL PARK

LASSEN NATIONAL PARK

WHISKEYTOWN NATIONAL RECREATION AREA

This scenic route highlights the beauty and majesty of the Pacific Northwest and includes several national parks, state parks and recreation areas. Beginning with a drive down the rugged Oregon cost, followed by a jaunt through California's giant redwoods, and concluding with a look at two vastly different volcanic sites, this drive showcases Mother Nature's power and diversity. Top it off with a visit to a peaceful mountain hot springs on the return loop and a post-trip stay in multicultural Portland, and you'll have memories—and photos—to last you a lifetime.

ROUTE

This route begins in Portland, Oregon and heads west to Tillamook. From there it follows Highway 101 South, along the Oregon Coast, across the California border, through Redwood National and State Park. Next it's east on Highway 299 to Whiskeytown National Recreation Area, and then on to Redding. Then follow Highway 44 east to Lassen National Park. To complete the loop, follow Highway 89 north to Interstate 5, and connect to Highway 97 to Klamath Falls; then head north to Highway 62 to Crater Lake National Park. Continue east to Interstate 5 North to Eugene, where you'll connect to Highway 126 east to Highway 20 east to Highway 22 north to Detroit and Breitenbush Hot Springs. Then it's back to Interstate 5, and north to Portland.

ALONG THE WAY

Redwood National and State Park

Collectively referred to as Redwood National and State Park, the North Coast old-growth redwoods span three California state parks as well as Redwood National Park. Jointly managed by the California Department of

Scenic Oregon Coast at Haceta Head near Florence, Oregon.

Parks and Recreation and the National Park Service, this World Heritage Site features dense redwood forests filled with giant trees averaging 500 to 700 years old. It's one of the most scenic drives in California, with fog usually blanketing the forest in the early mornings. There are also several accessible trails and viewpoints along the way.

Traveling south on Highway 101, you'll first pass through Del Norte Coast Redwoods State Park, which features eight miles of rugged coast filled with old-growth redwoods. Because of the coastline, there really aren't a lot of places to stop, so just enjoy the drive until you hit Prairie Creek State Park, where you'll find the majority of the accessible sites.

The first accessible trail in Prairie Creek State Park is the Big Tree Trail, which is just a short .16-mile level stroll through the redwoods. If you'd prefer a longer hike, then give the 1.5-mile Prairie Creek Trail a try. Located just across the street from the Big Tree Day Use Area, this level trek through the giant trees offers wheelers and slow walkers an in-depth look at the forest ecosystem. Last but not least, the .34-mile Campfire Center Trail, which is just down the road near the Elk Creek Prairie Campground, also offers level access to the big trees. After that, Highway 101 winds south through Redwood National Park, around Stone Lagoon and continues on to Eureka.

If you have time for a little detour on the north end of the drive, head east on Elk Valley Road and Howland Hill Road, after you pass through Crescent City. This windy road travels through Jedediah Smith Redwoods State Park, and passes through Stout Grove. And although the Stout Grove Loop Trail is not technically wheelchair-accessible, the first half-mile is level and doable for most folks. It's well worth the extra drive, as there's not much traffic on this road, because it's too windy for motorhomes and trailers.

Whiskeytown National Recreation Area

Located just eight miles west of Redding, Whiskeytown National Recreation Area is a great place to linger for a few days. Not only is Whiskeytown Lake very beautiful, but it also provides a wide variety of accessible recreational opportunities.

If you'd like to catch some trout for dinner, then head on down to the Whiskey Creek Fishing Platform or the Oak Bottom Marina. Both areas feature accessible parking and barrier-free access down to the water. Oak Bottom Marina also boasts an accessible picnic area, and it makes a great place for a lunch break.

If you'd prefer to spend some time in the water, then Brandy Creek Beach is just the place for you. There's plenty of accessible parking in Lot A, with an accessible path through the picnic area. At the end of the path, a cement ramp leads down to the water, so you can literally get your feet wet. There are also two accessible picnic sites, so pack a lunch and enjoy a full day at the beach.

And for some great fun on the water, sign up for the Special Access Kayak Program. This unique program pairs volunteers with participants in two-person kayaks, for a relaxing two-hour evening paddle on the lake. For more information about the program, give Ranger Nancy Quirus a call at (530) 242-3454. Advance registration is required, and all participants are interviewed to determine their access needs.

If you'd like to pitch your tent and overnight in the park, then check out the wheelchair-accessible tent sites at Oak Bottom Campground. Managed by Forever Resorts, the campground boasts two wheelchair-accessible tent sites, which are level and close to the restrooms. As an added bonus, one site even has electricity so you can recharge your wheelchair or scooter batteries. For reservations or more information call (530) 359-2269. And don't forget to mention your America the Beautiful Access Pass for a 50% discount.

Lassen Volcanic National Park

Lassen Volcanic National Park is a little off-the-beaten-path, but the diverse scenery makes it well worth the slight detour. The best way to see the park is on a driving tour, so be sure an pick up a park map at the information desk at the Loomis Museum, near the north park entrance. The drive through the park takes about an hour, but allow ample time for stops along the way. It's also a good idea to pack along a picnic lunch, as dining options in the park are somewhat limited.

Make sure and stop at the Devastated Area, just 10 miles south of the Loomis Museum, as it boasts one of the most accessible trails in the park. Signs of the 1915 eruption of Mt. Lassen, as well as the subsequent rebirth of the forest, are evident along the length of this very easy half-mile trail. As an added bonus, the trail was repaved in 2010, as part of a park-wide improvement project.

The South Summit Lake Picnic Area, which is just a few miles south of the Devastated Area, is the best choice for an accessible lunch stop. Not only does it feature good pathway access to the picnic tables, but this site also has wheelchair-accessible vault toilets. Plus it's pretty pleasant, with lots of shaded sites.

Sulphur Works is also a must-see along the driving route, as it's one of the most active geothermal areas in the park. There's accessible parking in the paved lot, with sidewalk access to nearby boardwalks that overlook an interesting collection of mud pots, steam vents and sulphur streams. Although other areas of the park boast these geothermal features, this is the only accessible option. And since it's right along the main road, you don't even have to get out of your car to get a good view.

And for an overnight stay in the park, check out the accessible camping cabins at Manzanita Lake, near the north park entrance. Each cabin is furnished with a bed, a heater, a bear box, a lantern, a fire ring and a picnic table. Accessible parking is located nearby, with level access to the cabins and the accessible community bathroom. For reservations or more information call (877) 444-6777 or visit www.LassenRecreation.com. Plan ahead, as these popular cabins sell out fast!

Crater Lake National Park

Located in Southern Oregon, Crater Lake is surrounded by the sheer rugged cliffs of the Mount Mazama caldera. This mountain lake was formed some 7,000 years ago when the volcano collapsed and created an enormous depression. Known for its deep blue waters, today Crater Lake provides some stunning views and includes a diverse ecosystem in the surrounding forest. It's a great place to get away from it all, kick back and enjoy Mother Nature.

The trail down to the shore is very steep and not accessible; however, you can get a great view of the lake from the 33-mile Rim Drive. This scenic route circles the caldera and boasts more than 20 wheelchair-accessible overlooks. And the views are simply spectacular. Take your time and enjoy the drive. Even if this is the only thing you do in the park, it's worth a visit.

Make sure and stop in at Rim Village along the drive, where you'll find an accessible cafeteria, gift shop and Visitor Center. There's also a paved path in front of the gift shop, which meanders around the edge of the lake and provides a great view the deep blue waters below.

Over on the east part of the Rim Drive, you'll find some accessible picnic sites at the Vidae Falls Picnic Area. The Crater Peak Trail also begins in this picnic area; and although it's not technically wheelchair-accessible, the first hundred yards is wide and level. This short stretch leads to a lovely patch of old-growth forest. Don't attempt this trail when it's wet though, as it gets very muddy and makes for some very rough—and messy—going.

Last but not least, the Godfrey Glen trail offers a very scenic hike through an old-growth hemlock and fir forest with some stunning canyon views. The trailhead is located between Mazama Village and Park Headquarters on Munson Valley Road. Rated as "accessible with assistance" the one-mile dirt trail features no cross slope, and although it's not entirely level it's doable for some manual wheelchair-users. Some folks may need a bit of assistance over the steeper patches on this loop trail, but give it a try and see how it goes.

Breitenbush Hot Springs

Located about 65 miles east of Salem, Breitenbush Hot Springs is one of Oregon's alternative getaway spots. This remote conference center is located

....

Office and dining building at Breitenbush Hot Springs.

on a 154-acre tract of forest land, and it's also open to leisure guests. It's in a beautiful setting, and it's quite rustic and pretty remote. That said they've upgraded two of their 1930s cabins to include some access features.

Both cabins feature ramp access and are furnished with two twin beds. Cabin B1 has a roll-under sink and a toilet with grab bars, while cabin B2 has no toilet or sink. A nearby community shower house has tiled roll-in showers without any grab bars or hand-held showerheads. These are community showers, without doors, so if you're shy, it's probably not the best option for you.

The cabins all have electricity; however, there's no cell phone reception. Additionally, many electric items like blow dryers, curling irons and coffee makers are on the Breitenbush "do not bring" list.

There's ramped access to the office, meeting rooms and dining area. Three hearty organic meals are served daily, and they're included in the room rate. The food is tasty, with vegetarian options available upon request. There's also a wheelchair for loan at the check-in desk.

It should be noted that the parking area is located some distance from the cabins, but luggage carts are available to transport your luggage. And if you can't manage the distance from the parking area, arrangements can be made to have someone bring you down, and then take you back to the parking area when you leave.

Access to the hot springs requires assistance, as there are two to three steps down to the pools. Additionally, some of the dirt paths are a little bumpy. It should also be noted that the hot springs are clothing optional; so again, if you're shy this probably isn't the place for you.

All in all, Breitenbush is probably best suited for slow walkers who use a power wheelchair or scooter, because of the distances around the camp. Still, it's a very unique site, and a great place to relax in the woods or to take some personal time to recharge and regroup, before heading back to the city.

TIMING

This is definitely a summer trip. Depending on the severity of the winter, the roads through Lassen Volcanic National Park and Crater Lake National Park may not open till June. Snow can also be very problematic in the Breitenbush area. Additionally, it's not uncommon for the Oregon Coast to experience heavy rains—and sometimes floods—in the winter and spring. Play it safe and stick to a summer visit, when you'll dodge the snow and have moderate temperatures.

GREAT EATS

Portland tops the food scene on this route, with their yummy food cart fare. There's over 500 food carts throughout the city with offerings from traditional pizza, pitas and sandwiches to more eclectic Cuban, Korean, Thai and Indian dishes. And the access is good, because you just roll-up and order. They are grouped in clusters called pods, and the best downtown choices are the two pods close to Pioneer Courthouse Square. There's one pod at 10th and Alder Streets and another at 5th and Stark Streets. So take some time to browse the carts, then bring your food back to the square to enjoy. It's the way to eat like a real Portlander.

DON'T MISS IT

I f you'd like to overnight along the dramatic Oregon Coast, then check out the Pana Sea Ah Bed & Breakfast (541-764-3368, www.panaseah.com) in Depoe Bay, just 12 miles north of Newport. The accessible Tuscany Suite features a tiled bathroom with a roll-in shower. It's a very roomy and private suite, and it's also pet friendly. The driveway is a bit steep, but innkeeper Mary Hauser is happy to open the garage door so you can park and unload on a level service. Give her a call—she's very accommodating.

LINGER ON IN THE GATEWAY

P ortland is a great choice for a post road trip stay. Not only does it boast a very accessible and affordable public transportation system, but there's also an abundance of accessible things to see and do in the City of Roses.

■ Visit the oldest museum on the West Coast—the Portland Art Museum (503-226-2811, www.portlandartmuseum.org). There's ramp access on the left side, with barrier-free access through the galleries. The museum is known for its impressive collection of English silver, graphic arts and Native American art. It's also a favorite local haunt.

■ Check out the Portland Farmers' Market (www.portlandfarmersmarket. org) at Pioneer Courthouse Square (www.pioneercourthousesquare.org). This food and farm marketplace is held on Mondays, Tuesdays and

Portland Farmers' Market at Pioneer Courthouse Square.

Thursdays during the summer. It also features some hot food vendors, so it's a good place for a quick breakfast or brunch. Built on a slope, there's level access to Pioneer Courthouse Square from 6th Street, and ramp access down from Morrison Street.

- Get your bearings on a Best of Portland walking tour, presented by Portland Walking Tours (503-774-4522, www.portlandwalkingtours.com). This 2.5-hour tour focuses on things that make Portland a great place to live, and travels over a wheelchair-accessible route from downtown to the waterfront.

- Ride the streetcar around the downtown area—it's free. All streetcars are equipped with retractable bridge plates and wheelchair-accessible seating areas. Just look for the Free Rail Zone sign, and hop on. A fare is only required if you travel outside of the free zone.

- Hop on Max Rail and head over to Washington Park and visit the Oregon Zoo (503-226-1561, www.oregonzoo.org). All MAX Rail trains feature roll-on access, and the zoo boasts barrier-free pathways to most areas.

- Take the Washington Park Shuttle to the other side of the park and visit the International Rose Test Garden (503-823-3636). The shuttle stop is located next to the Oregon Zoo entrance, and all buses are lift equipped. The International Rose Test Garden features more than 9,000 plants and features ramp access near the Rose Garden Store.

- Hit the town on your own in one of Radio Cab's wheelchair-accessible taxis. Just call (503) 205-3311 or e-mail specialneeds@radiocab.net to schedule your ride.

FLY-DRIVE OPTION

To make this a fly-drive vacation, fly to Portland International Airport (503-460-4234, www.flypdx.com), then rent an accessible van at Performance Mobility (888-707-0456, www.performancemobility.com), All in One Mobility (800-944-4935, www.allinonemobility-shop.com) or Wheelchair Getaways (800-642-2042, www.wheelchairgetaways.com).

ALTERNATE ENTRY POINTS

- From Seattle and Vancouver, take Interstate 5 south to Portland.

- From Sacramento, take Highway 99 north to Redding.

- From the San Francisco area, take Highway 101 north to Eureka.

VARIATION ON A THEME

For a long weekend getaway, plan a two-day or three-day trip to Lassen Volcanic National Park or Redwood National and State Park from San

Francisco. Breitenbush can also be done as a two-day or three-day retreat from Portland or Seattle. And if you'd like a longer road trip, then head north, and continue your journey on the Washington Wine Country driving route.

- IF YOU GO
  - Redwood National and State Park, (707) 464-6101, www.nps.gov/redw
  - Lassen Volcanic National Park, (530) 595-4480, www.nps.gov/lavo
  - Whiskeytown National Recreation Area, (530) 246-1225, www.nps.gov/whis
  - Redding Convention & Visitors Bureau, (530) 225-4100, www.visitredding.com
  - Humboldt County Convention & Visitors Bureau, (800) 346-3482, www.redwoods.info
  - Crater Lake National Park, (541) 594-3000, www.nps.gov/crla
  - Breitenbush Hot Springs, (503) 854-3320, www.breitenbush.com
  - Travel Portland, (503) 275-8355, www.travelPortland.com

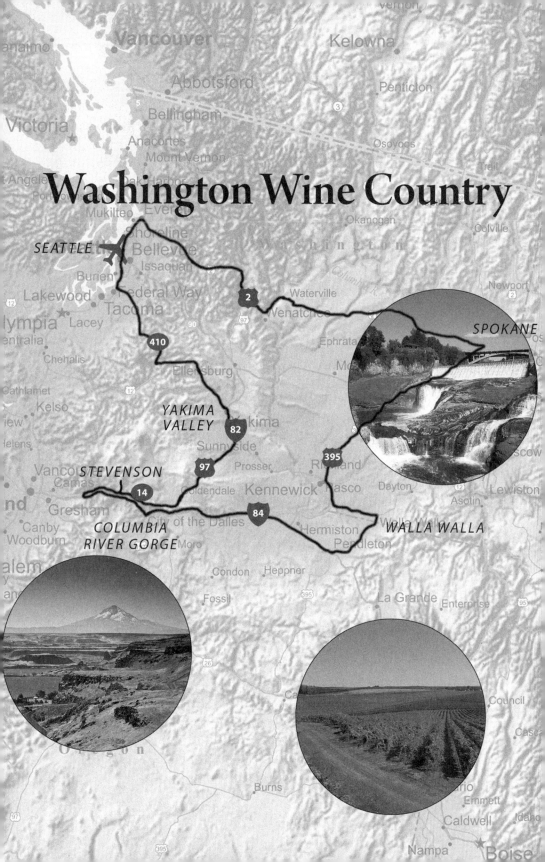

Washington Wine Country

This wine tasting route highlights three major Washington state appellations and features a scenic drive through the Cascade Mountains, the Columbia River Gorge and Yakima Valley and Walla Walla area vineyards. And although driving and wine tasting really don't mix, it's easy to base yourself in each area for several days; and take time to relax and soak in the ambiance of the area, spend more time at each winery and talk with the winemakers about their production process. And of course, don't forget to buy some wine along the way, so you can relive your trip once you return home.

ROUTE

This route begins in Seattle and travels east through the Cascades on scenic Highway 2, and on to Spokane. Then it's south on Interstate 90 to Highway 395 and Highway 12 to Walla Walla. Next, head south across the Oregon border on Highway 11 to Interstate 84 West. Follow the interstate along the Columbia River, with a slight detour on Highway 30 to Multnomah Falls. Then it's time to cross the Columbia River at the Cascade Locks and head east on Highway 14 and north on Highway 97 to Interstate 82 and on to Yakima. To complete the loop, follow scenic Highway 410 back to Seattle.

ALONG THE WAY

Spokane

Generally speaking, you usually don't find a lot of wineries in large metropolitan areas; however Spokane is definitely the exception to that rule. Billed as Washington's newest emerging wine region, Spokane boasts over 17 wineries which produce vintages from Walla Walla, Yakima and Columbia Valley grapes. Couple that with a winemaking community that embraces the hands-on process, and you have reason enough to linger for a few days and enjoy the fruits of their labors.

Barrister Winery (509-465-3591, www.barristerwinery.com) tops the Spokane list of unique boutique wineries. Located in a historic warehouse in the Davenport Arts District, this winery was definitely built on passion. What began as a basement operation with a five-gallon winemaking kit, soon blossomed into the award-winning winery it is today. Barrister specializes in reds and they are particularly well known for their Cabernet Franc.

Access is excellent throughout the tasting room, with a ramped entrance and plenty of room to wheel around. And with advance notice you can even arrange a private tour of their on-site production facility, which features good pathway access and elevator access down to the ageing room.

And although it lacks the curb appeal of the Barrister operation, the Lone Canary Winery (509-534-9062, www.lonecanary.com) produces some excellent Old World Style Italian and French varietals. Located in a business park, there's plenty of accessible parking and ramped access to the building.

Inside, the Lone Canary folks are very willing to talk about their wines, the grapes, the history of the winery and even how the winery was named. And if you visit during the fall crush, you might even get a sample of the grapes. Like most of the local winemakers, the folks at Lone Canary love what they do and they thoroughly enjoy sharing their passion with visitors.

Last but not least, don't miss Arbor Crest Wine Cellars (509-927-9463, www.arborcrest.com). Located on a historic estate outside the city, this winery simply oozes ambiance. The Cliff House, which was built in 1924, is the centerpiece of the property; and it's surrounded by the gate keeper's house, a sunken rose garden, terraced flower gardens and even a life sized checker board.

There is level access to the tasting room, which is located near the parking lot; and a paved pathway down to the Cliff House area. Arbor Crest is known for their Riesling as well as their Cabernet Sauvignon. And from June to September they also have Sunday evening concerts. You can pack your own picnic or buy something there. The music ranges form jazz and blues to country and even popular favorites. Bring a blanket, find a

Sunday evening concert at the Arbor Crest Winery in Spokane, Washington.

place on the grass and just enjoy. It's the perfect end to a Spokane wine tasting weekend.

Walla Walla

Moving south to the Walla Walla area, plan to stop at the Woodward Canyon Winery (509-525-4129, www.woodwardcanyon.com) to sample their award winning Cabernet Sauvignon or Merlot. Located just west of the city on Highway 12, this unique tasting room is housed in a restored 1870s farmhouse, complete with ramped access, wide doorways and plenty of room to navigate.

The Reininger Winery (509-522-1994, www.reiningerwinery.com), which is just a few miles down the road, is also worth a stop. Although this tasting room has a more contemporary design, the Reininger reds are not to be missed. Access is excellent there too, with a level entrance, accessible parking and good pathway access throughout the tasting room.

And if you'd prefer to forego the car for a day and simply wheel around the city to sample some wines, then plan to spend the night at the Marcus Whitman Hotel (509-525-2200, www.marcuswhitmanhotel.com)

Woodward Canyon Winery's unique 1870s farmhouse tasting room.

in Walla Walla. Built in 1927, this Walla Walla icon gets consistently high marks across the board—for access, ambiance and location.

The property features plenty of accessible parking, a level entry, wide doorways and good pathway access throughout the public areas. There is elevator access to all floors; and accessible rooms are available with either a tub/shower combination or a roll-in shower with a fold-down shower seat. Other access features include a hand-held showerhead, grab bars in the shower and around the toilet, a roll-under sink and a full five-foot turning radius in the bathroom. As an added bonus, the room tariff includes a delicious hot breakfast. And since the property is within rolling distance of many accessible tasting rooms, it's a great place to base yourself.

Columbia River Gorge

The Columbia River Gorge National Scenic Area, which skirts both sides of the Columbia River, is a must-do drive on any Washington wine country driving itinerary. With spectacular waterfalls and scenic gorge views dotting the south side, and rolling vineyards lining the north shore, there's certainly enough variety to warrant a leisurely drive through the area. But it's more than just a scenic drive, so make sure and allow ample time to stop and enjoy the sights along the way.

For a look at one of the most spectacular scenic wonders on this loop, take exit 35 off Interstate 84, and continue west on Highway 30 to Multnomah Falls. This 620-foot waterfall is the second tallest year-round waterfall in the nation and the showpiece of the Columbia River Gorge.

A word of warning though—the signs to Multnomah Falls direct visitors to exit 31, which leads to a remote parking lot. For best access take exit 35, so you can park directly in front of the falls. From this smaller parking area, you'll get a great view of the falls with very limited walking. Additionally, try and hit this top attraction as early in the day as possible, to avoid the crowds.

Continuing west on Highway 30, make sure and stop at Crown Point, about 8.5 miles from Multnomah Falls. This scenic viewpoint is located 733 feet above the river, and affords some spectacular gorge views. There is level access to the outside viewing area, and lift and ramp access to the first floor of Vista House. Known as the symbol of the Columbia River Gorge, this 1916 building houses a museum, interpretive exhibits, cafe and a gift shop. There is no admission charge, and the copper-domed octagonal structure is an architectural treasure by itself.

After you've taken in the view, continue west on Highway 30, until you rejoin Interstate 84 near Corbett. Follow the interstate back to the Cascade Locks, cross the river on the Bridge of Gods and continue east on Highway 14. The scenery is decidedly different along this side of the river, with several wineries and tasting rooms along the route.

The Maryhill Winery (877-627-9445, www.maryhillwinery.com), located near the end of the Columbia River Gorge National Scenic Area, is an excellent place to stop and sample the local wine. Although the winery looks unremarkable from the front, the view of the mountains, river and vineyards from the back deck will really wow you.

There is accessible parking near the entrance; and although the lot is gravel the accessible spaces are on cement slabs. The tasting room features level access, as does the patio and back deck. Sit down and enjoy a glass of one of their premium red wines out on the patio, or gather around the fireplace inside. Either way, Maryhill Winery makes a very pleasant stop.

Stevenson

Located midway along the Washington side of the Columbia River Gorge National Scenic Area, Stevenson is the perfect place to base yourself while you explore the area.

One of the larger properties in the area—the Skamania Lodge (509-427-7700, www.skamania.com)—is a great choice for wheelchair-users and slow walkers. It's situated on 175 acres of prime real estate, and features stunning river or mountain views from nearly every room.

There is an accessible pathway to the lobby from the nearby parking area, and a convenient drop-off area near the front entrance. The property features good pathway access to all the public areas, including the gift shop, restaurants, library and adjacent conference center. This 254-room mountain resort boasts 11 accessible rooms; including eight with tub/shower combinations and three with roll-in showers.

The accessible guest rooms all have good pathway access, a lowered peephole, lever handles and lowered closet rods. Access features in the spacious bathrooms include a hand-held showerhead, grab bars in the shower and around the toilet, a roll-under sink and a portable shower bench.

And don't miss the back gardens. There is level access to the patio, with ramp access down to the garden and back lawn area. Unfortunately, most of the lodge trails are not very accessible, as they are covered in crushed gravel and have undulations or other access obstacles. Still, the garden or patio area is a great place to just sit back, relax and take in the scenery.

If you'd really like to take a hike, then hop in the car and head over to the Sams-Walker Trail, just a few miles down the road. This 1.7-mile scenic loop features level access down to the river, and it's a great place for a picnic lunch or a short afternoon excursion. It's also a great vantage point for some spectacular gorge views.

Yakima Valley

The Yakima Valley is the perfect place wrap up your wine tasting road trip, as it's where a third of the state's wine grapes are grown, as well as home to a number of vineyard wineries. Best bet is to pack a picnic lunch to enjoy along this leg of the journey.

Yakima Valley grapevines viewed from Silver Lake Winery.

Start off with a visit to Bonaire Winery (509-829-6027, www.bonairwine.com), located in the Rattlesnake Hills area of the Yakima Valley. After all, it's hard to miss on ambiance when a duck pond sits between the parking area and the tasting room.

The winery features accessible parking on a cement pad, with barrier-free access around the pond, and ramp access to the tasting room. Inside, there's plenty of room to roll around, as well as a unisex bathroom off the tasting room. Bonaire Winery produces a wide variety of wines, with an emphasis on wine and food pairing. Save some time to linger and enjoy some wine on the deck.

Just up the road, you'll find Silver Lake Winery (509-829-6235, www.silverlakewinery.com), which also gets top marks for ambiance. Located at the top of a hill, the tasting room opens out onto a deck that offers great views of the surrounding vineyards. Accessible parking is located on the side, near the accessible entrance. Alternatively, if you can manage three steps, the main entrance is just around the corner. The tasting room features a lowered counter, and if you're in the mood for barbeque, then stop by on Saturday, when they fire up the grill.

And for the absolute best view of the Yakima Valley, head up north to Windy Point Vineyards (509-877-6827, www.windypointvineyards.com), located just outside the Yakima city limits. This boutique winery limits production to just 3,000 cases annually, and they're especially known for their Cabernet Franc.

Accessible parking is available on a cement slab in the lot, with barrier-free access to the ramped tasting room. Windows line the front façade of the building, which affords patrons great views of the valley. And if you can't access the standard height tasting bar, then enjoy your wine from a comfortable sofa, an overstuffed chair or a one of the many dining tables. No matter where you sit, the view is terrific!

TIMING

F all is the ideal time for this driving route, as the fall colors are simply spectacular along the Columbia River Gorge. And since fall is crush time at the wineries, there are a lot of fun activities such as grape stomps, harvest festivals and even free concerts. Additionally, many wineries have special sales during this time, so watch their websites for harvest time deals.

GREAT EATS

F or a real culinary treat, hit Frank's Diner (509-747-8798, www.franksdiners.com) in downtown Spokane for breakfast. This kitsch restaurant is housed in a vintage railcar, with ramped access in back. Today the railcar is outfitted with booths and a counter; but it began life as an observation car and was later converted to a private railcar for the railroad president. You can either eat in your wheelchair seated at the end of a booth, or transfer to the booth for your meal. If the latter is your choice, the staff will happily store your wheelchair in the back until you need it. They also have large accessible restrooms—larger than I've ever seen on a train before. Known for their Eggs Benedict, Frank's Diner serves up comfort food at its best. And don't forget to ask for gravy and onions on your hash browns—it's a house specialty.

DON'T MISS IT

For a taste of Britain along the Columbia River, don't miss Maryhill Stonehenge. Located just past the Highway 97 junction on the south side of Highway 14, this full-size replica of Stonehenge was erected as a memorial to local soldiers who died in World War I. There's no striped parking, but you can park close to the monument. Most of the areas are pretty level and quite wheelable, and unlike the original Stonehenge you can walk around the Maryhill version and actually touch it. It's kind of fun, and much easier to access than the one in Wiltshire. Plus, like everything else along the gorge, it boasts a spectacular view.

LINGER ON IN THE GATEWAY

Seattle makes a great post road trip add-on, as it's a culturally diverse community with a wide range of attractions. And despite some hilly areas, it's still relatively easy to get around the Emerald City on a nicely accessible public transportation system.

■ Stop in at Pike Place Market (www.pikeplacemarket.org) where you'll see vendors hawking fresh fish, flowers, vegetables and fruits. There are wide level pathways throughout the market, and elevator access from the street above.

- Take the Seattle Center Monorail (206-905-2620, www.seattlemonorail. com) from Westlake Mall over to Seattle Center. Although a bit outdated, in 1962 it was a vision of the future. Still it's fun—if not a bit nostalgic—to ride. There's a small gap between the platform and the train, but it's doable for most folks. Inside, you can just wheel into an empty space and stay in your wheelchair for the short trip.

- Go to the top of the Seattle Space Needle (206-905-2100, www. spaceneedle.com) for a great view of the city. Built for the 1962 World's Fair, this Seattle icon has an accessible observation deck and restaurant at the top, with elevator access from the lobby.

- Hop aboard the Seattle Streetcar (206-553-3000, www.seattlestreetcar. org) for a 2.6-mile loop through the downtown area. The streetcar features low floors, accessible platforms and ramped access, which makes boarding a snap.

- Get a full day of culture with a visit to the Seattle Art Museum (206-344-5275, www.seattleartmuseum.org) and the Seattle Asian Art Museum (206-654-3206, www.seattleartmuseum.org). Both museums feature level access, barrier-free pathways and accessible restrooms. The Seattle Art Museum also has free loaner wheelchairs near the coat check.

- Head down to Pier 59 and visit the Seattle Aquarium (206-386-4300, www.seattleaquarium.org), the seventh largest aquarium in the U.S. Opened in 1977, this waterfront favorite features themed exhibitions in a 18,000 square foot space. There's level access at the entrance with good pathway access to all exhibits.

- Don't miss the Boeing Future of Flight and Aviation Center Tour (360-756-0086, www.futureofflight.org) in nearby Everett. This 90-minute tour features a look inside the factory where Boeing 747, 767, 777 and 787 jets are assembled. Although the standard tour requires a lot of walking and climbing up and down stairs, advance arrangements can be made for a wheelchair-accessible tour. It's also important to note that visitors must be at least four feet tall in order to take the tour.

FLY-DRIVE OPTION

To make this a fly-drive vacation, fly to Seattle-Tacoma International Airport (206-787-5388, www. portseattle.org/seatac); then rent an accessible van at Absolute Mobility Center (425-481-6546, www.absolutemobilitycenter. com), Wheelchair Getaways (800-854-4176, www.wheelchairgetaways.com) or Kersey Mobility (877-507-7491, www.kerseymobility.com).

ALTERNATE ENTRY POINTS

- From Boise, take Interstate 84 west, then follow Highway 11 north to Spokane.

- From Portland, head east on Interstate 84, and begin your journey on the Columbia River Gorge.

- From Vancouver, take Highway 14 east to Stevenson.

VARIATION ON A THEME

The Columbia River Gorge route makes a nice weekend getaway from Portland or Vancouver. Add on some wine tasting in the Yakima Valley, and you have a nice three-night itinerary. And if you'd prefer a longer trip, then connect down to Boise and do the Way Out West route.

- IF YOU GO

  - Spokane Regional Convention & Visitors Bureau, (888) 776-5263, www.visitspokane.com
  - Tourism Walla Walla, (877) 998-4748, www.wallawalla.org
  - Columbia River Gorge Visitors Association, (800) 984-6743, www.crgva.org
  - Yakima Valley Visitors & Convention Bureau, (800) 221-0751, www.visityakima.com
  - Washington Wine Commission, 206-667-9463, www.washingtonwine.org

Mountain States

SAN FRANCISCO DE ASÍS

Left: Old Faithful at Yellowstone National Park.
Upper right: San Francisco de Asis in Ranchos de Taos, New Mexico.
Lower right: Cathedral Rock in Sedona, Arizona.

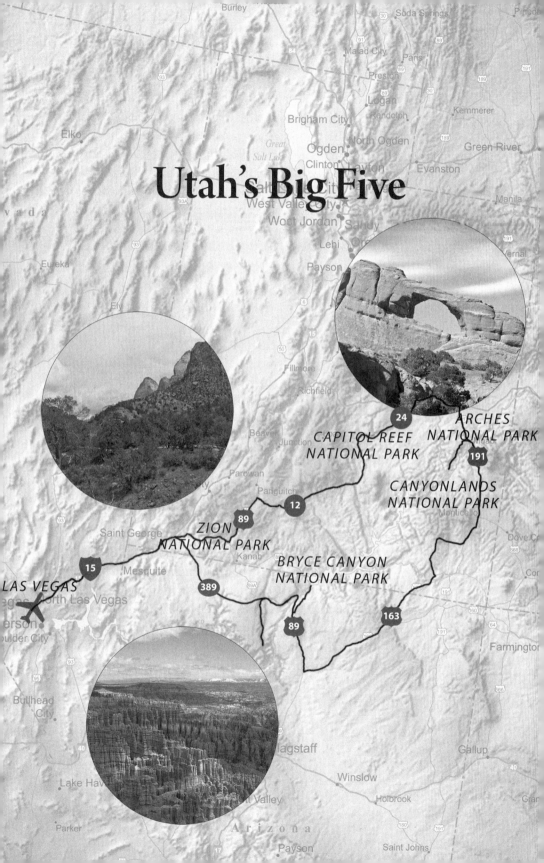

Utah's Big Five

ARCHES
NATIONAL PARK

CAPITOL REEF
NATIONAL PARK

CANYONLANDS
NATIONAL PARK

ZION
NATIONAL PARK

BRYCE CANYON
NATIONAL PARK

LAS VEGAS

Gorgeous scenery is in store for you along the length of this route, as it highlights five of Utah's national parks, takes a short jaunt through northern Arizona and concludes with a short detour to the north rim of the Grand Canyon. The landscape is awesome and varied, from Zion's massive canyon and Bryce's spire-like geologic features, to Capitol Reef's petroglyphs and the red rock formations in Arches and Canyonlands. And although the focus is on the outdoors, there's no shortage of comfortable accessible accommodations along the way. It's the best of both worlds—great scenery, plus all the creature comforts of home.

ROUTE

This route begins in Las Vegas and follows Interstate 15 into Utah, then continues east on Highway 9 to Zion National Park. Next it's out the east park entrance to Mt. Carmel Junction, where you'll take Highway 89 to Highway 12 to Bryce Canyon National Park. Continue east on Highway 12 with a brief detour along the Burr Trail, before picking up Highway 24 in Torrey to Capitol Reef National Park. Then it's out the east park entrance and north on Highway 24 to Interstate 70 East. Exit the interstate at Crescent Junction, and take Highway 191 South to Arches and Canyonlands National Parks. Continue south on Highway 191 to Highway 95 East, then head south on Highway 261 to Highway 163 to Monument Pass. After you cross into Arizona, continue on Highway 163, then take Highway 160 west to Highway 98, to Highway 89 to Jacob Lake. Turn south on Highway 67 for a short detour to the north rim of the Grand Canyon. To complete the loop, head back to Jacob Lake and turn left on Highway 389, which turns into Highway 59 after you cross back into Utah. From there, continue on to Hurricane, then head west on Highway 9 and catch Interstate 15 back to Las Vegas.

The Pa'rus Trail along the Virgin River in Zion National Park.

ALONG THE WAY

Zion National Park

Although you'll need a car to get to Zion National Park, personal vehicles are prohibited along most Zion Canyon roads. That said, there's free shuttle bus transportation up and down Zion Canyon Scenic Drive, from the Springdale Visitors Center. And the good news is, all buses are lift-equipped and they run about every six minutes.

A full loop of the canyon takes about 90 minutes, and although most folks get on and off along the route, you can also take it as an uninterrupted tour if you need to conserve your energy.

If you'd like to get active and try a little hiking, take the shuttle bus to the last stop—the Temple of Sinawava—and head off to your right to the Riverside Walk. This mile-long paved trail runs alongside the Virgin River; and although the full length isn't accessible, the first part is doable for most folks.

Lower Emerald Pool Trail—across from Zion Lodge—is also worth a visit. This 1.2-mile trail is wide, and for the most part fairly level; with the first section having mostly 1:6 grades. As you get near the end there are a few steeper sections, but even if you can't make it all the way, you'll still be rewarded with some nice views of the river below.

Last but not least, stop at Canyon Junction to explore the Pa'rus Trail, the most accessible trail in the park. This 1.8-mile trail, which runs along the Virgin River, is wide and flat and a good choice for all ability levels. It runs from the Canyon Junction shuttle bus stop all the way back to the Zion Canyon Visitors Center, so it's the perfect way to explore the park on foot.

The best way to enjoy Zion National Park is to overnight there; and to that end Zion Lodge (888-297-2757, www.zionlodge.com) has accessible guest rooms with roll-in showers or tub/shower combinations. And rest assured, you won't have to schlep your luggage on the shuttle bus if you opt to spend the night, because lodge guests receive permits to drive their cars to the lodge. Not only is Zion Lodge the most convenient lodging option; but it's also the most scenic choice, as the property is literally surrounded by Zion Canyon.

Bryce Canyon National Park

Bryce Canyon National Park is a required stop on any Utah driving itinerary; as the red rock spire-like hoodoos that seem to mystically rise from the canyon floor are indeed a spectacular sight.

Although personal vehicles are not prohibited in Bryce Canyon National Park as they are in neighboring Zion, it just makes sense to park your car and take the free park shuttle bus, especially during the busy summer months.

There's plenty of accessible parking at the Bryce Canyon Visitors Center and Bryce Canyon Lodge; and since the shuttle buses run every 15 minutes, it's easy to catch one. Additionally, since all of the shuttle buses are lift-equipped, you never have to wait for the next bus. All in all, it's the most convenient way to explore this beautiful park.

Hoodoos in Bryce Canyon National Park.

If you can only walk a few steps or tire easily, your best bet is take the shuttle bus as a loop driving tour. If you have a little more energy, then consider getting off at Sunset Point, Bryce Point or Inspiration Point, which all have paved access to at least one viewpoint.

If, on the other hand, you're up for a pleasant stroll, then give Rim Trail a try. Although the whole length of this paved trail is not accessible, a half-mile section near the lodge offers good access. The best way to get to it is from nearby Sunset Point. From there, it's a level walk or roll along the canyon rim to Sunrise Point; with some beautiful views of the Queen's Garden and the Bryce Amphitheater along the way.

For a good education on Bryce Canyon geology and wildlife, join a park ranger for a 1.5-hour interpretive program or a half-hour Geology Talk. Both programs start at Sunset Point, and they're available from spring to fall. Best of all, they're free.

And if you're still around after sunset, then stop by the Sunset Campground campfire circle for their evening program. There's a paved pathway from the shuttle bus stop to the seating area, and the rangers always put on a good show.

Overnighting in the park is highly recommended, and the Lodge at Bryce Canyon (877-386-4383, www.brycecanyonforever.com) has accessible rooms with roll-in showers or tub/shower combinations. The accessible rooms, which are located on the ground floor of the new Sunset Building, feature barrier-free pathways to all areas, including the private decks. All in all it's a very comfortable, quiet and accessible lodging option.

Capitol Reef National Park

Capitol Reef National Park boasts the best of both worlds—spectacular sandstone formations, cliffs and canyons, paired with some historic Native American cultural treasures.

Be sure and stop at the Visitors Center for a park map and a great view of The Castle; an appropriately named formation that towers over the building. There is accessible parking and level access to the Visitors Center, which houses interpretive exhibits and a park information center.

From there, follow the signs along the 20-mile roundtrip scenic drive, where you'll see plenty or red rocks and canyons. The route passes Grand Wash, Slickrock Divide and ends at Capitol Wash. There are plenty of pull-outs along the way; and even if you can't negotiate the gravel surface, you can still get a great windshield view.

Once you are back up on Highway 24, be sure and stop to see the petroglyphs. There's only a wide spot in the road that serves as a parking area, but it is paved, and there is level access to the nearby boardwalk. From the viewing platform near the parking area you can get a good look at the petroglyphs on the adjacent canyon walls, through the wheelchair-height viewing scopes. There's also a shaded boardwalk trail along the canyon, which makes for a very accessible quarter-mile roll or stroll.

If you'd like to overnight near the park, then check out the Torrey Schoolhouse Inn (435-633-4643, www.torreyschoolhouse.com), located in nearby Torrey. This historic property features 10 guest rooms, including the accessible Garden Room, which has a roll-in shower. And since it's just a few minutes away from Capitol Reef, you'll be able to get an early start on your day and hit the park before the crowds pour in.

Arches National Park

With over 2,000 sandstone arches dotting the landscape, Arches National Park is appropriately named. Think of it as a place to let your imagination

Balanced Rock in Arches National Park.

run wild, with a vast collection of pinnacles, spires and windblown cliffs that resemble animals, buildings or otherworldly forms.

For a good general orientation, stop at the Visitors Center, located just off Highway 191, near the park entrance. There is plenty of accessible parking in front, with level access to the building. Inside, you'll find accessible restrooms, a number of interpretive exhibits and a ranger information station.

From the Visitors Center head north, past the petrified dunes and the rock pinnacles until you reach Balanced Rock. There is accessible parking near the .3-mile trail that leads around this unique formation. Bear right as you approach the loop trail, as this accessible section features paved access out to the overlook, where you'll snag some great views of the La Sal Mountains.

Back on the main road, continue north and take a right at the first intersection to visit the Windows Section of the park. Take time to stop for the great windshield views, as you pass by Ham Rock and the Parade of Elephants and other formations that are easily spotted from the road.

Once you've made your way back out to the main road, continue north and take the next right to Delicate Arch, the most photographed formation in the park. The trail out to this arch is not accessible, but you can get a great view of it from the Lower Delicate Arch Viewpoint.

To wrap up your scenic drive, head back towards the park entrance on the main road, but save some time for a stop at the Park Avenue Viewpoint. There's accessible parking near the short trail out to the viewpoint; and although the trail has a slight incline, it's doable for most folks. It's an excellent place to enjoy the sunset.

Canyonlands National Park

Save another day for a visit to Canyonlands National Park, located just north of Arches, off of Highway 191. The most accessible section of the Park— Islands in the Sky—is a large mesa wedged in between the Green and Colorado Rivers.

The best place to start your visit is at the Visitors Center, which features accessible parking, a level entry and accessible vault toilets. Inside, there are a few interpretive exhibits, but the main reason for this stop is to pick up the self-guided CD audio tour in the gift shop. It's only $10, and it includes nice bits of history about the park. Make sure and stock up on water here too, because outside of the Visitors Center, there's none available in the park.

When you're all stocked up, pop in your CD audio tour and begin your scenic drive through the park. Best bet is to head directly out to the end of the road and take in the view at Grand View Point Overlook. There's plenty of accessible parking and a paved trail out to the overlook, where you'll get a panoramic view of the park.

As you work your way back towards the park entrance, be sure and stop at Buck Canyon Overlook and Green River Overlook for more spectacular canyon views. Buck Canyon Overlook features accessible parking and a 200-foot paved pathway that leads out to the overlook. Although there's a slight incline, it's doable for most folks. Green River Overlook also has accessible parking, with level access out to a great canyon view.

Last but not least, take a little detour over to Upheaval Dome. Although there's no wheelchair access at this site, you can get some great windshield views by driving slowly through the picnic area. The small dome actually sits inside a larger crater, and it's yet another example of the geologic diversity found in Utah's national parks.

If you'd like to spend the night in the area, then check out Red Cliffs Lodge (866-812-2002, www.redcliffslodge.com). Located about 14 miles off Highway 191, the lodge is well off the beaten path. The drive there is beautiful, as it travels over a two-lane road along the Colorado River.

The accessible riverside king suite (Room 101) features a roll-in shower with grab bars, good pathway access and level access to a private back deck. And don't forget to stop by the Moab Museum of Film and Western Heritage, just off the main lobby. The accessible entrance is located around the back, and the museum contains memorabilia from the over 120 movies shot in the area. There's no admission charge and it's a fun stop for film buffs.

TIMING

Although Bryce National Park is simply stunning after a winter snowfall, the optimal time to drive this route is from late spring to early fall. Summer can get pretty warm, so shoot for the fringe of that window if you have issues with the heat. Highway 67 to the north rim of the Grand Canyon is barricaded and closed from late October to mid May, and it's not unusual to get snow in Zion and Bryce in April. Not matter when you travel, take along tire chains or cables.

GREAT EATS

For a fun Western-themed dinner, head down to the north rim of the Grand Canyon and enjoy the Grand Canyon Cookout Experience. Held at the Grand Canyon Lodge North Rim (877-386-4383, www.GrandCanyon Forever.com), this nightly event features a chuck wagon dinner and lots of fun cowboy entertainment. Dinner is served in a remote tent where you'll chow down on slow cooked beef brisket, roasted chicken and all the trimmings. There's lift-equipped tram transportation to and from the lodge, with level access to the tent.

Truth be told, this isn't exactly a short detour or even a day trip, so plan to stay a few days and enjoy this remote part of the park. Accessible cabins with roll-in showers or tub/shower combinations are available at the lodge; and you just can't beat the view from the back deck.

DON'T MISS IT

Located midway between Bryce Canyon and Capitol Reef, the Burr Trail features a scenic drive trough Long Canyon with spectacular views of Circle Cliffs and Waterpocket Fold. Just make a right turn off Highway 12 in Boulder and follow the signs. This 30-mile drive winds through Grand Staircase-Escalante National Monument along a paved road, before it turns into a four-wheel drive road near Capitol Reef. Pack along a lunch and enjoy it at the wheelchair-accessible picnic shelter near the end of the paved road. You'll probably have it all to yourself, and the scenery is breathtaking.

LINGER ON IN THE GATEWAY

Save some time for a post road trip stopover in Las Vegas. From the glitz and glamour of the strip, to the rugged beauty that dots the surrounding landscape, there's no shortage of fun in this Entertainment Capital of the World.

■   Go anywhere you want, as all Las Vegas cab companies have wheelchair-accessible vehicles. Although accessible cabs are ubiquitous throughout the city, heavy traffic makes getting around pretty slow, so plan ahead and give yourself plenty of extra time.

■ Try your luck at the casinos. Most of the hotel casinos along the strip have accessible slot machines and many have lowered gaming tables.

■ Hop on the Las Vegas Monorail (702-699-8299, www.lvmonorail.com). It features roll-on access and it's a good way to get to the Las Vegas Convention Center from the strip.

■ Catch a ride on the Las Vegas Strip Trolley (702-382-1404). Most of the trolleys are lift-equipped, and they stop at the major strip hotels.

■ Enjoy one of the free outdoor shows along the strip. The Fountains at Bellagio features dancing waters accompanied by lights and music, while the Sirens of TI (Treasure Island) has more of a pirate theme. Both shows can be seen from level viewing areas on the street.

■ Get our of town and take a tour of Hoover Dam (702-494-2517, www.usbr.gov/lc/hooverdam). The one-hour Power Plant Tour is wheelchair accessible, and there's elevator access up to the Visitors Center Overlook, where you'll catch a great view of the Dam.

■ Top off your Las Vegas visit with a rafting trip on the Colorado River with Black Canyon Adventures (702-294-1414, www.blackcanyonadventures.com). There is ramped access to the dock, and the large raft features a 37-inch wide center aisle, which makes the trip doable for many people.

FLY-DRIVE OPTION

To make this a fly-drive vacation, fly to McCarran International Airport (702-261-5211, www.mccarran.com); then rent an accessible van at Ability Center (866-405-6806, www.abilitycenter.com), Better Life Mobility

Center (702-876-9606, www.betterlifemobility.com) or Wheelchair Getaways (888-824-7413, www.wheelchairgetaways.com).

ALTERNATE ENTRY POINTS

- From Flagstaff, take Highway 89 north to Jacob Lake, visit the north rim of the Grand Canyon, then head north to Bryce and Zion National Parks.

- From Denver, take Interstate 70 east to Crescent Junction, then go south to Arches and Canyonlands National Parks.

- From Salt Lake City, take Interstate 15 south to Highway 9 to Zion National Park.

VARIATION ON A THEME

The north rim of the Grand Canyon portion of this route can easily be done as a three or four day side trip from Flagstaff. Likewise, a visit to Arches and Canyonlands National Parks is a very doable short getaway from Salt Lake City. And if you'd like a longer trip, then head south to Kingman, Arizona from Las Vegas and connect to the Essential Arizona route.

- IF YOU GO
  - Zion National Park, (435) 772-3256, www.nps.gov/zion
  - Bryce Canyon National Park, (435) 834-5322, www.nps.gov/brca
  - Capitol Reef National Park, (435) 425-3791 ext. 111, www.nps.gov/care
  - Arches National Park, (435) 719-2299, www.nps.gov/arch
  - Canyonlands National Park, (435) 719-2313, www.nps.gov/cany
  - Las Vegas Convention and Visitors Authority, (702) 892-7575, www.visitlasvegas.com

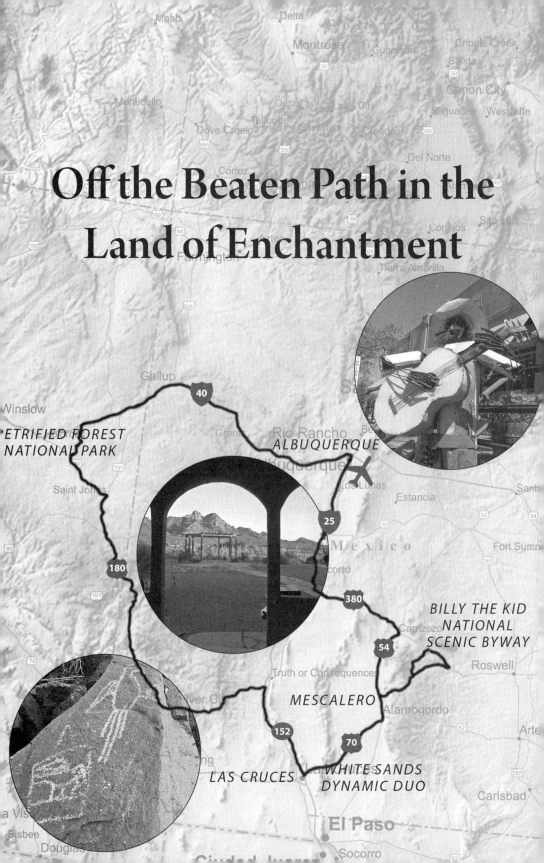

Off the Beaten Path in the Land of Enchantment

PETRIFIED FOREST NATIONAL PARK

ALBUQUERQUE

BILLY THE KID NATIONAL SCENIC BYWAY

MESCALERO

LAS CRUCES

WHITE SANDS DYNAMIC DUO

Although this route begins in Albuquerque, once you hit the road you'll enjoy some of the less touristed areas of New Mexico and Arizona. From Las Cruces to Mescalero and Billy the Kid Country, you'll enjoy quiet mountain towns and vast desert landscapes. Add in the Petrified Forest National Park, Acoma Pueblo and the White Sands Missile Museum, and you have a diverse, entertaining and somewhat quirky itinerary.

ROUTE

This route begins in Albuquerque and follows Interstate 25 south, then heads east on Highway 380 to Carrizozo. Next take Highway 54 south to Tularosa, and Highway 70 east to Mescalero. From there you can take a nice day trip on the Billy the Kid National Scenic Byway, through Ruidoso, Capitan and Hondo. Once you're back in Mescalero, head west on Highway 70, past White Sands National Monument to Las Cruces. Next take Interstate 25 north to Highway 152 to Santa Clara, where you'll connect to Highway 180 and cross over into Arizona. Continue north along Highway 180, then follow the signs through the Petrified Forest National Park to Interstate 40. To complete the loop, go east on Interstate 40, cross back into New Mexico and head towards Albuquerque.

ALONG THE WAY

Mescalero

Located just a short drive from Ruidoso, Mescalero makes a perfect home base for a visit to Billy the Kid Country. And the Inn of the Mountain Gods (800-545-9011, www.innofthemountaingods.com) is the ideal Mescalero lodging choice. Perched on the shore of Lake Mescalero, this mountain resort is comfortable, accessible and definitely off the beaten path.

Shopping in Old Town in Albuquerque, New Mexico.

The 273-room property is decorated with Native American artwork and features 10 accessible guest rooms. Access features include wide doorways, lever handles, lowered closet rods and good pathway access. All of the accessible rooms feature a lake or forest view, and each has a private balcony with a threshold ramp.

Eight of the accessible rooms have a bathroom with a tub/shower combination, while the other two have a roll-in shower. Bathroom access features include grab bars in the shower and around the toilet, a hand-held showerhead, a roll-under sink and a full five-foot turning radius. A portable shower chair is available upon request. All in all, the accessible rooms are very comfortable, and great attention was paid to even the smallest access details—such as the lowered robe hooks in the bathrooms.

There's no shortage of things to do at the resort, as it boasts a casino, several restaurants and even a conference center. There is barrier-free access to all the public areas, including the lobby and patio, where you can get some great mountain, lake and forest views. And if you'd like to explore the great outdoors, then check out the nicely accessible level trail around the lake.

Whatever your choice, you won't be disappointed with this quiet, comfortable and very accessible property.

Billy the Kid National Scenic Byway

Save at least one day for a leisurely drive along the Billy the Kid National Scenic Byway. The official route begins in Ruidoso and follows Highway 70 to Hondo, then turns on Highway 380 and travels through Lincoln and Capitan, before coming full circle with a short drive down Highway 48 back to Ruidoso. Not only is this route one of the most picturesque drives in New Mexico, but as Billy the Kid's former stomping grounds, it also boasts numerous reminders of that colorful era.

Make the Billy the Kid Visitors Center the first stop along your route. It's located near Ruidoso Downs on Highway 70. There's level access to the Visitors Center, with barrier-free pathways to the inside galleries. It's a great place to pick up some maps and get a good overview of the area.

The Hubbard Museum of the American West (505-378-4142, www. hubbardmuseum.org), which is located next door, is also worth a stop. Just follow the signs to the accessible parking area in the lower lot. The museum features wide doorways, good pathway access and elevator access to all levels. Inside there are a variety of exhibits on the old West, with equal emphasis on the Native American, Hispanic and Pioneer cultures.

Located about 35 miles from Ruidoso, Lincoln is also worth a stop. The town remains largely as it was in the 1800s, when Billy the Kid made his famous last escape from the Lincoln County Courthouse. For a good overview of the town, stop in at the Anderson Freeman Museum and Visitors Center, which features level access to the main entrance and barrier-free access inside. And don't miss the old Lincoln County Courthouse, as it's the most interesting site in town. There is ramped access in the back, but you need to tell the clerk to unlock the door. Although the second floor is only accessible by stairs, you can still get a good feel for the era by exploring the first floor.

Last but not least, don't miss the Smokey Bear Historical Park (505-354-2748, www.smokeybearpark.com), just up the road in Capitan. The museum is dedicated to Smokey, who was found in the nearby Capitan Mountains after a wildfire destroyed his home. The Visitors Center features exhibits about the history of Smokey Bear, while the boardwalk nature trail includes vegetation from six different climate zones. And of course, Smokey's grave is prominently located along the trail.

All in all it's a very scenic drive, with lots of interesting and accessible stops along the way; so pack a picnic lunch, and enjoy your day in Billy the Kid Country.

White Sands Dynamic Duo

Although they share part of a name, White Sands National Monument and the White Sands Missile Range Museum are vastly different entities. One showcases the natural beauty of the area, while the other focuses on the nuclear history; but both are worth a visit on the drive from Alamogordo to Las Cruces.

White Sands National Monument (505-679-2599, nps.gov/whsa/index.htm) is a great place to get a close look at the snow white sand dunes and learn about the delicate desert ecosystem. The Visitors Center features a variety of interpretive exhibits and includes accessible parking, level access to the building and accessible restrooms.

The best way to see the park is in your car, so just follow Dune Drive out to the end of the road. Along the way there are a number of interpretive exhibits and a nicely accessible boardwalk across the dunes. At the end of the drive, there's a large parking lot, accessible restrooms and a number of accessible picnic tables. Additionally, there's a very small nature center which has ramped access.

Admittedly the dunes are not wheelchair-accessible, but they seem to be a big attraction for kids with snow saucers. It's fun to watch, but to be honest the drive is worth the price of admission. It's really a great way to get a closer look at the unique desert landscape.

The White Sands Missile Range Museum (575-678-8824, www.wsmr-history.org) is located 16 miles down Highway 70 on the base. There's no admission charge, but the easiest way to access it is to walk on the base. There's accessible parking near the gate, and a barrier-free pathway over to the museum.

There's level access to the main museum building which presents a comprehensive history of the atomic age, plus some interesting displays about prehistoric inhabitants and the Wild West in southern New Mexico. Exhibits include everything from vintage telecom equipment and old cameras used to

An assortment of rockets at the White Sands Missile Museum.

film missile tests, to weather equipment, bomb shelter supplies and missile models and plans.

Across the parking lot, the wheelchair-accessible V-2 Building features a V-2 rocket with a number of interpretive signs. And outside in Missile Park, you'll find everything from Patriot and Pershing missiles to a Howitzer missile launcher and even a Huey helicopter. There's a paved pathway through the park, and it's a great place to learn about military history. Plus, it's not very touristed, so you'll rarely find any crowds there.

Las Cruces

Las Cruces is a great place to spend a few days and soak up the local culture. And if you're in the market for some turquoise jewelry, you'll also find good deals there. That's two good reasons to linger on in Las Cruces.

The best place to begin your visit is at the Branigan Cultural Center (575-541-2155, www.lascruces-culture.org). Located in the downtown mall on Water Street, it houses historical objects, old photographs and artwork by local artists. There is level access to the main entrance and barrier-free access to all of the galleries.

Next door you'll find the Museum of Art (575-541-2137) which features contemporary work by local artists. There is level access to the gallery, and as with the Branigan Cultural Center, there's no admission charge.

If you are looking for some locally crafted merchandise, then hit the mall on Wednesday and Saturday mornings for the Farmers & Crafts Market (www.lascrucesfarmersmarket.org). You'll find good deals on silver and turquoise jewelry, and ample space to navigate around the booths.

Save some time to visit the Bicentennial Log Cabin and the New Mexico Railroad and Transport Museum while you're downtown. Built in the late 1800s, the Bicentennial Log Cabin (505-541-2155) features ramp access and it's just across the street from the mall. There's no admission charge, but reservations are required.

The New Mexico Railroad and Transportation Museum (505-541-2155) is located several blocks from the mall, on the corner of Mesilla Street and Las Cruces Avenue. Located in the old Santa Fe Depot it's a must-see for train buffs. It boasts exhibits which focus on the history of train travel in the area, including old train memorabilia, photographs, logs and a model freight train. There is level access to the depot and there's no admission charge. Plan ahead though, as this museum is only open on Saturday mornings.

Last but not least, don't miss the New Mexico Farm & Ranch Heritage Museum (575-522-4100, www.frhm.org), which focuses on the history of farming and ranching in the region. Located off Interstate 25 near the University exit, this interactive museum features plenty of accessible parking, level access to the entrance, accessible restrooms and barrier-free access to all of the inside galleries. Loaner wheelchairs are available at the front desk, and outside there's also level access around the yard exhibits.

And for a very accessible place to rest your head, book a few nights at the Dream Catcher Inn (505-522-3035, www.dreamcatcherinn.com). This three-room property is located in the middle of the desert, and features two accessible rooms with roll-in showers and one with a tub/shower combination. The access is very nicely done, and the daily breakfast is to die for. It's a combination you just can't beat.

Petrified Forest National Park

The Petrified Forest National Park is an ideal choice for wheelers and slow walkers, as there are a number of short trails and scenic vistas located along the main park road. The 28-mile drive takes about an hour, but save some time to stop along the way to get a closer look at the world's largest collection of petrified wood.

To begin your journey, just follow the signs to the south park entrance from Highway 180. For a good overview of the park, make sure and stop at the Rainbow Forest Museum, located just past the entrance station. There are a number of interpretive exhibits inside, but the Giant Log Trail out back is the big attraction at this stop. It's a great place to get a close look at some large petrified logs; and although this loop trail isn't technically wheelchair-accessible, the first half-mile is do-able, as it's fairly level and devoid of steps.

Located a little father north of the museum, the Crystal Forest Trail is also worth a stop. Although the right side of the .75-mile loop is a bit of an uphill climb, the area to the left, is level, paved and pretty close to some sizable petrified logs. Even if you can't go the whole way, you'll still be able to see some remnants of this ancient forest.

For a great driving tour through the desert be sure and take the Blue Mesa Loop, located just off the main road, a little north of the Crystal Forest Trail. This 3.5-mile spur features spectacular views of the colorful badlands, several log falls and even some massive pedestal logs.

Another must-do is the Puerco Pueblo trail, located near the north entrance. This .3-mile loop winds around the ruins of a 100-room pueblo, which dates back some 700–1200 years. As an added bonus, the rocks along the south end of the trail are dotted with pertroglyphs. Although the trail is paved, there are some cracks and uneven pavement along the way, so some wheelchair-users may need a little help. There is also a step up to one of the petroglyph viewing spots; however, you can easily see them without taking the step.

And don't miss the Painted Desert Inn, located just shy of the north park entrance. Once a popular stop for weary Route 66 travelers, the inn is now a National Historic Landmark. You can get a good glimpse at the inn from outside, but the best part of this stop is the wheelchair-accessible overlook behind the inn. Just take the paved trail to the right of the inn, for a stunning view of the Painted Desert badlands. After you've had your fill, head out the north park entrance and continue east along on Interstate 40 to Albuquerque.

Timing

You'll likely hit snow in Billy the Kid Country in winter, so that's really not the best season for this drive. Likewise, summers are dreadfully hot in Southern New Mexico, so that's another time to avoid. Fall and spring are pleasant, with fall getting top billing. The fall colors are stunning along the Billy the Kid National Scenic Byway, and harvest festivals are ubiquitous during that time of year. A word of warning though—if you don't like crowds, avoid Albuquerque during the first week of October, as visitors flock to the very popular Albuquerque Balloon Fiesta.

Great Eats

For some authentic New Mexican cuisine, stop in at El Pinto Restaurant (505-898-1771, www.elpinto.com) in Albuquerque. Opened in 1962 as a one room restaurant, today this Albuquerque institution is the largest restaurant in the state. But large doesn't mean impersonal, as the atmosphere is intimate and relaxed; with a fountain studded courtyard and secluded nooks for that special lunch or dinner date. Access is good, with plenty of accessible parking and level access to the inside dining area and courtyard. There is one step down in the bar area, where part of the lunch buffet is set up, but the staff is happy to assist if you can't manage it. The El Pinto lunch buffet is a local favorite, and their Sunday brunch features Eggs Benedict with a red chili Hollandaise Sauce. And don't forget to buy some El Pinto salsa for the road—their jalapeno variety is delicious.

Don't Miss It

Located 45 miles west of Albuquerque, the Acoma Pueblo (800-747-0181, www.acomaskycity.org) is well worth a visit, if only for the scenery along the way. Nicknamed Sky City, this ancient village is perched on top of a 367-foot sandstone bluff, and is considered the oldest continually inhabited pueblo in the US. Private vehicles are not allowed on pueblo land, but there is space in front of the tour bus for a folding wheelchair. They have a modified tour for slow walkers that lasts approximately 25 minutes and stops at the church, the plaza and at a few vendors. It's important to note that the ground may be bumpy and uneven in some places, but it's doable for some folks, and a great opportunity to tour an inhabited pueblo.

Acoma Pueblo—"Sky City"—is the oldest continually inhabited pueblo in the US.

Linger on in the Gateway

Albuquerque is the perfect place to get a taste of New Mexican culture, before or after your road trip. So linger on and enjoy the food, learn about the history of the area and shop for some Native American jewelry. There's certainly plenty of accessible things to do in this Southwestern cultural Mecca.

- Take a History, Legends and Lore walking or rolling tour of Old Town with Tours of Old Town (505-246-8687, www.toursofoldtown.com). This leisurely one-mile walk is an excellent option for wheelers and slow walkers, with a level route and several opportunities to sit and rest along the way.

- Shop till you drop in Old Town, at the outdoor vendor area across the street from the Old Town Plaza on San Felipe Avenue. There's level access to the area, where you'll find local artists selling handcrafted jewelry and pottery. The quality is excellent, and the prices are very reasonable.

- Visit the Albuquerque Museum of Art & History (505-243-7255, www.cabq.gov/museum). This top-rated museum features art and artifacts that chronicle over 400 years of Southwestern history, and includes an impressive sculpture garden. Access is excellent throughout, with plenty of accessible parking, level access to the building and barrier-free access to the galleries and sculpture garden.

- While you're in the area, walk across the street and explore the New Mexico Museum of Natural History (505-841-2800, www. nmnaturalhistory.org). This Albuquerque mainstay features barrier-free access throughout the building, which boasts eight permanent exhibit halls, a theater and a planetarium. Don't miss "Startup," a fascinating exhibit that chronicles the personal computer revolution, which got its start in Albuquerque.

- Learn about ballooning—an integral part of the local culture—at the Abruzzo Albuquerque International Balloon Museum (505-768-6020, www.cabq.gov/balloon). Located next to Balloon Fiesta Park, this eclectic museum features barrier-free access to the galleries, elevator access to all levels and plenty of accessible parking.

- Check out the art museum at the Natural Hispanic Cultural Center (505-246-2261, www.nhccnm.org). With level access and barrier-free pathways throughout the exhibition space, the museum hosts a variety of exhibits with a focus on Hispanic artists and culture. Slow walkers should note that it's a long walk from the parking lot, so plan to bring along a wheelchair if you have one.

- Learn about the 19 pueblos of New Mexico at the Indian Pueblo Cultural Center (505-843-7270, www.indianpueblo.org). There is barrier-free access throughout the complex, with plenty of accessible parking in front. Inside, interpretive exhibits chronicle the history of the Pueblo Indians; and individual exhibits showcase pottery, jewelry and other handcrafted pieces from each tribe.

FLY-DRIVE OPTION

To make this a fly-drive vacation, fly to Albuquerque International Sunport (505-244-7700, www.cabq.gov/airport); then rent an accessible van at

New Horizon Vans (505-884-2492, www.newhorizonvans.com) or Wheelchair Getaways (800-408-2626, www.wheelchairgetaways.com).

ALTERNATE ENTRY POINTS

- From Santa Fe, take Interstate 25 south to Albuquerque.
- From El Paso, take Interstate 10 to Interstate 25, to Las Cruces.
- From Amarillo, head west on Interstate 40 to Albuquerque.

VARIATION ON A THEME

If you only have a week, spend four days in Albuquerque and then head down to Mescalero and explore the Billy the Kid National Scenic Byway for the balance of your time. The Albuquerque and Acoma parts of this itinerary also make a nice three-day add-on to a Santa Fe visit. If you'd like a longer trip, then take Interstate 25 north to Santa Fe and continue along on The Rockies and Beyond route.

- IF YOU GO
    - Billy the Kid National Scenic Byway, (877) 784-3676, www.billybyway.com
    - Las Cruces Convention & Visitors Bureau, (505) 541-2444, www.lascrucescvb.org
    - Petrified Forest National Park, (928) 524-6228, www.nps.gov/pefo
    - Albuquerque Convention & Visitors Bureau, (800) 284-2282, www.itsatrip.org

Essential Arizona

GRAND CANYON
NATIONAL PARK

HISTORIC
ROUTE 66

SEDONA

SCOTTSDALE

PHOENIX

SAN
DIEGO

TOMBSTONE

Kartchner
Caverns

This scenic drive through the Grand Canyon state features all the essential elements of the quintessential family vacation. From the Wild West shootouts in Tombstone and the Native American cliff dwellings at Montezuma Castle National Monument, to the red rocks of Sedona and the magnificent Grand Canyon vistas, this itinerary is packed full of family fun, great scenery and off-the-beaten-track finds. Top it off with a drive along an original stretch of the Mother Road, for a fitting end to a perfect road trip.

ROUTE

This route begins in San Diego and follows Interstate 8 east across California and into Arizona, before merging with Interstate 10 and continuing on through Tucson. Next it's south on Highway 90 to Kartchner Caverns, then on to Tombstone on Highway 80. Continue the loop and rejoin Interstate 10 and head east to Highway 191; then take Highway 70 east to Highway 60, and continue on to Phoenix. From there take Interstate 17 north to Highway 179 to Sedona, with a side trip out to Montezuma Castle National Monument and Clarkdale. Next, continue north along Highway 89, then head west on Interstate 40 to Williams, where you'll connect with Highway 64 to the Grand Canyon. After your canyon visit, continue west along Interstate 40 to Historic Route 66 in Seligman, then rejoin Interstate 40 in Kingman and continue back into California. To complete the loop take Highway 95 south, then head west on Interstate 10, to Interstate 15 to San Diego.

ALONG THE WAY

Tombstone

If you'd like to learn a little about the old west, then plan to stay a few days in Tombstone. Located in southern Arizona, the historic part of the city is closed off to vehicle traffic, so it's perfectly acceptable to walk or roll right

OK Corral Gunfight site in Tombstone, Arizona.

down the middle of the street. Additionally the boardwalk sidewalks have curb-cuts at every corner, and many of the shops and restaurants have a level entry.

If you'd prefer a guided tour, then try a Tombstone Trolley Tour (520-995-3090, www.tombstonetrolleytours.com). There is lift access to the trolley, with space to park two wheelchairs aboard. The tour departs from the trolley office at Fourth and Toughnut Streets, passes by the historic sites, and then stops briefly at the Boothill Graveyard. And along the way you'll learn about the true history of Tombstone and how the OK Corral gunfight really went down.

The Rose Tree Museum (520-457-3326), located just across the street from the trolley office, is also worth a visit. The museum takes its name from the giant rose tree planted in back, and features a well-curated collection of vintage clothing, weapons, photographs, mining tools and historic documents. And even though it's located in a historic building there's level access to the front door, with adequate space to maneuver a wheelchair inside; and ramp access to the back porch, where you can view the rose tree.

For a good primer on Tombstone history, the Tombstone Courthouse (520-457-3311, www.pr.state.az.us/Parks/TOCO/index.html) is a mandatory stop. This historic building, which formerly housed the courtroom, jail and gallows, now features some excellent interpretive exhibits on the Tombstone area. There are two steps at the front entrance; but there's a wheelchair-lift just to the right. Inside, there's barrier-free access throughout the first floor, however the second-floor exhibits can only be accessed by a flight of stairs. And although there are nine steps down to the gallows out back, employees are happy to open the accessible side gate upon request.

Last but not least, you just can't leave Tombstone without a visit to the Boothill Graveyard. There is accessible parking near front entrance, with level access through the gift shop to the graveyard. Although it's fairly level at the top, the gravel surface may be a challenge for some wheelchair-users. And if you can't manage the pathways, you can still get a good view from the parking lot.

Phoenix-Scottsdale

Plan to linger on a few days in the Phoenix-Scottsdale area to soak up the culture, do a little shopping and enjoy the desert landscape.

Frank Lloyd Wright's Taliesin West (www.franklloydwright.org) tops the cultural must-see list in Scottsdale. Although this architectural masterpiece wasn't built to be accessible, today there's ramp access to the gift shop and a barrier-free route on all the house tours. The tours are excellent, and it's a rare opportunity for wheelchair-users to go inside a Frank Lloyd Wright structure.

If you'd like to do little gallery hopping and shopping, then head over to Old Town Scottsdale. Located in the middle of the downtown area, this historic oasis offers a wide selection of galleries, jewelry shops and artisan boutiques. This pedestrian friendly area features wide sidewalks, ubiquitous curb-cuts, accessible shops and a free lift-equipped shuttle. And don't miss the Thursday evening Art Walks, where participating galleries showcase their creations and provide light snacks and entertainment. Visit www.ScottsdaleGalleries.com for Art Walk schedules.

There are also a good number of cultural attractions in neighboring Phoenix, with the Pueblo Grande Museum and Archaeological Park

(602-495-0900, www.pueblogrande.com) topping the list. This archeological museum takes an in-depth look at the Hohokam Indians, and features barrier-free access to all of the interpretive exhibits. Outside there's a wide paved trail through the archeological site, with reproductions of Hohokam homes and a ballcourt. Hit this site early in the day though, to beat the heat.

For an interesting look at the desert ecosystem, check out the Desert Botanical Garden (480-941-1225, www.dbg.org). Located on 1,450 acres near the Phoenix Zoo, this Phoenix mainstay features more than 50,000 plants, a butterfly pavilion and five themed interpretive trails. Access is good throughout the complex, with level access on most of the trails.

And if you only have time for one Phoenix museum, make it The Heard Museum (602-252-8840, www.heard.org). Billed as *the* place to learn about Southwestern Native American cultures, it features accessible parking and barrier-free access throughout the galleries. Best bet is to spend a whole day there, with a noon-time lunch break in the relaxing courtyard café.

Sedona and Beyond

Sedona is a place to get away from it all, enjoy the scenery and do a bit of gallery hopping. You'll start to get a taste of the spectacular scenery just a few miles south of the city, when you enter red rock country. For a great view of it all, stop at Bell Rock Overlook, located at milepost 309.8, just a mile north of Tequa Plaza. The upper part of Bell Rock Trail is wide, level and made of hard-packed dirt. It's doable for most wheelchair-users, but even if you can't manage it, you'll still get a great view from the overlook.

On the cultural scene, there's no shortage of galleries in Sedona; but the Tlaquepaque Arts and Crafts Village (928-282-4838, www.tlaq.com) is one of the most popular gallery hopping spots. There is level access to most of the shops, plenty of accessible parking and lots of room to wheel around the peaceful courtyards. It's a fun place to spend the day, do a little shopping, visit with the artists and get a bite to eat.

Save at least one day for a trip into the surrounding countryside and a ride on the Verde Canyon Railroad (800-528-7245, www.verdecanyonrr.com). The train departs from the old mining town of Clarkdale, which is located south of Sedona on Highway 89. There is lift access to the train; and although the lift has some weight restrictions, loaner wheelchairs are available, and the staff is very creative and accommodating. It's a great day trip and probably the most accessible way to enjoy the beautiful red rock formations that surround Sedona.

After your train ride, take Highway 89 to Highway 260, cross Interstate 17 and follow the signs to Montezuma Castle National Monument (928-567-3322, www.nps.gov/moca). This five-level cliff dwelling was constructed by the Sinagua Indians over 600 years ago, and it's viewable from a paved trail around the ruins. The first quarter-mile of the trail is accessible, but after that it gets a bit steep. Still, you can still get a good look at the site from the accessible part of the trail.

And for a very accessible place to overnight in Sedona, check out the Lodge at Sedona (800-617-4467, www.lodgeatsedona.com). Surrounded by red rock formations, the property includes the accessible Meadow Breeze Suite with a private entrance and a roll-in shower. This spacious suite is furnished with a king-sized bed, a fireplace and a two-person Jacuzzi tub. And breakfast is a grand affair here, with a full five course meal served al fresco on the wheelchair-accessible deck.

Grand Canyon National Park

The south rim of the Grand Canyon—which is definitely worth a visit—is the most accessible area of this popular national park. That said, it's also the most congested, with private vehicles prohibited on some park roads. The good news is, the free shuttle bus system is now 100% accessible. Visitors with a disabled parking placard can also pick up a permit to drive on the restricted roads at the Visitors Center; which makes this site a good choice for wheelers and slow walkers.

There's plenty to do on the South Rim, starting with the accessible Rim Trail, which runs alongside the canyon. This wide paved trail is mostly level and very wheelable, from the Hopi House to just past the Arizona Grill. The Arizona Grill makes an excellent lunch stop; and if you are seated at the right table, you can get a pretty good canyon view. The side entrance has a few steps, but the canyon-side entrance is accessible.

If you want to overnight in the park, Xanterra Resorts (888-297-2757, www.grandcanyonlodges.com) offers several accessible choices. Thunderbird Lodge has accessible guest rooms with roll-in showers, while El Tovar Lodge and Kachina Lodge feature accessible rooms with tub/shower combinations and grab bars. Maswik Lodge and Yavapai Lodge offer accessible rooms with either bathroom configurations.

Save at least one day to explore the East Rim Drive, as it offers some great windshield views and it's one of the less touristed areas in the park. There are several overlooks between Yaki Point and Grandview Point where you can just pull in and enjoy the view; but there are plenty of other stops along the way, where you can get out and explore.

Grandview Point features accessible parking with level access to the canyon overlook, while BuggeIn Hill has an accessible picnic area with a good view. There is accessible parking at Moran Point, with level access out to the overlook; however, there's one step down to the end viewpoint.

Don't miss the Tusayan Museum & Ruins, which features artifacts from the Pueblo Indians. There is level access to the small museum; however, it can get a bit crowded. Outside there is a paved .1 mile trail through the ruins. It's nicely done—level with lots of benches along the way.

The last stop on the drive, Desert View, offers the most services, including a gift shop, a store, a service station and accessible restrooms. The ground floor of the Desert Watchtower is wheelchair-accessible, but the tower itself is only accessible by stairs. Still, there are some great views from the overlook in front of the building.

Historic Route 66

There's no better way to wrap up a road trip, than with a short drive along Historic Route 66. Known as the Mother Road, this Chicago to Los Angeles route was America's first interstate highway. Today it's largely abandoned; however, this Arizona slice of the historic road is paved, passable and worth the slight detour.

Finding Historic Route 66 is easy. Just take exit 123 off Interstate 40, about 30 miles west of Williams. Then follow the signs, through Seligman and continue west on the historic route.

One kitschy stop worth a visit along the way is Grand Canyon Caverns (928-422-3223, www.gccaverns.com). Located a mile or so off the road between Seligman and Peach Springs, it's a fun photo stop. It's a true old fashioned roadside attraction in every sense of the definition.

The Hackberry General Store on Historic Route 66 in Hackberry, Arizona.

Unfortunately the caverns themselves are not accessible, however the adjacent restaurant is.

Once back on Historic Route 66, you'll pass by some old Burma Shave Signs, cross a Hualapai Indian reservation and pass through Peach Springs, Truxon and Valentine, before you roll into Hackberry. Here you'll find the Hackberry General Store (www.hackberrygeneralstore.com), which features a vintage gas station, a soda fountain and another great photo opportunity.

There's just a dirt parking area in front, but it's usually not that crowded, so there's plenty of room. Outside there's a treasure trove of memorabilia including some rusted out old cars, signs, tools and a nicely restored 1957 Corvette.

There's level access to the soda fountain and souvenir shop, which is packed with more memorabilia. Don't forget to take a gander in the men's restroom, which is tastefully decorated with vintage pinup posters. Once you've had your fill of nostalgia, continue on to Kingman.

Once you hit Kingman, check out the Powerhouse Route 66 Museum (928-753-5001), before you hop back on the interstate. Housed in a former substation, it features photos from the Dust Bowl era, information on the origin of those ubiquitous Burma Shave signs, and a movie about the rise, fall and the rebirth of the Mother Road. There's accessible parking in front with elevator access in the museum. Additionally, the museum boasts some very nice accessible restrooms, which are somewhat scarce along the historic section of the Mother Road.

TIMING

· ·

Although the roads along this route are all passable in the summer, it's far from the ideal time to visit. Large crowds in the Grand Canyon, coupled with high temperatures in the south, can somewhat take away from the whole summer experience. On the other hand, fall and spring are excellent times to visit, but try and avoid the Grand Canyon from November to March. During this time, the weather can be unpredictable and snow and ice can make driving a real challenge.

GREAT EATS

· ·

For a touch of nostalgia—and a great milkshake— stop in at Mrs. D'z Route 66 Diner (www.mrdzrt 66diner.com), across the street from the Powerhouse Route 66 Museum in Kingman. There's accessible parking in front, with level access to the front door. Inside, there's good pathway access, but no accessible restrooms. The décor is retro, the food is filling and the service is good. The menu includes the usual burger and sandwich fare, along with a decent selection of pizzas, pasta dishes and dinner specials. And if you're in

Mr. D'z Route 66 Diner in Kingman, Arizona.

between meals, try a banana split, a hot fudge sundae or even a popsicle float. Outside seating is also available, and it's a great place to sit back and watch vintage cars cruise along the Mother Road.

DON'T MISS IT

Located approximately 1½ hours southwest of Tucson, Kartchner Caverns (520-486-4100, http://pr.state. az.us/parks/KACA) is a required stop on any Arizona itinerary, as these newly discovered caves were developed with wheelchair access in mind. And although you can't totally ramp Mother Nature, the 1½-hour cave tours travel along paved pathways, with plenty of places to rest along the way. For the most part the pathways are fairly level and doable for wheelchair-users, however there are alternative viewing points for those who can't make it up some of the steeper grades. The tram that transports visitors up to the cave entrance is also ramped, so you can stay in your wheelchair for the ride.

Wheelchairs and scooters are permitted in the cave, as long as they are less than 30 inches wide and 40 inches long. Crutches and walkers are prohibited, but rubber-tipped canes are permitted. Loaner wheelchairs are also available. Don't miss the accessible hummingbird garden in front of the Visitors Center, which features paved pathways and interpretive signs—and of course plenty of colorful hummingbirds.

LINGER ON IN THE GATEWAY

San Diego—which has picture perfect weather year round—is a great place for a relaxing post road trip break. And thanks to the efforts of local advocates and Accessible San Diego, there's a wide choice of accessible activities in this Southern California playground.

- Take the Old Town Trolley (619-298-8687, www.oldtowntrolley.com) through San Diego, and stop along the way to visit Old Town, the Gaslamp Quarter, Balboa Park and Coronado Island. You can start the tour at any trolley stop, and hop on and off of the lift-equipped trolley as you please.

- Enjoy an exciting land and water adventure on a Seal Tour (619-298-8687, www.sealtours.com). This 90-minute narrated tour focuses on military history and splashes down into San Diego Bay for the last twenty minutes of the tour. It's a fun tour for all ages, with lift access to the tour vehicle.

- Go wild at the famous San Diego Zoo (619-234-3153, www.sandiegozoo.org). Although there are a number of steep areas in the zoo, a free shuttle service for disabled visitors is also available.

- Visit the San Diego Wild Animal Park (760-747-8702, www.wildanimalpark.org), located about 30 miles northeast of downtown San Diego.

Although there are a few patches of rugged terrain in this rural park, a free courtesy shuttle is available to the steeper areas. The park also publishes an access map, which highlights the most accessible routes.

- Enjoy the shows at Sea World (619-226-3901, www.seaworld.com). Access is excellent throughout most of the park, including barrier-free access to the restaurants, shows, gift shops and restrooms.

- Hit the beach and cruise around in a motorized beach wheelchair. They're available at lifeguard stations at Coronado, Oceanside, Mission Beach, Silver Strands and Imperial Beach.

FLY-DRIVE OPTION

To make this a fly-drive vacation, fly to San Diego International Airport (619-400-2404, www.san. org); then rent an accessible van at Ability Center (866-405-6806, www.abilitycenter.com), Better Life Mobility Center (619-474-4072, www.betterlifemobility.com) or Wheelchair Getaways (619-474-4883, www.wheelchairgetaways.com).

ALTERNATE ENTRY POINTS

- From Las Vegas, take Highway 93 to Kingman, then continue east on Historic Route 66.

- From Albuquerque, take Interstate 40 west to Flagstaff, then continue west to the Grand Canyon.

- From San Francisco, head east and then take Highway 5 south to San Diego.

VARIATION ON A THEME

I f your time is limited, you can easily do the Sedona leg of this trip as a two or three night side trip from Phoenix. Likewise, it's easy to connect from Las Vegas to Kingman to do the Grand Canyon portion of the route. The Tombstone and Kartchner Caverns loop is also a very doable two or three night trip from Tucson. If you'd prefer a longer road trip, then take Interstate 40 east in Flagstaff, and connect to the Off the Beaten Path in the Land of Enchantment route in the Petrified Forest National Park.

- IF YOU GO
  - Tombstone Chamber of Commerce, (888) 457-3929, www.tombstonechamber.com
  - Greater Phoenix Convention & Visitors Bureau, (877) 225-5749, www.phoenixcvb.com
  - Scottsdale Convention & Visitors Bureau, (800) 782-1117, www.scottsdalecvb.com
  - Grand Canyon National Park, (928) 638-7888, www.nps.gov/grca
  - Accessible San Diego, (619) 325-7550, www.asd.travel
  - San Diego Convention & Visitors Bureau, (619) 236-1212, www.sandiego.org

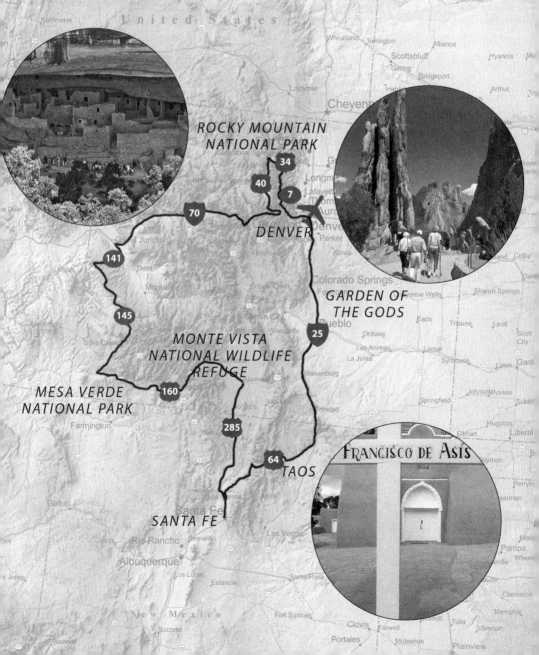

The Rockies and Beyond

ROCKY MOUNTAIN
NATIONAL PARK

DENVER

GARDEN OF
THE GODS

MONTE VISTA
NATIONAL WILDLIFE
REFUGE

MESA VERDE
NATIONAL PARK

FRANCISCO DE ASÍS

TAOS

SANTA FE

Although this trip presents an ambitious itinerary, with several stretches of long drives; you'll be rewarded with some spectacular scenery along the way. From the grandeur of the Rocky Mountains to the intense beauty of the Northern New Mexican landscape, variety is the key word along this route. Add in a good dose of Native American culture at the Taos Pueblo and Mesa Verde National Park, plus some relaxing spa time at Ojo Caliente, and you've got a road trip that will surely please all your senses.

ROUTE

This route begins in Denver and follows Interstate 25 south into New Mexico, then continues west on Highway 64 to Taos. Then it's south on Highway 518 and Highway 76, to Highway 285 to Santa Fe. Next it's north on Highway 285, through Ojo Caliente and back into Colorado, to Highway 160 to Monte Vista. Continue west on Highway 160 with a slight detour south to Mesa Verde National Park near Cortez. Next take Highway 145 to Highway 141 to Interstate 70. Head east on the interstate to Highway 40 to Granby, then connect to Highway 34 through Rocky Mountain National Park to Estes Park. To complete the loop, follow Highway 7 south, then connect to Highway 72 and take Highway 119 south to Interstate 70, and head east to Denver.

ALONG THE WAY

Taos

There's certainly no shortage of cultural diversions in the Taos area. At the top of the list is the Taos Pueblo (575-758-1028, www.taospueblo.com), which is located just outside of town. These multi-storied adobe buildings have been inhabited for over 1,000 years, and although it's a National

Historic Landmark, it's still doable for most folks in dry weather. There are level dirt pathways throughout the pueblo, but some of the buildings have narrow doorways or steps. Still, it's worth a visit for a glimpse of Pueblo life.

Another must-see is the Millicent Rogers Museum (575-758-2462, www.millicentrogers.org), located near Highway 64 and Taos Ski Valley Road. Housed in a 1940s adobe, the museum features an impressive collection of Native American jewelry, textiles and pottery. And even though it's a historic structure, it features a ramped entry and level access to most of the galleries. And for a great mid-day break, pack along a picnic lunch and enjoy it out back.

While you're in the neighborhood, don't miss the view from the Rio Grande Gorge Bridge, just a 10-minute drive away. Although you have to be able to climb up a foot-high step to access the walkway across the bridge, the view is just as impressive if you drive over the bridge.

Back in town, be sure and stop in at the Kit Carson Home and Museum (505-758-4945, www.kitcarsonhomeandmuseum.com), located just off the Plaza. The main entrance is in back; but just ask someone to unlock the more accessible front entrance. From there you can access the majority of the rooms and get a good primer on Southwestern history.

And don't miss the historic San Francisco de Asis Church, which is located just south of town, near the post office. This Taos icon features plenty of parking in the dirt parking lot, with level access to the sanctuary.

For a fun day excursion, hop on the historic Cumbres & Toltec Scenic Railroad (888-286-2737, www.cumbrestoltec.com). The train departs from the Antonito Depot—which is just an hour from Taos—and travels along the Colorado-New Mexico border to Charma. Passengers are then bussed back to Antonito; and both the bus and the train are lift-equipped. The staff is very accommodating; and it's a great opportunity to see an 1880s locomotive in action.

And for an accessible place to overnight, check into the San Geronimo Lodge (575-751-3776, www.sangeronimolodge.com). Rooms 4 and 5 feature wide doorways, level thresholds, good pathway access, open-framed beds and roll-in showers. Both of them also include kiva fireplaces for those chilly evenings. Top it all off with a tasty breakfast, and it's hard to pass up overnighting in this historic adobe lodge.

Santa Fe

Although there's no shortage of lodging in Santa Fe, it's best to base yourself near the Plaza. This cultural heart of the city is surrounded by museums and historic attractions, and features numerous benches throughout the small park.

Located just minutes from the Plaza, the Don Gaspar Inn (505-986-8664, www.dongaspar.com) is a great choice. The accessible Olive Tree Room features good pathway access and a spacious bathroom with a roll-in shower. It's a fun historic inn, with a very accommodating staff. And although the breakfast area is only accessible by steps, the innkeeper is happy to deliver a tray to your room if you can't manage them.

You can spend days exploring the Plaza museums, all of which are within easy walking distance of one another. At the top of the list is the Palace of the Governors (505-476-5100, www.palaceofthegovernors.org), located just across the street from the Plaza. This one-time regional head-quarters for the Spanish government now boasts good access and barrier-free pathways to exhibits about New Mexico history. And just outside, you'll find an impressive collection of Native American vendors selling their hand-crafted creations.

Next door, The Museum of Fine Arts (505-476-5072, www.mfa santafe.org) showcases local talent and contains traditional as well as contemporary pieces. There is ramp access to the historic building and freight elevator access to the second floor. Don't miss the WPA murals in the courtyard.

Just down the street, the Georgia O'Keeffe Museum (505-946-1000, www.okeeffemuseum.org) is dedicated to the art of O'Keefe and to the study of American Modernism. Access is excellent throughout the single level gallery, with free loaner wheelchairs available at the front desk.

And if you still haven't had your fill of museums, catch the accessible M Line (505-955-2001) bus up to Museum Hill. The bus stops on Sheridan Street, just around the corner from the Museum of Fine Arts; and the fare is just $1.

Up on Museum Hill the bus stops in front of Milner Plaza, where you'll find the Museum of International Folk Art (505-476-1200, www. internationalfolkart.org), the Museum Cafe and the Museum of Indian Arts & Culture (505-476-1250, www.miaclab.org). There is elevator access up to the plaza level, and all of the museums offer barrier-free access.

Wide, smooth pathways and sweeping vistas at Monte Vista National Wildlife Refuge.

And if you're up for a short walk, check out the Wheelright Museum of the American Indian (505-982-4636, www.wheelwright.org) and the Museum of Spanish Colonial Art (505-982-2226, www.spanishcolonial. org). They both feature good access, but they are located next door and across the street from Milner Plaza. Truth be told, you could also spend several days exploring Museum Hill!

Monte Vista National Wildlife Refuge

Located in Southern Colorado, approximately 50 miles north of the New Mexico border, Monte Vista is a pretty unremarkable town—unremarkable except for the very unique Monte Vista National Wildlife Refuge. Technically the refuge is located just south of town—on Highway 15—but Monte Vista is really the closest town, and a good place to overnight. And overnighting is essential, so you can get up at the crack of dawn for prime bird watching opportunities.

The great thing about the refuge is that it's relatively untouristed; however, that doesn't mean it's devoid of avian life. Quite the contrary.

During the spring and fall thousands of sandhill cranes and migrating waterfowl descend on the surrounding wetlands; while song birds, shore birds and water birds nest there in the summer. Spring and summer are especially colorful seasons, as many of the residents sport their breeding plumage.

Although most of the refuge can easily be seen from an automobile, there's also a short accessible trail near the entrance. This wide level pathway winds alongside the marsh, and continues for approximately 100 yards, out to an accessible overlook. The trail is covered in crushed granite, and there is a bench midway along the route. And if you'd like to bring breakfast, there's also a picnic table located near the trailhead.

The bulk of the refuge is devoted to the 2.5-mile auto loop. There are interpretive signs posted along the route, and an accessible overlook that extends out over the adjacent pond. Red-winged blackbirds, yellow-headed black birds, herons, ducks and ibis are commonly sighted along the route. Don't forget the insect repellent though, as the mosquitoes can get pretty thick at the overlook.

So, take some time to explore this relatively undiscovered gem as you drive through Southern Colorado. It's a great place to get away from the tourist crowds!

Mesa Verde National Park

Located in Southwestern Colorado, Mesa Verde was once the home to the Ancestral Pueblo people. Today this national park—which features the remains of cliff dwellings, pueblos and pithouses—is very doable for wheelers and slow walkers.

Make your first stop the Far View Visitors Center, to get your bearings and pick up a map. Then head down to the south end of the park, and explore the sites on the Mesa Top Loop. This scenic six-mile drive features a variety of archeological sites grouped in chronological order, and offers a good representation of the variety of housing styles used by the Ancestral Pueblo people.

Recommended stops on the Mesa Top Loop include the first pithouse, the pithouses and pueblos site and the first, second and third mesa top villages. All of the sites feature accessible parking and paved trails to the ruins. There is also a small picnic area, complete with accessible restrooms, located next to the mesa top sites. It's a great spot for a mid-day break.

Cliff dwellings at Mesa Verde National Park.

Located just north of the Mesa Top Loop, near the Chapin Mesa Archeological Museum, Spruce Tree House is also worth a stop. Although the site is rated as accessible with assistance because of the slope; it's really only doable for power wheelchair-users. So make sure you can make it back up the hill before you head down the trail. And if it's more than you can handle, there's a more accessible viewing area behind the Chief Ranger's Office, next to the Chapin Mesa Archeological Museum.

Last but not least, save some time for a stop at the Far View Sites, located back near the park entrance. Unfortunately, uneven terrain prevents accessible travel to all of the ruins, but the Far View House is doable for most folks. It's located close to the level dirt parking area; and if you've had your fill of walking for the day, you can still get a good view from your car. It's a nice way to end the day.

And for a very accessible place to overnight, check out the Best Western Turquoise Inn (970-565-3778, www.bestwesternmesaverde.com) in nearby Cortez. Their accessible suite (307) boasts a nice roll-in shower and is furnished with a queen-sized sleeper sofa in the living room, and a queen-sized bed in the bedroom. It's very roomy and can easily accommodate four people. Plus you just can't beat the location—near Mesa Verde.

Rocky Mountain National Park

Rocky Mountain National Park is a must see on any drive through the Centennial State, as it boasts a number of accessible trails, pullouts and a nice accessible backcountry camp. Additionally, the drive over Trail Ridge road is breathtaking—even if you don't get out of your car.

At the top of the accessible trail list is the Coyote Valley Trail, located five miles from the Grand Lake entrance. This mile-long trail parallels the Colorado River and is covered with decomposed granite. It's a great place to spot elk and moose in the early morning or evening.

The Beaver Ponds Boardwalk, located on the eastern side of Trail Ridge Road is doable for many people. There's no accessible parking, but if you can deploy your lift on the sidewalk, you'll be good to go. The top half of the trail is a bit steep, but the boardwalks over the beaver ponds are nice.

Bear Lake Road also boasts two accessible trails. The half-mile trail around Sprague Lake is fairly level and covered with decomposed granite, with benches and fishing platforms along the way. You can get a great view of the Continental Divide from this trail. Accessible restrooms, parking and a picnic tables are also available there.

If you'd like to overnight in the park, the Sprague Lake Backcountry Camp is a good choice. Located about a half-mile from the trailhead, it includes an accessible vault toilet, picnic tables and a fire ring. It can accommodate up to 12 campers, including five wheelchair-users. Remember you'll have to pack everything in and out, so it's a good idea to bring along a cart for supplies. Call (970) 586-1242 for reservations.

Another trail that will work for many people is located at Bear Lake. This half-mile trail travels around the lake, and although it's covered with decomposed granite, it's a bit steep in a few places. Give it a try—if you can't manage, you can always turn back.

And don't forget to stop at Lily Lake, located just six miles south of Estes Park. A level ¾-mile trail covered in decomposed granite runs around the lake and through the adjacent wetlands. There's also an accessible vault toilet, picnic tables and a fishing pier there. The area is especially scenic in late spring and early summer, when you'll find it filled with wildflowers.

TIMING

Because of the heavy snows in the higher elevations of Rocky Mountain National Park, the best time to drive this route is from mid summer to early fall. That said, you'll find more crowds in July and August, so aim for September if you want a quieter experience. Additionally, the weather in Northern New Mexico is especially pleasant in the fall.

GREAT EATS

Stop by Maria's New Mexican Kitchen (505-983-7929, www.marias-santafe.com) in Santa Fe for some authentic New Mexican cuisine. Located just a few miles from the Plaza, there is ramp access to the front door, with a barrier-free pathway to the front dining room and restrooms. This Santa Fe mainstay features tasty blue corn enchiladas and yummy tamales. And you just can't leave without sampling one of their famous margaritas—they have over 100 to choose from!

DON'T MISS IT

Although it's hard to pick out highlights along this route, Garden of the Gods (719-634-6666, www.gardenofgods.com) consistently tops my must-see list. Located near Colorado Springs, this 480-acre parcel is filled with

Dramatic views and towering red rocks at Garden of the Gods near Colorado Springs, Colorado.

scenic red rock formations and features a 1.5-mile wheelchair-accessible trail through the heart of the park. And when you've had your fill of walking, meander along the main park road for some equally impressive views. Pack a picnic lunch and make a day out of it. Best of all—there's no admission charge!

And if you'd like to visit a very unique hot springs, then drop by Ojo Caliente (800-222-9162, www.ojocalientesprings.com). Located two hours north of Albuquerque, this five star resort features natural lithia, iron, arsenic and soda hot springs. They also have an accessible Plaza Cottage (Room 7), Pueblo Suite (Room 47) and Cliffside Suite (Room 53); which are all equipped with roll-in showers. The spa area features level access around all of the outdoor pools; however, there are steps into each pool. Still it's a great place to go and enjoy the beautiful scenery, even if you opt not to take the waters.

LINGER ON IN THE GATEWAY

· ·

There are plenty of accessible things to do in the Mile High City, so linger on for a few days and enjoy them all.

■ Take a self-guided tour of the Colorado State Capitol and see the ornate decorations made of Yule marble and Colorado Rose Onyx marble, as well as the impressive gold dome. The accessible entrance is located on the south side of the building (14th and Sherman) in the basement, with elevator access to the other levels.

■ Visit the Denver Art Museum (720-865-5500, www.denverartmuseum. org) and enjoy the world's greatest collection of Native American art, an impressive Old Masters collection, and even some interesting Old West classics. There's barrier-free access throughout all galleries, with loaner wheelchairs available on a first-come basis.

■ Have lunch and enjoy the exhibits at the Downtown Aquarium (301-561-4450). The aquarium features underwater exhibits that highlight ecosystems around the world, while the Aquarium Restaurant serves up a tasty lunch or dinner seven days a week. Access is excellent throughout the facility, with barrier-free pathways, spacious galleries and accessible restrooms.

■ Walk on the wild side at the Denver Zoo (303-376-4800, www.denver zoo.org), where you'll find wheelchair access to all the exhibits, plus a hand-carved carousel that features two accessible chariots.

■ Enjoy the ambiance of the 16th Street Pedestrian Mall, where you'll find outdoor cafes, retail stores and glass walled skyscrapers. There's level access to most buildings and curb-cuts at every corner. And if you get tired, the free wheelchair-accessible MallRide bus will take you from one end to another.

■ Stop and smell the roses at the Denver Botanic Gardens (720-865-3585, www.botanicgardens.org), which features 23 acres of plants in the middle of the city. Most of the areas are wheelchair-accessible, with loaner wheelchairs available at the information desk.

■ Take a tour of the Denver Mint (www.usmint.gov). Advance reservations are required, but the tours are free. The entire tour is wheelchair-accessible, so everyone can enjoy it. The only downside is that they don't give away free samples!

FLY-DRIVE OPTION

To make this a fly-drive vacation, fly to Denver International Airport (303-342-2000, www.flydenver.com); then rent an accessible van at Wheelchair Getaways (303-674-1498, www.wheelchairgetaways.com), Wheelers Van Rentals (800-456-1371, www.wheelersvanrentals.com) or Performance Mobility (800-868-3067, www.performancemobility.com).

ALTERNATE ENTRY POINTS

■ From Albuquerque, take Interstate 25 north to Santa Fe, then follow the route up to Ojo Caliente.

■ From Amarillo, take Interstate 40 west to Tucumcari, then connect to Highway 104 to Las Vegas, and follow Interstate 25 to Santa Fe.

■ From Kansas City, take Interstate 70 west to Denver. Be aware that this drive makes for a long day, so consider breaking it up into two or three days and include a little sightseeing along the way.

VARIATION ON A THEME

You can easily do Rocky Mountain National Park as a three-day getaway from Cheyenne, Wyoming. Likewise, you can do the Mesa Verde and Monte Vista portion of this itinerary as a nice three- or four-day side trip from Salt Lake City. And if you fancy a longer road trip, then head east on Interstate 70 to Abilene, and connect to the Head 'Em Up and Move 'Em Out route.

- IF YOU GO
  - Taos Chamber of Commerce, (575) 751-8800, www.taoschamber.com
  - Santa Fe Convention & Visitors Bureau, (505) 955-6200, www.santafe.org
  - Monte Vista National Wildlife Refuge, (719) 589-4021, www.fws.gov/alamosa
  - Mesa Verde National Park, (970) 529-4465, www.nps.gov/meve
  - Rocky Mountain National Park, (970) 586-1206, www.nps.gov/romo

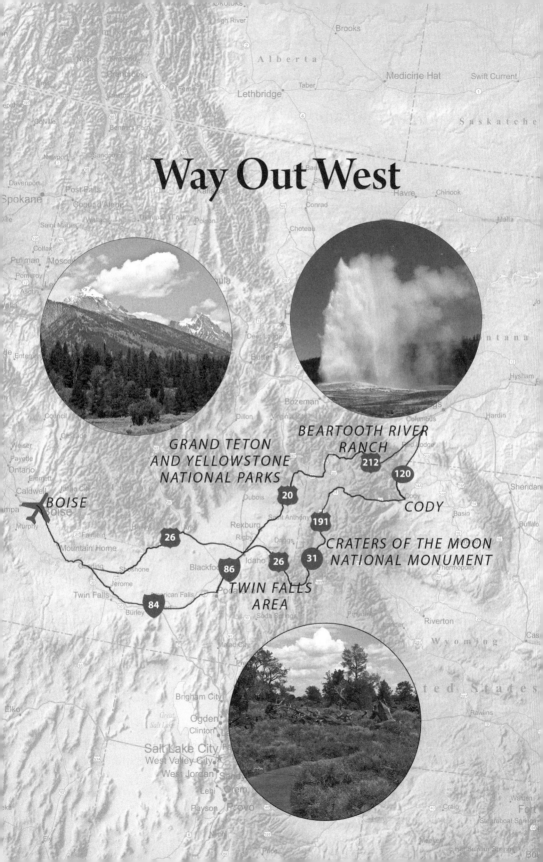

Way Out West

GRAND TETON
AND YELLOWSTONE
NATIONAL PARKS

BEARTOOTH RIVER
RANCH

212

120

20

BOISE

26

191

CODY

26   **31**

CRATERS OF THE MOON
NATIONAL MONUMENT

86

84

TWIN FALLS
AREA

This route highlights the untamed west from a variety of perspectives. From the historic sites on the Oregon Trail near Twin Falls, to the roaming buffalo and majestic beauty of Yellowstone National Park, and the Wild West atmosphere of Cody, Wyoming, this itinerary runs the full gamut of the Wild West experience. Top it off with a dude ranch stay and a scenic drive through the rugged landscape of Craters of the Moon National Monument, and you have a nicely accessible road trip that showcases the many faces of the wild and wooly west.

ROUTE

This route begins in Boise and follows Interstate 84 east through Twin Falls, then travels along a short stretch of Interstate 86 and connects to Interstate 15 North. Next it follows Highway 26 and continues on Highway 31, Highway 33 and Highway 22 to Jackson. Then it's time to head through Grand Teton National Park on Highway 191, and connect with Highway 287 though Yellowstone National Park. Next it's out the east park entrance, past Pahaska Tepee, and along the Buffalo Bill Scenic Byway to Cody. Then head north on Highway 120, cross over into Montana and continue along Highway 72 to Belfry. From there follow Highway 72 to Highway 310 North, to Highway 212 South, and loop back through Yellowstone. Finally, exit the park at West Yellowstone and follow Highway 20 to Highway 26 to Craters of the Moon National Monument. To complete the loop, continue along Highway 26 to Interstate 84, and head back to Boise.

ALONG THE WAY

Twin Falls Area

The Twin Falls area is a good place to stop and learn a little bit about the Oregon Trail, as there are several interesting sites, as well as a stretch of the

Idaho's State capitol in Boise.

old trail in the area. It's estimated that over 300,000 Americans immigrated out west on the wagon rutted trail, which stretched from Independence, Missouri to Oregon City, Oregon.

There's no better place to get an introduction to the Oregon Trail, than at the old Rock Creek Station and Striker Home Site (208-423-4000, www.friendsofstricker.yolasite.com). Located about 15 miles west of Twin Falls, there's a small interpretive center there, along with what remains of the old store and home. There's ramped access to the interpretive center, and although you have to be able to do a few steps to go inside the historic buildings, you can still get a good look from the outside. The best part of this stop is that you can actually walk or roll along a piece of the Oregon Trail.

Up the road in Burley, the Cassia County Museum (208-678-7172)—on the corner of Main and Highland—is also worth a visit. Although not specific to the Oregon Trail it contains an eclectic collection of historic

Historic artifacts at the Cassia County Museum in Burley, Idaho.

artifacts including an old one-room schoolhouse. Access is good too, with level access to the main building, and barrier-free access to the outbuildings.

Round out your Oregon Trail tour with a visit to the City of Rocks, located near Almo. This branch off the Oregon Trail took immigrants south to the Raft River and over the Sierra Nevada range to Northern California. Those early settlers named this area City of Rocks, for the granite rocks which rise abruptly out of the around. As one pioneer put it, it looked like a rock-built city of the stone age.

There's level access to the Visitors Center, which features interpretive exhibits about the quarter-million immigrants who passed through Almo, beginning in 1843. Although there aren't any accessible trails in the City of Rocks National Reserve (208-824-5901, www.nps.gov/ciro), it still makes an excellent driving tour, with some spectacular windshield views.

And if you'd like to overnight in the area, check out the nearby Almo Inn (208-824-5577, www.almocreek.com), which features an accessible cabin (# 6) with a roll-in shower. It's nicely done, and the old west décor really adds to the ambiance of it all. There's also an accessible restaurant next door.

Grand Teton and Yellowstone National Parks

Take a few days to explore Grand Teton and Yellowstone National Parks. Begin your visit with a stop at the Laurance S. Rockefeller Preserve in Grand Teton National Park, for a short stroll through the forest on a hard-packed dirt trail. The trail ends at the nature center, which features barrier-free access and a variety of interpretive exhibits. Next, head up to South Jenny Lake, where you'll find the ¾-mile Lakeshore Loop Trail, located behind the Visitor Center. Although this paved trail has some undulations, it's still doable for many people.

Last but not least make sure you stop at Coulter Bay Village for the excellent David T. Vernon Indian Arts Museum, which boasts an impressive collection of Native American jewelry, baskets, beadwork, weaving and clothing. There's level access at the front museum entrance, but if you can't do stairs, you'll need to use the back door to access the lower level. There's also a nice barrier-free trail along the lakeshore, just behind the museum. Just park near the amphitheater and follow the path down to the lake.

Up in Yellowstone, Old Faithful puts on a daily show that's not to be missed. There's level access to the Visitor Center, which has information about the next eruption; and plenty of room for wheelchairs in the geyser viewing area. There's also a .7-mile boardwalk and asphalt trail around the geyser.

After the show, take the barrier-free asphalt trail in front of the general store to Upper Geyser Basin. Even if you don't want to do the whole 1.5-mile length, Castle Geyser and Crested Pool are just a short walk away.

Don't miss the most dynamic thermal area in the park—Norris Geyser Basin. There's level access to the small museum, and although the trail around the Back Basin isn't technically accessible, it's doable for some folks. Even if you can't manage the trail, there's a great view from the accessible overlook behind the museum.

Top off your visit with a drive down South Rim Drive for a spectacular view of the Grand Canyon of the Yellowstone River. There's a paved pathway out to the overlook at Artist Point for a view of Lower Falls; and a boardwalk and hard-packed dirt trail out to the edge of Uncle Tom's Overlook, for a look at Upper Falls. Both are worth a stop.

Laurance S. Rockefeller Preserve in Grand Teton National Park.

Cody

The Cody area is alive with remnants of the old west, and there's no better place to start your visit than at the Pahaska Tepee (307-527-7701, www. pahaska.com), located just outside the east entrance to Yellowstone National Park. It's a fitting introduction to the area, as this historic structure was once Buffalo Bill's hunting lodge. Today it boasts a restaurant and a gift shop as well as some hotel rooms; and even if you're not hungry it's worth a stop for a look at the Buffalo Bill memorabilia.

There's ramp access up to the historic building which now houses the gift shop and restaurant. The Lodgepole Room is a site to see with the old knotty pine paneling lining the walls; and although it offers a pretty basic menu, the food is hot and the service is good. Plus it makes a nice break along the road from Yellowstone.

From there, just follow the Buffalo Bill Scenic Byway through the Wapiti Valley, along the North Fork of the Shoshone River and past the Buffalo Bill Reservoir to Cody.

The Buffalo Bill Historical Center (307-587-4471, www.bbhc.org) is a must-see in Cody as it has five galleries dedicated to the old west, including the impressive Buffalo Bill Museum. Other galleries include the Whitney Gallery of Western Art, the Plains Indian Museum, the Cody Firearms Museum and the Draper Museum of Natural History—all of which have level access, and present a comprehensive picture of the old west. There's also level access to the Cashman Greever sculpture garden, where Buffalo Bill's boyhood home is on display. Although there are three steps up to the cabin, you can still get a good look at it from the garden.

If you'd like a little cowboy entertainment, get tickets to Dan Miller's Cowboy Music Revue (307-272-7855, www.cowboymusicreview.com). Located downtown, just across the street from Buffalo Bill's Irma Hotel, this Branson style music show features lots of old cowboy tunes. There's level access to the theater with plenty of wheelchair seating up front. It really puts you in that "old west" mood. After the show save some time to stroll around the downtown area, as it's fairly level with wide sidewalks and curb-cuts at every corner.

And if you're looking for an accessible place to overnight, the Holiday Inn Cody (307-587-5555) features some nice accessible rooms with roll-in showers or tub/shower combinations. Best of all, it's just five blocks from the Irma hotel.

Beartooth River Ranch

Located in the shadows of the Beartooth Mountains, about 50 miles north of Cody. Beartooth River Ranch is a great place to spend a few days and soak up a little cowboy culture. This working ranch is a bit off-the-beaten-path, and to be honest, it's a challenge to find. On the plus side, if you pay attention and follow the directions, you'll be rewarded with good access and a fun place to hang your hat.

Access is nicely done at the ranch, with ramp access up to the porch and barrier-free access to the living area and dining room. This large common area is equipped with a computer for guest use, lots of reading material, and comfy nooks to kick back and relax. It's also where the family-style meals are served; I guarantee you won't go away hungry.

The sleeping accommodations are just as inviting and accessible. The accessible Yellowstone Suite features wide doorways and good pathway access. It's furnished with a 20-inch-high king-sized bed, as well as a fold-out sleeper sofa. The bathroom includes a roll-in shower with grab bars and a hand-held showerhead, grab bars on the back and right toilet walls (as seated) and a roll-under sink. The adjoining Cottonwood Room is furnished with a double bed and has a bathroom with a low-step shower, and it's a good choice for folks traveling with kids or an attendant. All in all, it's a very comfortable and accessible suite.

And although they don't have any adaptive riding programs, guests can instead opt to explore the area on day trips. They do have plenty of evening activities though, including cowboy music night and an excursion into town to watch the pig races at the Bear Creek Saloon. Although there's no guarantee you'll pick the winning pig, there's level access to the venue.

Of course you can just sit back and enjoy nature, including an abundant bird population. From Sandhill Cranes, Blue Herons and hawks in the summer to wild turkeys, pheasants and geese in the fall, there's always something to see. And then again, you can do absolutely nothing, and just enjoy the fresh air and the wide open spaces.

Craters of the Moon National Monument

Located approximately 18 miles east of Arco on Highway 26, Craters of the Moon National Monument boasts an eerie lunar-like landscape. Although the last eruption was some 2,000 years ago, it's filled with old lava flows and other remnants of past geologic activity. There are several accessible trails in the park, so it's really worth a short side trip on your way back to Boise.

There's level access to the Visitor Center, which features a few interpretive exhibits, and some very clean accessible restrooms. Additionally there's a regularly scheduled ranger talk, which focuses on the geology, the eruptions and the natural history of the park.

From there a scenic seven-mile drive loops through the park. Although you'll certainly get some spectacular windshield views along the drive, it's highly recommended that you park the car and get an up-close-and-personal look at some of the unique geological formations.

The North Crater Flow Trail makes a nice stop, as this quarter-mile trail winds out past one of the newest lava flows in the park. There are plenty of interpretive signs along this three-foot-wide paved trail; and although there are a few undulations in it, it's very doable for wheelchair-users and slow walkers. There's also a bench mid-way along the trail; but be forewarned there are no shade structures. And although the trail narrows to 28–30 inches in a few places, it's still plenty wide for most folks.

Just up the road, the Devils Orchard Trail is also a good choice for wheelchair-users and slow walkers. There's accessible parking near the trailhead, and a wheelchair-accessible pit toilet across the parking lot. This half-mile three-foot-wide paved loop trail winds through a sea of cinders filled with lava fragments, trees and logs. There are a few undulations, but it's still very accessible. There's also an accessible picnic table across form the trailhead, so pack along a lunch and enjoy.

And although it's technically not accessible, the first part of the Spatter Cone Trail is worth a try. If you can make it up the first 8% grade, you'll do OK, as that's the toughest part. It also gets pretty windy up there, and most wheelers will need some assistance. It's just 247 feet to the miniature volcano known as the Sugar Cone, which still has snow at the bottom in early summer. Give it a try, as it's a very interesting formation.

TIMING

· ·

The best time to drive this route is in September, just after Labor Day. That way you'll dodge the huge summer crowds in Yellowstone, yet still make it through the park before the roads close in early November. The roads usually open up in late April, although in some years it has snowed in Yellowstone in May and even June; so it's always wise to carry chains on this route.

GREAT EATS

· ·

If you've got a hankering for something sweet, then stop by the Clover Leaf Creamery (208-543-4272, www. cloverleafcreamery.com) in Buhl, Idaho. Well off the tourist track, it's considered the Ted Drewes of the Twin Falls area. There's level access to the store, where you can order a scoop or two of their ice cream; and with advance notice they're also happy to give you a tour of the production facility out back. This family-run business has some great flavors from Cowboy Crunch and Huckleberry Swirl to Elk Tracks, Egg Nog and even Apple Strudel. Just a short drive west of Twin Falls, it's a great stop on the way from Boise.

DON'T MISS IT

For a bird's eye view of the Tetons, take a ride on the Jackson Hole Aerial Tram at Jackson Hole Mountain Resort (307-733-2292, www.jacksonhole.com). Located in Teton Village, just two miles from the Granite Canyon Entrance to Grand Teton National Park, it's the perfect introduction to the Tetons.

Access is good too, with plenty of accessible parking, level access to the ticket window and elevator access up to the boarding platform. Boarding is easy—you just roll right on to the gondola. The nine-minute ride to the top of Rendezvous Mountain features some great views; but nothing compared to the view you'll get from the top. Be sure and take a jacket though, as it can get chilly on the mountain top, even in the middle of summer. It's a great way to view the Tetons.

LINGER ON IN THE GATEWAY

Save a few days to explore some of Boise's numerous cultural attractions. Not only will they give you a good feel for the history and culture of the area, but most also have excellent wheelchair access.

- Visit the Idaho State Historical Museum (208-334-2120, www.history. idaho.gov/idaho-state-historical-museum), for a good primer on Idaho history—from the Oregon Trail to the Victorian era. Access features include a level entrance, good pathway access and plenty of room to wheel around in the galleries.

- Stroll through the Boise Art Museum (208-345-8330, www.boiseart museum.org), which boasts a permanent collection of 2,300 works, with an emphasis on Pacific Northwest art, American Realism and ceramics. Access is excellent throughout the museum, with loaner wheelchairs available at the front desk.

- Learn about African American history at the Idaho Black History Museum (208-433-0017, www.ibhm.org), located in the historic St. Paul Baptist Church. There's ramp access on the side of this one-room museum, which features exhibits about the culture and history of African Americans, with a emphasis on Idahoan African Americans.

- Hit the bricks and explore the downtown entertainment district (BODO) on foot. From the state capitol to Capitol Boulevard, it's a very accessible area with wide level sidewalks and curb-cuts at every corner. Pick up a map at the Visitors Center on the east side of Boise Centre, and hit the streets.

- Head out to the World Center for Birds of Prey (208-362-8687, www. peregrinefund.org), which features interpretive exhibits and presentations about raptors. Access is excellent throughout the facility, with level access to the gift shop and the interpretive center; and wide level pathways around the cages in the outdoor area.

- Take a trek over to the Warhawk Air Museum (208-465-6446, www. warhawkairmuseum.org) at the Nampa Municipal Airport. It boasts a substantial collection of World War II memorabilia along with some nicely restored vintage war planes. It's also nicely accessible with a level entrance and barrier-free access throughout the 17,000 square-foot hangar.

- Stroll through the Idaho Botanical Garden (208-343-8649, www.idaho botanicalgarden.org)—a 15-acre oasis in the shadow of a former prison guard tower. For best access, park in the upper parking lot and enter through the level pathway to the English Garden. There's good access throughout the garden as most of the dirt pathways are fairly level and doable in dry weather.

- Save some time to pop in next door and tour the Old Idaho Penitentiary (208-334-2844, www.history.idaho.gov/old-idaho-penitentiary). Although there are some rutted walkways and uneven pavement in this historic prison, there's also level access to the first-floor cell blocks and some out buildings. It's definitely worth a visit.

FLY-DRIVE OPTION

To make this a fly-drive vacation, fly to Boise Airport (208-383-3110, www.cityofboise.org/Departments/Airport); then rent an accessible van at Wheelchair Getaways (800-630-8267, www.wheelchairgetaways.com).

ALTERNATE ENTRY POINTS

- From Salt Lake City, head north to Highway 86, and pick up the route just west of Twin Falls.

- From Spokane, head south to Pendleton, Oregon; then follow Interstate 84 to Boise.

- From Helena, take Interstate 15 south to Idaho Falls, and take the Highway 26 exit to Jackson, Wyoming.

VARIATION ON A THEME

If you only have three nights, you can easily visit the Twin Falls sites and Craters of the Moon National Monument from Salt Lake City, while the Cody–Beartooth

River Ranch–Yellowstone loop makes a nice week-long trip from Cheyenne. If you'd like an even longer road trip, then head over to Denver and connect to The Rockies and Beyond route. Although it's a 12-hour drive, if you break it up into two days, you'll also have time for a side trip to the Bonneville Salt Flats, near Wendover.

- IF YOU GO
  - Grand Teton National Park, (307) 739-3300, www.nps.gov/grte
  - Yellowstone National Park, (307) 344-7381, www.nps.gov/yell
  - Buffalo Bill's Cody and Yellowstone Country, (800) 393-2639, www.yellowstonecountry.org
  - Beartooth River Ranch, (406) 664-3181, www.beartoothriverranch.com
  - Craters of the Moon National Monument, (208) 527-1300, www.nps.gov/crmo
  - Boise Convention & Visitors Bureau, (208) 344-7777, www.boise.org

Left: The Riverwalk in San Antonio, Texas.
Upper right: McGee's Landing in Henderson, Louisiana.
Lower right: Minnie Pearl's memorabilia at the Grand Ole Opry Museum.

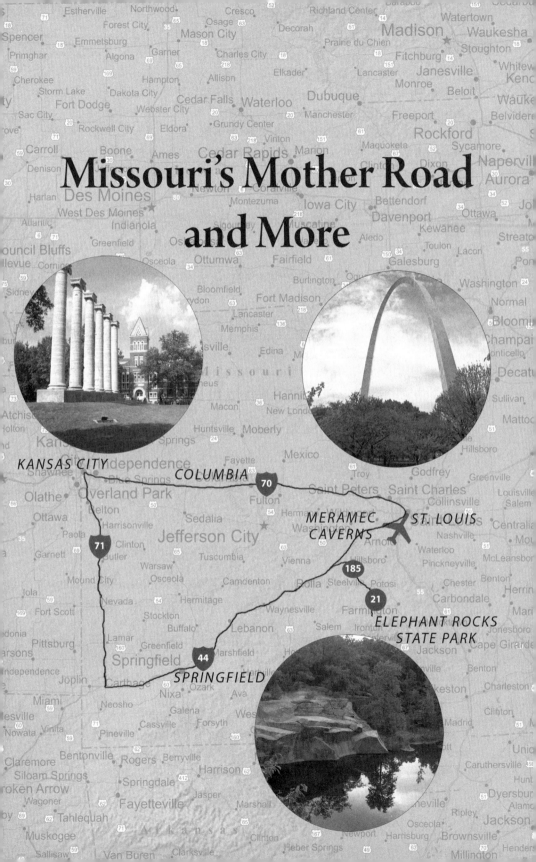

Missouri's Mother Road and More

KANSAS CITY

COLUMBIA

70

ST. LOUIS

MERAMEC
CAVERNS

71

185

21

ELEPHANT ROCKS
STATE PARK

44

SPRINGFIELD

This footloose and fancy free route features a nostalgic jaunt along the Missouri stretch of Route 66, coupled with the cultural attractions of Kansas City and St. Louis, and capped off with the Main Street USA ambience of rural Columbia. Between the iconic roadside attractions, unique museums and even a nice country winery, you'll experience the full breadth of diverse attractions and must-see offerings of the Cave State.

ROUTE

This route begins in St. Louis and follows Interstate 44 east past Meramec Caverns; then takes a slight detour on Highway 185 to Polosi, and continues on to Highway 21 to Elephant Rocks State Park. Back on Interstate 44, the route then travels west to Springfield, and continues on to Highway 71, north to Kansas City. Then it's time to head east on Interstate 70 to Columbia, before traveling on to St. Louis to complete the loop.

ALONG THE WAY

Meramec Caverns

It's kind of hard to miss Meramec Caverns, as billboards directing folks to this iconic attraction are plastered along the interstate; while signs painted on the sides of old barns in 14 states serve as constant reminders of what's ahead. Located about 60 miles west of St. Louis off Interstate 44, this roadside attraction was a must-see during Route 66's heyday; however, it's still a fun stop today. The caverns are just as beautiful, and the tour is fairly wheelchair-accessible—a winning combination in my book.

The caves also have a colorful past, as according to historians, they were the one-time hideout for Jesse James and his gang. As legend has it, a posse tracked James and his cohorts to the cavern entrance, only to find the gang's abandoned horses. They searched the caverns to no avail, as the gang had already escaped through an underground river passage.

As far as caves go, Meramec Caverns offers fairly good access. There are paved walkways throughout the caverns, with plenty of room for wheelchairs to maneuver. The lower level of the caverns is fairly level; however, because of the very steep grade, most manual wheelchair-users will have a tough time with the ramp to the upper level. Still with a little assistance it's doable for most people.

On the plus side, the trails through the caverns are very doable in a scooter or a power wheelchair. Abbreviated tours of the caves are also available for wheelchair-users who can't access the upper level, or manage the 1¼-mile distance of the regular tour.

It's definitely worth a stop no matter what your ability level, as the lower caverns offer some spectacular formations, crystal clear streams and Mirror River—an 18-inch deep pool which reflects a great hollow overhead dome. All in all, it's a fun and educational stop, and it serves as a great introduction to the Cave State. After all it's still billed as the "greatest show under the earth."

ELEPHANT ROCKS STATE PARK

To be honest, Elephant Rocks State Park is more than a just slight detour off Interstate 44. It's a good 1½-hour drive from Stanton—more if you get lost—but it's definitely worth the extra drive. Although it's only 60 miles south of Stanton off of Highway 185, we're not exactly talking super highways here. Still, it's a fun off-the-beaten-path day trip.

Billed as one of the most curious geological formations in Missouri, the granite boulders at Elephant Rocks State Park stand end-to-end like a train of circus elephants. The formations date back 1.5 billion years to the Precambrian Period, and the giant red boulders provide the perfect backdrop for a leisurely afternoon picnic. As an added bonus, the site is well off the usual tourist track, so it's nicely devoid of crowds. In fact, don't be surprised if you have it all to yourself.

Quarry Pond at Elephant Rocks State Park.

Access is excellent as well, with plenty of accessible parking and accessible pit toilets nearby. Additionally, the one-mile path around the giant boulders was designed with access in mind; in fact it's the site of Missouri's first wheelchair-accessible Braille trail. The four-foot wide asphalt trail leads around the formations, up to Quarry Pond, and back to the picnic area. It's a very pleasant stroll, with some unique scenery along the way.

It should be noted that there are no services available at this park, but to be honest you don't really need any. Just pack along a picnic lunch and some drinks, and you're good to go for a day at Elephant Rocks State Park.

SPRINGFIELD

Located three-quarters of the way along the Missouri stretch of the Mother Road, Springfield is definitely worth a stop, as it boasts more than a few unique attractions. At the top of the list is the Springfield Bass Pro (417-887-7334, www.basspro.com). Granted it's basically an outdoor store; however, it's a popular stop on nearly every Route 66 itinerary, which means you'll likely spot some classic rides in the parking lot.

There's plenty of accessible parking in the Bass Pro lot, with level access to the front door, and barrier-free access throughout the massive store. To be honest, it's much more than just a store—I like to think of it as "Midwest sports outlet meets Disneyland." There's certainly no shortage of merchandise; however, there's also a shooting gallery, a waterfall and a newly renovated aquarium in the store.

And while you're there, don't miss Wonders of Wildlife (417-890-9453, www.wondersofwildlife.org), located right across the parking lot. This hybrid mix of an aquarium, zoo and interactive museum just underwent a major renovation and expansion project; and although the exhibition hall and wildlife galleries were recently reopened, the grand reopening date for the rest of the facility is set for December 2012. It's even worth a stop during the construction period, as there's still plenty to see. Access is good too, with level access to the front door and barrier-free pathways through all the galleries.

Located off Interstate 44, just north of town, Fantastic Caverns (417-833-2010, www.fantasticcaverns.com) is also worth a visit. Billed as America's only ride-through cave, it's also wheelchair-accessible; as visitors are transported through the cave in a jeep-drawn tram. There is ramp access to the tram, so it's easy to roll aboard for the 55-minute narrated tour. The tram follows an ancient riverbed and gives visitors a great look at some of the magnificent stalactite and stalagmite formations in the cave. The gift shop and visitors center are also nicely accessible with tile floors, level entries, accessible bathrooms and plenty of room to maneuver.

Last but not least, don't forget to stop at the Best Western Route 66 Rail Haven (417-866-1963, www.bwrailhaven.com) on your way out of town. This piece of Route 66 history is worth a stop even if you don't overnight there, as it offers a nostalgic glance at a bygone era. Plus there are usually some pretty cool cars in the parking lot.

Kansas City

For a change of pace, plan to spend several days in Kansas City to soak up a little culture and enjoy some good barbeque. The best place to begin your visit is at The Nelson-Atkins Museum of Art (816-751-1278, www.nelson-atkins.org). Not only does it offer free admission and audio tours, but it's one of America's top general art museums, with over 33,500 pieces in their permanent collection. There's lots of accessible parking in the museum lot, with elevator access to the lobby from the garage. Inside, there's barrier-free access throughout the spacious galleries; with loaner wheelchairs available at the Coat Check in the Bloch Building.

Don't miss the 22-acre Kansas City Sculpture Park out front, as it's home to the largest collection of Henry Moore bronze sculptures, as well as some whimsical pieces such as the iconic shuttlecocks that adorn the front lawn. There is an accessible pathway through the park with a few steps here and there to get to some of the sculptures. Still, you can get a good view of most pieces from the pathway.

Save some time for the Kemper Museum of Contemporary Art (816-753-5784, www.kemperart.org), which is just a few blocks away. There's no admission charge to this excellent museum, which houses over 1,000 works in a wide range of media, dating back to 1913. Access is good here too, with plenty of accessible parking and barrier-free access to the galleries.

Round off your museum hopping tour with a visit to the 18th & Vine historic district to see the Negro Leagues Baseball Museum (816-221-1929, www.nlbm.com) and the American Jazz Museum (816-474-8463, www.americanjazzmuseum.com). Both museums have level access to the front entrance with barrier-free access throughout the galleries. Although they are must-sees for jazz fans and baseball buffs, they also serve as a great introduction to both subjects.

Save some time to stroll around the Country Club Plaza shopping district, enjoy the Spanish architecture and take a gander at the J.C. Nichols fountain at night. This 15-block district boasts more than 150 shops and dozens of fine restaurants, and it's a great place to get your barbeque fix. And with level sidewalks and lots of curb-cuts, it's very easy to navigate.

And for a very accessible place to rest your head, check out Southmoreland on the Plaza (816-531-7979, www.southmoreland.com), which features the accessible August Meyer room. This first-floor room has a tub/shower combination with a hand-held showerhead, grab bars and a built-in corner shower seat. It's a great room for slow walkers, and a unique opportunity to stay in a historic mansion.

COLUMBIA

• •

Round out your Missouri road trip with a stop in Columbia, located halfway between Kansas City and St. Louis. It's a great place to hop off the fast track, enjoy a little nature and meander through the quaint downtown area. And the good news is—it's very accessible.

As an added bonus, Columbia is also connected to the wheelchair-accessible Katy trail by the equally accessible MKT Trail. This eight-mile multi-use trail spur begins at 4th and Cherry Streets in downtown Columbia and connects to the Katy Trail near McBaine. It's wide, flat and very rollable. MKT trailheads with accessible parking are located at Stadium, Forum and Scott Boulevards. The Stadium Boulevard trailhead also features the wheelchair-accessible Martin Luther King Memorial Garden.

Another good place to enjoy Missouri's natural beauty is at Shelter Gardens. This five-acre garden space, which is located on the grounds of the Shelter Insurance Company, features a wide selection of native and exotic plants including a shade garden, conifer garden, rock garden and sensory garden. Wide paths and level walkways make the gardens nicely accessible; and it's the perfect venue for the free Sunday evening concerts in June and July.

Save some time for a stroll through the downtown area, which features wide level sidewalks and a large variety of eateries and shops. Be sure and pop in to the Candy Factory (573-443-8222, www.thecandyfactory.biz) at 7th and Cherry Streets. This Columbia mainstay is nicely accessible with a zero-step entry and lift access to the upstairs area. Not only is it a chocolate-lover's paradise, but you can also get a look at the whole production process upstairs.

Last but not least, head out the University of Missouri for a look at two excellent museums, both of which feature good wheelchair access. Located in historic Pickard Hall, the MU Museum of Art and Archeology (572-882-3591, www.maa.missouri.edu) features over 14,000 artifacts, including a collection of Greek and Roman casts, several galleries of ancient Mediterranean and West Asian works, and the Samuel H. Kress Collection of 14 Old Master paintings.

University of Missouri in Columbia, Missouri.

Next door in Swallow Hall, you'll find the equally impressive Museum of Anthropology (573-882-3573, www.anthromuseum.missouri.edu), which features a permanent exhibition on Native American cultures, plus rotating exhibits focusing on cultures around the world. Both are must-sees on any Columbia visit.

TIMING

The summers can be sweltering in Missouri, so it's best to avoid the peak summer season in the Cave State. April and October offer pleasant weather, with fewer crowds. The former is great for the spring blooms, while the latter is better if you like the fall colors. And although winters typically get more ice than snow, it's still not the optimal time to visit.

GREAT EATS

L ocated at the Le Bourgeois Winery in Rocheport, the Blufftop Bistro (573-698-2300, www.missouri wine.com) serves up some tasty provincial fare that includes house-smoked meats, fresh seafood and local produce. Make sure you reserve a table on the deck, which boasts a nice view of the river below— it's especially beautiful at sunset. It's just 15 minutes from Columbia, and with level access to the front door, valet parking, and a barrier-free pathway to the deck, it's well worth the short drive.

DON'T MISS IT

F or a nostalgic drive along an old section of Route 66, exit Interstate 44 at exit 58, then go west through Paris Springs to Spencer. Not only is this part of Route 66 very scenic, but it also contains a rare stretch of the original concrete road. Spencer is just a ghost town these days, but it's also worth a quick stop. The hard-packed ground is pretty level, and although there are no designated parking spaces, it's pretty deserted, with plenty of space to pull over and park. Just up the road there's a very scenic truss bridge over Johnson Creek, that's definitely worth a photo stop, before heading on to Carthage.

LINGER ON IN THE GATEWAY

E xtend your time in Missouri with a pre or post road trip stay in St. Louis. There's no shortage of fun attractions, most of which offer good access.

A rare stretch of the original concrete road that made up Route 66.

- Spend the day at the St. Louis Zoo (314-781-0900, www.stlzoo.org), which features the flight cage from the 1904 World's Fair, the Monsanto Insectarium and the Zooline Railroad. There's ramped or level access to most of the exhibits, wide level pathways throughout the property and a ramped car on the Zooline Rail Road.

- Act like a kid at the City Museum (314-231-2489, www.citymuseum.org). This interactive children's museum features lots of spaces to crawl, roll or climb, with elevator access to all levels and good pathway access throughout this quirky fun house.

- Visit the Museum of Westward Expansion (314-655-1700, www.nps.gov/jeff) at the base of the iconic Gateway Arch. Although there is no wheelchair access to the arch, there's barrier-free access throughout the museum.

- Check out the Museum of Transportation (314-615-8668, www.museum oftransport.org), which features 70 locomotives, a vintage horse-drawn streetcar and Bobby Darin's dream car. Located on 150 acres at Barton Station, the museum features barrier-free access to all the indoor exhibits, an accessible path through the rail yard, and even ramp access up to the train car viewing areas.

- Sample some beer and feed the animals at Grant's Farm (314-843-1700, www.grantsfarm.com), operated by St. Louis-based Anheuser-Busch. There's ramp access to the tram tour of the 281-acre deer park, and level pathways to most of the animal enclosures at the Tier Garden. After you work up a thirst, top off your visit with a free sample of your favorite Anheuser-Busch adult beverage.

- Visit the St. Louis Art Museum (314-721-0072, www.slam.org) and the Missouri History Museum (314-746-4599, www.mohistory.org) in Forest Park. Both venues feature top notch exhibits, an accessible entrance and restrooms, elevator access to all floors and plenty of room to navigate through the galleries.

- Stroll through the Missouri Botanical Gardens (314-577-5100, www.mobot.org). There are level pathways throughout the gardens, plus a wheelchair-accessible tram tour of the 79-acre property.

- Shop till you drop at Union Station (314-421-6655, www.stlouisunionstation.com). This former train station houses over 100 shops and restaurants; with good pathway access throughout the shopping center and level access to the individual shops.

- Top off your St. Louis visit with a thick and creamy milkshake at Ted Drewes Frozen Custard stand (314-481-2652, www.teddrewes.com). This Route 66 landmark features roll-up access, and the milkshakes are so thick that they're served upside down.

FLY-DRIVE OPTION

To make this a fly-drive vacation, fly to Lambert-St. Louis International Airport (314-890-1333, www.lambert-stlouis.com); then rent an accessible van at Wheelers Van Rental (314-621-4180, www.wheelersvanrentals.com), United Access (314-549-8014, www.unitedaccess.com) or Kersey Mobility (877-507-7491, www.kerseymobility.com).

ALTERNATE ENTRY POINTS

- From Tulsa, take Interstate 44 just past Joplin, then hop on Highway 71 and head north to Kansas City.

- From Chicago, take Interstate 55 south to St. Louis.

- From Indianapolis, take Interstate 70 west to Kansas City.

VARIATION ON A THEME

The Route 66 segment of this drive makes a nice three- or four-night getaway, and can easily be done from Little Rock or Memphis. Likewise, the Columbia and St. Louis portion of the route makes a perfect long weekend from Des Moines. If you're up for an even longer road trip, then head on over to Abilene from Kansas City, and drive the Way Out West in Kansas route.

- IF YOU GO
  - Meramec Caverns, (573) 468-2283, www.americascave.com
  - Elephant Rocks State Park, (573) 546-3454, www.mostateparks.com/park/elephant-rocks-state-park
  - Springfield Missouri Travel and Tourism, (417) 881-5300, www.springfieldmo.org
  - Kansas City Convention & Visitors Bureau, (800) 767-7700, www.visitkc.com
  - Columbia Visitors Bureau, (573) 875-1231, www.visitcolumbiamo.com
  - St. Louis Convention & Visitors Commission, (800) 325-7962, www.explorestlouis.com

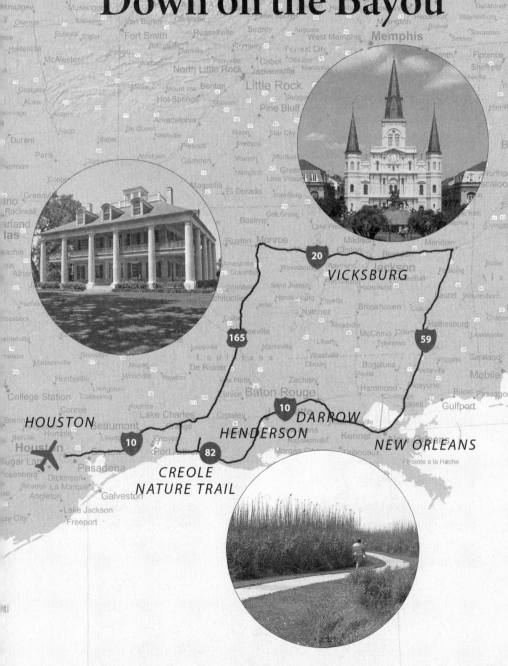

Down on the Bayou

VICKSBURG

HOUSTON

DARROW

HENDERSON

NEW ORLEANS

CREOLE
NATURE TRAIL

This fun and fanciful route takes you into the heart of the Louisiana bayou, through some lightly traveled back roads and deep into Cajun country, before it loops up through Mississippi for a look at a few historic sites. And although parts of the drive are pretty remote, they're not without wheelchair access, as there's a swamp tour, a plantation and even a few nature trails that are doable for many wheelchair-users and slow walkers. Add in a taste of excitement in New Orleans, some great scenery along the Creole Nature Trail and a dab of history on the Natchez Trace Parkway and you have all the ingredients for an accessible and adventurous road trip.

ROUTE

T his route begins in Houston, then heads east on Interstate 10 into Louisiana, before it branches off to the Creole Nature Trail in Sulphur. After it rejoins Interstate 10 in Rayne, it continues east to New Orleans, with stops in Henderson and Darrow. Then it's north on Interstate 59 to Meridian, Mississippi; and west on Interstate 20 to Vicksburg. Finally the route heads south on Highway 165 in Monroe, before it rejoins Interstate 10 and circles back to Houston.

ALONG THE WAY

Creole Nature Trail

Located in Southwestern Louisiana, the Creole Nature Trail offers a great opportunity for an up-close-and-personal look at the bayous and marshlands bordering the Gulf of Mexico. It's easy to find too—just take Highway 27 south in Sulphur, and follow the signs.

Accessible viewing platform on the Blue Goose Walking Trail along the Creole Nature Trial.

There's also a downloadable audio tour available at www.Creole NatureTrail.org, which offers a good history and overview of the area. Additionally, a free Smartphone app is available at the iTunes App Store and the Android Market; while a new GPS hand-held tour can be checked out at the Southwest Louisiana Convention & Visitors Bureau.

The first accessible trail you'll come upon is the Blue Goose Walking Trail, located just past the boat launch in the Sabine National Wildlife Refuge. The paved mile-long trail meanders along the edge of Calcasieu Lake, and presents some great birding opportunities. The area is teeming with waterfowl in February, and it's an excellent place to spot neotropical songbirds in the spring and fall. And if you can't manage the trail, there's also an accessible viewing platform near the parking area.

Just up the road, the equally accessible Wetlands Walkway features a 1½-mile boardwalk and paved trail through a wetlands area, with an accessible viewing platform located midway along the trail. This is prime gator habitat, and you'll most likely spot one or two alongside, or even on, the trail.

For more accessible wildlife viewing, head east on Highway 27 towards Cameron. After you cross the canal on the small Cameron Ferry, bear left and continue along on Highway 27 towards Creole, then continue north to the Cameron Prairie National Wildlife Refuge Visitors Center. There's plenty of accessible parking out front, with level access to the building. Inside, you'll find a wide variety of interpretive exhibits, plus some nice accessible restrooms. And don't miss the boardwalk trail surrounding the center, as it's a great place to spot some native wildlife.

To round out your tour of Louisiana's Outback, head south on Highway 27 to the Pintail Wildlife Drive. This three-mile long driving loop is a great place to spot birds year round. And the newly constructed Wetland Walkway boardwalk is nicely accessible, and offers wheelers and slow walkers an excellent up-close-and-personal viewing opportunity.

To complete this scenic driving loop through the bayou, follow Highway 27 south to Oak Grove, go west on Highway 82 to Highway 35, and connect back to Interstate 10 in Rayne. It's a bit off-the beaten-path, but it makes for an interesting drive.

Henderson

Located just a short hop off Interstate 10, Henderson, Louisiana is definitely worth a stop. Not only is it a scenic drive on a rural road, but it's also the home of McGee's Landing—a great place for a Cajun lunch and a swamp tour of the Atchafalaya Basin.

It's somewhat of a challenge to find, but definitely worth the effort. Just take exit 115 off of Interstate 10 and go south to Highway 347, and east on Highway 352. Turn right on Henderson Levee Road and travel about 2½ miles, until you see a sign marking the left turn over the levee to McGee's Landing. Although the directions are pretty straightforward, the turn is easy to miss. Be forewarned though, your GPS will lead you astray in this area, so it's best to rely on your own navigational skills.

Although the parking lot isn't paved, there's accessible parking on an asphalt slab near the entrance, and ramp access up to McGee's Bar & Cafe. Inside, there's good pathway access in the restaurant and gift shop, with level access out to the patio that overlooks the Atchafalaya Basin. The decidedly Cajun menu boasts southern staples such as alligator, crawfish etoufee, seafood gumbo, boiled crabs and fried shrimp. It's a local favorite and you just can't beat the surroundings.

After lunch, save some time for a swamp tour. Although it's not technically wheelchair-accessible, many wheelers and slow walkers will be able to manage the tour. There's a two-inch step up to the dock, with ramp access to the pontoon boat. The ramp is only 21 inches wide—too narrow for most power wheelchairs—but some slow walkers, scooter-users and manual wheelchair-users will be able to manage it.

And the tour through the Atchafalaya Basin—the overflow region of the Atchafalaya River—is excellent. The boat cruises by moss draped trees, while the guide regales passengers with tales of the region, and educates them about the native flora and fauna. It's a very popular tour, so advance reservations are highly recommended.

Even though there are a few access obstacles on the boat, McGee's Landing is definitely worth a visit, if only for lunch. Even if you can't access the boat, you'll still come away with a real feel for what's billed as one of America's greatest river swamps.

Darrow

Plan to spend at least a day in Darrow to visit the beautiful Houmas House (225-473-9380, www.HoumasHouse.com) plantation estate. Billed as the crown jewel of Louisiana's River Road, this historic home features excellent wheelchair access. The oldest part of the home dates back to 1710, but Wade Hampton made some substantial additions in the 1820s. Today it's Kevin Kelly's home, and as such it's free of the velvet ropes and Plexiglas panels found in most other period homes.

Unlike McGee's Landing, it's pretty easy to find too. Just take exit 179 off of Interstate 10 and go south on Highway 44 to Highway 942. Take a right on Highway 942, and you'll find Houmas House about a half-mile up the road on your right.

There's plenty of accessible parking, with level access to the gift shop; where you can buy mansion tour tickets. From there, there's level access to the 38-acre garden filled with ponds, sculpture and some of the largest oak trees I've ever seen. The accessible restroom is located behind Burnside Cafe, and the pathways through the garden are wide and level, with lots of benches to rest along the way.

Houmas House in Darrow, Louisiana.

    The mansion is also very accessible, as it boasts ramp access, barrier free pathways and an elevator. The tour is fascinating, as it's sprinkled with tidbits of local history. And everywhere you turn there's something unique; from the massive three-story spiral staircase, to a clock once owned by Marie Antoinette. And if that isn't enough, Houmas House even served as the filming location for *Hush...Hush, Sweet Charlotte*; and the preserved room where Bette Davis stayed is also included on the tour.

    But the mansion tour isn't the only reason to visit Houmas House; as it's also a great place to dine. Cafe Burnside features level access and serves up sandwiches, southern favorites and salads for lunch; while the more elegant Latil's Landing, which is located inside the accessible mansion, is *the* place for that special dinner. And then there's the Le Petite Houmas Restaurant, which has level access and offers a Sunday brunch with a definite southern twist; with dishes like Eggs Creole and Grits and Grillades. No matter what your dining choice, you won't be disappointed at Houmas House; in fact, it's reason enough to visit this former sugar plantation.

Saint Louis Cathedral on Jackson Square in New Orleans, Louisiana.

New Orleans

New Orleans is a must-see on any bayou itinerary; and there's no better place to base yourself than in the historic French Quarter. Granted, access is variable; however, the most accessible route runs along Decatur Street, where you'll find curb-cuts and well maintained sidewalks. Additionally, the Riverwalk, which runs along the Mississippi River, is wide, level and nicely accessible. And if you tire of walking, just hop on the wheelchair-accessible Riverfront Streetcar, which runs from the French Market to the Convention Center.

The best way to explore the French Quarter is to pick up a map at the Ann Street Visitors Center, near Jackson Square, and set out on foot. This walking tour is fairly accessible, and you can do it at your own pace. Be sure and stop in at the Presbytere (504-568-6968), right behind Jackson Square. There's a ramp access to this historic building which houses the Louisiana State Museum. Next door, there are more historic exhibits at the Cabildo (504-568-6968), which boasts level access to the front entrance, good pathway access inside, and elevator access to all floors.

Don't forget to stop at Cafe Du Monde (504-525-4544, www.cafedu monde.com), just across from Jackson Square. This New Orleans mainstay features level access, and it's *the* place to get cafe au lait and beignets in the Crescent City.

If you'd prefer a more organized tour of the city, try the Gray Line (504-569-1401, www.graylineneworleans.com) Super City Tour, which can be conducted in a wheelchair-accessible bus, given 48-hours notice. Alternatively, the Friends of the Cabildo (504-523-3939, www.friendsofthe cabildo.org) offers an excellent French Quarter walking tour, which can follow a wheelchair-accessible route if needed. And if you'd like to hear some tales of the ghostly residents of the French Quarter, the New Orleans Ghost Tour (504-628-1722, www.neworleansghosttour.com) is just what the doctor ordered. These night tours cover less than a mile, and the guides are happy to alter the route for wheelchair-users and slow walkers.

Last but certainly not least, plan to overnight at the Hotel Monteleone (504-523-3341, www.hotelmonteleone.com), located in the heart of the French Quarter. This 570-room property features 18 accessible rooms, including six with roll-in showers. As an added bonus, it also features a number of resident ghosts—most of whom prefer the 14th floor.

Vicksburg

For a little change of pace, plan a short stay in Vicksburg along your route. It's the perfect place to soak up some Civil War history, and enjoy the small town feel of the downtown area.

The best place to begin your tour is at the Visitors Center at Vicksburg National Military Park (601-636-0583, www.nps.gov/vick). There's plenty of accessible parking, level access to the building and barrier-free access around the exhibits inside.

Be sure and pick up a map of the park, which features a 16-mile loop drive with 15 designated tour stops. Although not all of the stops are fully accessible, there is space to pull off and get a good view at most of them. Additionally, a free cell phone tour is available at designated stops. Just dial the phone numbers listed on the plaques and listen to the commentary. The average driving time through the park is about two hours, but that's dependent on how long you spend at each stop.

Located about halfway along the drive, the USS *Cairo* Museum and Gunboat is definitely worth a stop. There is good access throughout this museum, which features exhibits about Civil War naval operations and life on the USS *Cairo*. It also includes a short video about the sinking, discovery and salvage of the historic gunboat.

After you finish your tour of the military park, head on over to the downtown area for a look into Vicksburg's past. Pop into the Corner Drug Store, located at 1123 Washington Street, and take a gander at the old pharmacy supplies, apothecary jars and civil war artifacts in this working drug store. There is level access from the street, and room for wheelers to get down most aisles.

Just up the street, the Biedenharn Coca-Cola Museum (601-638-6514) is doable for some slow walkers. This former candy store is the place where Coca-Cola was first bottled; and today it's filled with old equipment, signs and other Coca-Cola memorabilia. Although it's not wheelchair-accessible, slow walkers who can do at least eight steps should be able to manage it.

Last but not least, stop in at the Old Courthouse Museum (601-636-0741, www.oldcourthouse.org), just up the hill. There's ramp access on the left to this stately old building, and a wheelchair-lift up to the second floor. Constructed in 1858 by slaves, this National Historic Landmark is filled to the brim with exhibits; from pre-Columbian implements and Native American arrowheads, to Victorian china and dresses. They also have an excellent collection of Civil War artifacts. Save some time for a stroll around the block on the sidewalk below, as you'll get an entirely different view of the historic building from each side.

TIMING

· ·

It's best to avoid this route during the summer, as it can get very hot and humid. And although New Orleans is crowded during the peak Mardi Gras season, it's a little more manageable during the New Orleans Jazz & Heritage Festival held in late April and early May. Other events worth attending are the Rayne Frog Festival in November; and the Louisiana Southern Fried Festival, held in West Monroe in late May.

GREAT EATS

For some good home cooking stop by Hollier's Cajun Kitchen (337-527-0061) in Sulpher, Louisiana before you hit the Creole Nature trail. This local favorite specializes in steaks and seafood cooked the Cajun way, with regional favorites such as fried catfish and jambalaya topping the menu. They also have a daily seafood buffet, and a weekly barbeque buffet. There is level access to the front entrance with room enough to maneuver inside. It's far from fancy, but it's the place to go for good food at reasonable prices.

DON'T MISS IT

Take a drive on the Natchez Trace Parkway (800-305-7417, www.nps.gov/natr) while visiting Vicksburg. This scenic driving route stretches from Natchez to Nashville and passes by Civil War battle sites, some beautiful scenery, and a number of secluded picnic areas. From Vicksburg, head east on Interstate 20 and pick up a map at the Natchez Trace Parkway Visitors Center in Clinton; before heading south on the parkway. Pack a lunch and stop at the picnic area at Deans Stand. There's no accessible parking there, but it's pretty secluded and there's plenty of room to pull up near the picnic tables. To complete your loop, head south to Port Gibson, then take Highway 61 and circle back to Vicksburg. And if you like what you see, consider exploring the entire length of the parkway on your next trip.

LINGER ON IN THE GATEWAY

Save a few days to soak up a little culture in Houston after your drive through Louisiana and Mississippi. There's a bounty of wheelchair-accessible cultural attractions, and most are within walking distance of one another.

- Visit the Contemporary Arts Museum Houston (713-284-8250, www.camh.org), which features ramp access, barrier-free access to the galleries and elevator access to the lower floor. This Houston icon features a large collection of international, national and regional art, dating back to the 1980s.

- Walk across the street to the Museum of Fine Arts, Houston (713-639-7300, www.mfah.org), which features over 56,000 works and boasts an accessible entrance, good pathway access and elevator access to all levels.

- Stop for a bite to eat at Bodega's Taco Shop (713-528-6102, www.bodegas tacoshop.com), which features ramp access on the side. This hidden gem of the Museum District serves up made-to-order Mexican favorites and top-notch margaritas.

- Drive over to The Health Museum (713-942-7054, www.thehealth museum.org), which features a ramped entrance and plenty of room to roll around. This interactive museum boasts a 27½-foot intestine, a colossal walk-in eyeball and a large collection of other educational exhibits.

- For more kid fun, head next door to the Childrens Museum (713-522-1138, www.cmhouston.org), which has barrier-free access to 90,000 square feet of interactive and educational exhibits.

- Drive over to the Holocaust Museum (713-942-8000, www.hmh.org) for a look at exhibits that chronicle the Holocaust; including a rail car that was used to transport Jews to concentration camps and a boat that was used to rescue them. There's plenty of accessible parking in the adjacent lot, with level access to the museum and ramp access to the rail car and the boat. Loaner wheelchairs are also available at the entrance.

- Check out the Houston Center for Contemporary Craft (713-529-4848, www.crafthouston.org), which features accessible parking near the entrance and barrier-free access to galleries filled with contemporary works in a wide variety of mediums.

- Chow down at the Downtown Aquarium Restaurant (713-223-3474, www.aquariumrestaurants.com) which serves up some of Landry's favorites in a dining room surrounded by a 150,000-gallon aquarium. After dinner, save some time to stroll through the adjacent aquarium, visit the rainforest exhibit and see the white tiger. There's barrier-free access throughout the aquarium and restaurant, with plenty of accessible parking nearby.

■ Save a day for a visit to Space Center Houston (281-244-2100, www.spacecenter.org), located about 45 miles south of town. There's level access to the building and roll-on access to the tram that takes visitors to Mission Control, the Space Vehicle Mockup Facility and Rocket Park.

FLY-DRIVE OPTION

To make this a fly-drive vacation, fly to William P. Hobby Airport (713-640-3000, www.fly2houston.com) or George Bush Intercontinental Airport (281-230-3100, www.fly2houston.com); then rent an accessible van at Handi-Cab (713-723-8618, www.handicapvans.net), Wheelchair Getaways (866-616-8267, www.wheelchairgetaways.com), AMS Vans (800-775-8267, www.amsvans.com) or Accessible Vans of Northwest Texas (888-553-6003, www.adaptivedriving.com).

ALTERNATE ENTRY POINTS

■ From Dallas, take Interstate 45 south to Houston.

■ From Memphis, take Interstate 55 south to Vicksburg.

■ From Mobile, take Interstate 10 west to New Orleans.

VARIATION ON A THEME

T he New Orleans, Darrow, and Henderson portions of this route can be easily done on a three-night trip from Mobile; while the Vicksburg and Natchez Trace Parkway segment makes a good weekend getaway from Little Rock. For an extended trip, head east to Birmingham from Meridian and drive the Deep Southern Delight route.

- IF YOU GO

  - Southwest Louisiana Convention & Visitors Bureau, (337) 436-9588, www.visitlakecharles.org
  - McGee's Landing, (337) 546-3453, www.mcgeeslanding.com
  - Houmas House, (225) 473-9380, www.HoumasHouse.com
  - New Orleans Convention & Visitors Bureau, (504) 767-7700, www.neworleanscvb.com
  - Vicksburg Convention & Visitors Bureau, (800) 221-3536, www.visitvicksburg.com
  - Greater Houston Convention & Visitors Bureau, (713) 437-5200, www.visithoustontexas.com

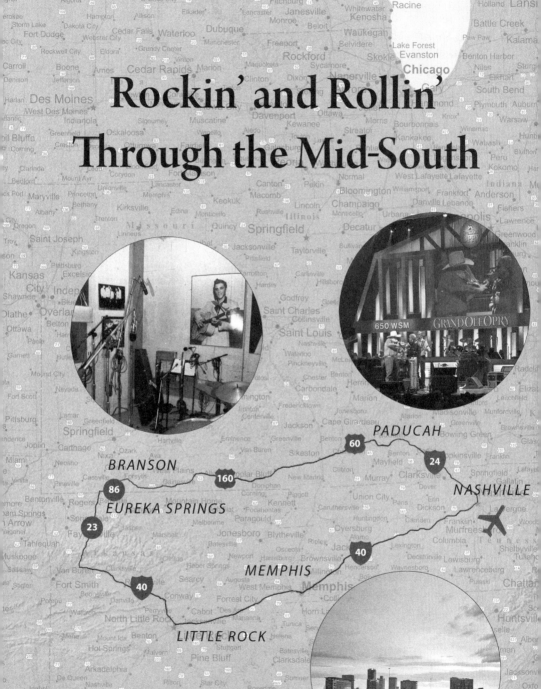

Rockin' and Rollin' Through the Mid-South

BRANSON

EUREKA SPRINGS

PADUCAH

NASHVILLE

MEMPHIS

LITTLE ROCK

This route is a must-do for music lovers, as it hits the live music trifecta of the Mid-South—Nashville, Memphis and Branson. And when you tire of the music there's the cultural diversions in Little Rock, a scenic drive through the Ozarks, a ghost hunting opportunity in Eureka Springs, and an extensive quilt collection in Paducah. Along the way, you'll find a variety of wheelchair-accessible sights, lots of friendly people and some good old fashioned home cooking—and that's a combination that's hard to beat.

ROUTE

Этиs route begins in Nashville and travels west on Interstate 40 through Memphis and Little Rock. It then continues along Interstate 40, and follows Highway 23 north to Eureka Springs. Next it continues north on Highway 23, crosses into Missouri, picks up scenic Highway 86, and connects with Highway 65 North to Branson. Then it's time to hop on Highway 160 and travel across Southern Arkansas, then take Highway 60 to Paducah, Kentucky. To complete the route, follow Highway 24 back to Nashville.

ALONG THE WAY

Memphis

Memphis is a great place to linger on for a few days, enjoy a little live entertainment and learn about the city's colorful musical history. The best place to begin your Memphis visit is on Beale Street—the true music hot spot of the city. Access is good along the street with wide sidewalks and plenty of curb-cuts, and barrier-free access to about 50% of the venues.

Located just a block from Beale Street, the Memphis Rock 'n' Soul Museum (901-205-2533, www.memphisrocknsoul.org) is also worth a visit.

A discrete ramp provides front door access to the mansion at Graceland.

This excellent museum has a level entry and barrier-free access; and features exhibits that chronicle the evolution of the infamous Memphis sound.

Of course no Memphis visit is complete without a pilgrimage to Graceland (901-332-3322, www.elvis.com/graceland), the long time home of Elvis Presley. Although the mansion was built in 1939, access features have been added over the years, so today it's an excellent choice for wheelchair-users and slow walkers. Lift-equipped busses shuttle folks up to the mansion, and the home itself features ramp access and barrier-free pathways along most portions of the tour route. The one exception is the basement, which can only be accessed by steps; however, a video of the area is available. Plan to spend an entire day at Graceland, as there's a lot to see and do.

And if you'd like to see where Elvis got his start, then head on over to Sun Studio (800-441-6249, www.sunstudio.com). Billed as the birthplace of rock and roll, it's the place where Elvis launched his career when he recorded "That's All Right Mama." By night, this historic location is still a working recording studio, but during the day it's open for tours. There is level access to the first floor, but only stairway access to the second floor. Still, it's an excellent tour, even if you can only do the first floor, as it includes some great stories about the early days of rock and roll.

For a very accessible place to spend the night, head on over to the Peabody Hotel (901-529-4000, www.peabodymemphis.com). Known for the pampered ducks that grace the lobby fountain, this Memphis icon features wheelchair-accessible rooms with a roll-in showers or tub/shower combinations. Even if you don't stay there, be sure and stop by to see the ducks march to and from their penthouse digs at 11 A.M. and 5 P.M. every day. It's a true Memphis tradition.

Little Rock

For a change of pace, stop over in Little Rock for a few days and enjoy some of the cultural attractions in this Arkansas capital city. The Old State House Museum (501-324-9685, www.oldstatehouse.com) is the perfect place to start your visit. Although this building served as the first Arkansas state capitol, today it houses a number of historic exhibits; including a collection of Arkansas First Ladies' gowns and Bill Clinton's saxophone. There is ramped access to the main entrance, elevator access to the upper floor and plenty of room to wheel around in the spacious galleries.

For a little more history, head on over to the Historic Arkansas Museum (501-324-9351, www.historicarkansas.org), just a few blocks away, on 3rd Street near Cumberland. The museum features six galleries and five historic buildings that present a good overview of Arkansas history, art and culture. There is level access at the front entrance, good pathway access to the galleries and elevator access to all floors. And although there is level pathway access around the property, not all of the historic buildings are accessible. Still it's worth a visit, as the indoor exhibits are excellent.

Of course you can't leave Little Rock without a visit to the crown jewel of the River Market District, The William J. Clinton Presidential Library (501-374-4242, www.clintonpresidentialcenter.org). Featuring a massive 20,000 square feet of exhibition space, the building boasts excellent access to all of the galleries, sleek wood floors, accessible restrooms and loaner wheelchairs available at the front desk. This anchor attraction houses a large collection of exhibits which chronicle the Clinton presidency; including a replica of the oval office (including the moon rock), items from Bill's childhood, and even a collection of Saturday Night Live clips featuring Clinton impersonations. Plan to spend the whole day there, as it's massive.

Displays at the Old State House Museum in Little Rock, Arkansas.

Last but not least, save some time for a stroll through the River Market District, which spans the entire length of President Clinton Avenue, along the Arkansas River. Throughout this revitalized 10-block area, you'll find a wide variety of galleries, shops, restaurants and bars; as well as a summer and fall farmers market. There are curb-cuts and wide sidewalks throughout the district, so it's a fun place to browse your dining options, window shop or even enjoy an adult beverage or two.

Eureka Springs

Truth be told, Eureka Springs isn't exactly the most accessible city in the world; however, it's worth a stop to visit the Crescent Hotel—also known as America's most haunted hotel. The drive through the Ozarks is pretty scenic too, and it's just a short jog off the main route up to Branson.

Built in 1886, the Crescent Hotel served as a hotel for over 20 years, before it was converted to a boarding school, and finally a cancer hospital. It was only after it reverted back to a hotel that the ghostly apparitions began. Today, guests report a steady stream of sightings and "unusual events" on the hotel's website. Are they real or simply the result of overactive imaginations and the power of suggestion? The best way to answer that question is to take the Eureka Springs Ghost Tour (479-253-6800, www.eureka-springs-ghost.com) and decide for yourself.

The tour starts in Room 212 and lasts for about two hours. Best bet is to drive to the hotel, as there's accessible parking in front, with ramp access to the lobby. From there, just take the elevator to the second floor.

The tour begins on the second floor, with tales of the Irish stonemason who haunts Room 218, and the little boy who plays in the second floor hallway. Up on the third floor, you'll hear about Annabelle who walks through the wall near Room 319. And then of course, there's Theodora in Room 419, who gets very upset with messy guests.

But by far, the creepiest part of the tour is the visit to the basement, which served as the morgue for the Baker Cancer Cure Hospital. Corpses were reportedly stored there until hearses came in the dead of night to collect them. The reason for all the secrecy was that Doctor Baker didn't want folks to know that his cancer cures had failed and his patients had died. It's also rumored that some bodies were cremated there.

There is good pathway access to all areas on the tour, and although there are stairs to the basement, advance arrangements can be made for an additional guide to escort you along an accessible route.

Head over to the Best Western Inn of the Ozarks (479-253-9768, www.innoftheozarks.com), for accessible overnight accommodations in Eureka Springs. Located just a mile from the Crescent Hotel, there's level access to the public areas; and Rooms 131 and 151 both have nicely done roll-in showers. It's an affordable, relaxing and very accessible place to stay.

Branson

Variety is the key word in Branson—in both the entertainment offerings and the attractions. Dolly Parton's Dixie Stampede (417-366-3000, www.dixiestampede.com) tops the entertainment list. This high energy dinner show takes place in a 35,000-square-foot arena and features everything from trick riding and musical production numbers, to toilet seat tossing and ostrich racing. It's also very accessible, with plenty of wheelchair seating and barrier-free access to the outside stable area.

If you're up for a little shopping, then head on over to Branson Landing (www.bransonlanding.com), which offers more than 100 retail shops in a dynamic waterfront setting. Not only are there no curbs or lips on the

Curbless sidewalks at Branson Landing.

sidewalks in this pedestrian mall, but an accessible trolley transports visitors from one end to another.

The Titanic Museum (417-334-9500, www.titanicbranson.com) is also worth a visit, especially for history buffs. Located near the intersection of Highway 76 and Highway 165, the building is shaped like the ill-fated luxury liner, complete with an iceberg and a replica of Waterloo Train Station in the foreground. There's plenty of accessible parking in front, and level access to the main museum entrance. Inside, there's barrier-free access throughout the spacious galleries, which house over 400 Titanic artifacts.

Don't miss the Branson Ducks (877-887-8225, www.bransonducks.com), a fun Branson tour with a unique twist. The 1½-hour tour is conducted in a WWII amphibious vehicle, that travels through the entertainment district and heads to the hills, before it finally splashes down into Table Rock Lake. There's elevator access up to the boarding level, but you have to be able to walk up a few steps in order to board the vehicle. Still, it's a fun tour if you can manage it.

Finally, if you'd like an accessible taste of the great outdoors, then check out Table Rock Lake. Just head west on Highway 76 until it dead ends, then go east on Shepherd of the Hills Expressway. When you hit Highway 265, turn left, cross the lake and continue on to the Dewey Short Visitors Center. There's level access to the building, which contains a number of interpretive exhibits, and a two-mile barrier-free trail outside. It's especially scenic in the spring when the dogwoods are blooming; but it makes for a pleasant stroll throughout the year.

And if you'd like a little variety in your Branson overnight accommodations, then check out David Neitz's wheelchair-accessible town homes (866-384-5783, www.bransontownhomes.com) in Stonebridge Village. These three-bedroom units are located next door to one another, and they each feature good pathway access and have an accessible master suite with a roll-in shower. Best of all, they're located in a quiet gated community, which offers a welcome retreat after a long day of sightseeing.

TIMING

. . . .

Spring and fall are absolutely beautiful in the Ozarks. The dogwood blooms burst forth in the spring, and the changing leaves put on a grand show in the fall. And although the weather isn't exactly ideal during the holidays, it's a good time to visit Branson if you want to take in some of the special Christmas shows.

GREAT EATS

. . . .

Make plans to dine on the Showboat Branson Belle (800-475-9370, www.showboatbransonbelle. com), when visiting Branson. There's good access throughout the boat, with elevator access to all decks, and spacious accessible restrooms aboard. Most of the seating is wheelchair-accessible too, so make sure and specify your needs when you make your reservation. The two-hour cruise on Lake Branson features a delicious three-course meal and a live show. The food is prepared on board from scratch, and it's fresh, flavorful and filling. It's just a fun way to enjoy an afternoon or evening meal.

DON'T MISS IT

B e sure and stop in Paducah, Kentucky for a visit to the Museum of the American Quilter's Society (207-442-8856, www.quiltmuseum.org). This massive museum features a large core collection of contemporary quilts, augmented by a smattering of visiting exhibitions. Even non-quilters will enjoy the pieces for their artistic value. The museum is nicely accessible too, with a level entrance and barrier-free access throughout the spacious galleries. And since the museum makes new acquisitions ever year, it's also worth a repeat visit, because you'll never see the same show twice.

LINGER ON IN THE GATEWAY

S ave a few days to explore Nashville and learn about the musical heritage of Music City USA. Most of the hot spots offer good wheelchair access, and it's a fun place for music lovers of all genres.

■ Start your Nashville visit with a Gray Line trolley tour (615-883-5555, www.graylinenashville.com). A lift-equipped trolley is available with 48-hours notice; the one-hour tour takes in the downtown area, the state capitol, Music Row and the Parthenon.

■ If you'd prefer to hoof it, try the Gray Line walking tour instead. The two-block tour travels along an accessible route in the downtown area, and features tales of famous song writers, musicians and celebrities.

■ Visit the Country Music Hall of Fame and Museum (615-416-2001, www.countrymusichalloffame.com), which has a ramped entrance on

Fifth Avenue and excellent wheelchair access throughout the museum. This comprehensive museum is filled with interpretive exhibits that chronicle the history of country music, including memorabilia from artists who had a hand at shaping the industry.

■ Take the Studio B Tour for a glimpse into Nashville's recording history. Operated by the Country Music Hall of Fame Museum, the tour includes lift-equipped transportation to Studio B. The historic recording studio, which played host to Roy Orbison, the Everly Brothers, Dolly Parton and even Elvis, features an accessible entrance, and plenty of room to roll around inside.

■ Stroll along the Music City Walk of Fame, located in Hall of Fame Park, just across the street from the Country Music Hall of Fame. There are paved level pathways throughout the park, and plenty of benches along the way.

■ Attend a performance of the Grand Ole Opry (615-871-6779, www.opry.com). For most of the year the show is based at the Grand Ole Opry House, but some performances are held at the historic Ryman Auditorium. Accessible seating with adjacent companion seats are available at both venues.

■ Check out the Grand Ole Opry Museum, just to the right of the Grand Ole Opry House. There's plenty of accessible parking near Opry Plaza, with level access to the museum, which contains exhibits that chronicle the history of the Opry.

■ Explore Fort Nashborough in Riverfront Park. This reconstruction of Nashville's first settlement features an accessible entrance on the south side and paved pathways through the complex. Although most of the buildings have steps, you can still get a good view of the interiors from the outside.

■ Visit the Charlie Daniels Museum, located on Second Avenue, just a few doors down from the Hard Rock Cafe. Manual wheelchair-users may need a little assistance over the lip at the entrance; but after that there's level access through the gift shop to the museum. This eclectic site houses a bevy of Charlie Daniels photos, concert memorabilia, costumes and instruments.

- Enjoy a lunch break at Jack's Bar-B-Que (615-254-5715, www.jacks barbque.com) on Broadway, where you can get a big old plate of BBQ, two sides and bread for a very reasonable price. There is level access to the first-floor dining area, but only stair access to the top floor, where the restrooms are located.

- Stroll through Hatch Print, just down the street from Jacks. As one of America's oldest letter-press poster print shops, they've printed concert posters for top artists like Bruce Springsteen, Johnny Cash and Coldplay. Old posters are available to purchase, but it's fun just to browse and take a short trip down memory lane. The shop itself is pretty small, but there's level access and enough room to navigate.

- For some free musical entertainment, go to church. Nashville insiders insist it's one of the best places to hear some great free music. Pick a larger church for a better musical program, and make sure to inquire if the sanctuary is wheelchair-accessible before your visit.

FLY-DRIVE OPTION

To make this a fly-drive vacation, fly to Nashville International Airport (615-275-1675, www.nash intl.com), then rent an accessible van at Wheelchair Getaways (866-762-1656, www.wheelchairgetaways.com) or Wheelers Van Rentals (931-881-2033, www.wheelersvanrentals.com).

ALTERNATE ENTRY POINTS

- From Atlanta, take Interstate 24 west to Nashville.
- From Louisville, take Interstate 65 south to Nashville.

■ From St. Louis, take Interstate 55 south to Interstate 57, then go east to Highway 60 to Paducah.

VARIATION ON A THEME

. . . .

The Branson and Eureka Springs portion of this route makes a good three-night getaway from Kansas City; while the Memphis and Nashville segment can be easily done as a week-long trip from Birmingham. If you fancy a longer road trip, then drive to Springfield from Branson and connect with the Missouri's Mother Road and More route.

- IF YOU GO
    - Memphis Convention & Visitors Bureau, (901) 543-5300, www.memphistravel.com
    - Little Rock Convention & Visitors Bureau, (501) 376-4781, www.littlerock.com
    - Branson Lake Area Chamber of Commerce, (800) 296-0463, www.explorebranson.com
    - Nashville Convention & Visitors Bureau, (615) 259-4700, www.visitmusiccityusa.com

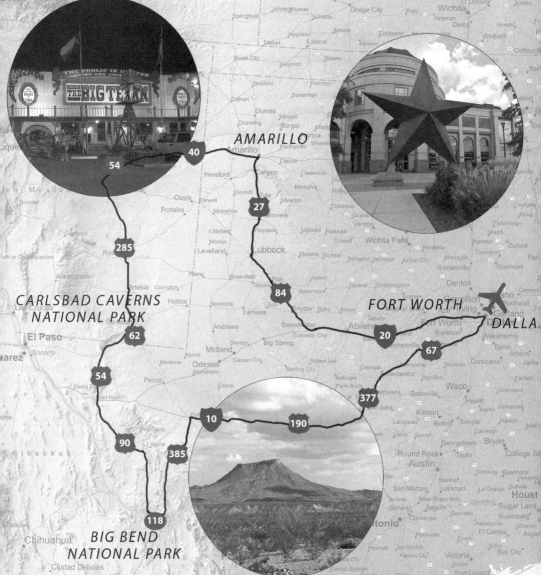

Cowboys, Indians
and New Mexicans

AMARILLO

FORT WORTH

DALLAS

**CARLSBAD CAVERNS
NATIONAL PARK**

**BIG BEND
NATIONAL PARK**

Although this is a rather ambitious route, it's packed full of cowboy culture, natural wonders, Native American history and great scenery. Add in a little Route 66 history and the cultural attractions of Dallas and Fort Worth, and you'll return home with some fond memories, fun stories and great photographs.

ROUTE

T his route begins in Dallas and heads west on Interstate 20 to Fort Worth, then continues west along the interstate to Highway 84, to Interstate 27 to Amarillo. From there it heads west on Interstate 40, crosses into New Mexico and connects with Highway 54, Highway 285, Highway 62 and Highway 7, before it dead ends at Carlsbad Caverns National Park. Back out on the main road, Highway 62 crosses back into Texas, before it's time to head south on Highway 54, then follow Highway 90 and Highway 118 to the Study Butte entrance of Big Bend National Park. Finally the route heads out the Marathon park gate and travels north on Highway 385 to Interstate 10 East. The final segment of the journey follows Highway 190 to Highway 377, to Highway 67, before it loops back to Dallas.

ALONG THE WAY

Fort Worth

Although it's often lumped together with nearby Dallas, Fort Worth deserves recognition as a cultural destination in its own right. Not only does the downtown cultural district boast a healthy smattering of world class museums, but the historic stockyards offer visitors a unique opportunity to soak up a little cowboy culture.

The Texas Whitehouse B&B in Fort Worth, Texas.

The best place to begin your Fort Worth visit is in the stockyard district. Located just north of downtown, this area was once the headquarters for Armour and Swift meat packing companies. Today the meat packers are long gone, but the stockyard history still remains. And although you'll find some high curbs and uneven brick pavement throughout this historic district, there are alternate accessible routes to most areas. Pick up a map at the visitors Center at 130 E. Exchange Avenue, and strike out on your own— you'll find something interesting around every corner.

And don't miss the Fort Worth Herd (www.fortworthherd.com), the twice daily cattle drive up Exchange Avenue. It's great fun and a good chance to get a close look at some real Texas longhorns.

Save at least a day to explore the downtown cultural district. The museums all have excellent wheelchair access, and they're located within walking distance of one another. And with wide sidewalks and plenty of curb-cuts, it's an easy area to explore on foot.

Top cultural picks include the Amon Carter Museum (817-738-1933, www.cartermuseum.org), the Kimbell Art Museum (817-332-8451, www.kimbellart.org), the Modern Art Museum of Fort Worth (817-738-9215, www.mamfw.org), the Fort Worth Museum of Science and History (817-255-9300, www.fwmuseum.org) and the National Cowgirl Museum and Hall of Fame (817-336-4475, www.cowgirl.net).

And although it's located well out of the cultural district, the C.R. Smith Museum (817-967-1560, www.crsmithmuseum.org) is also worth a visit. Named for the former President of American Airlines, the museum is dedicated to the history of commercial aviation and American Airlines. There is plenty of accessible parking outside, with barrier-free access to all areas of the museum, except for the restored DC-3. Best of all, admission is free.

And for a fun and accessible place to overnight, check out the Texas White House B&B (817-923-3597, www.texaswhitehouse.com). It's just a short drive from the cultural district, and this historic property features the nicely accessible Longhorn Room. Located in the carriage house, this comfortable room includes wide doorways, wood floors and an accessible bathroom with a roll-in shower. And although the historic house can only be accessed by steps, innkeeper Grover McMains is happy to deliver breakfast to the room if you can't manage them.

Amarillo

Located in the Texas Panhandle, Amarillo offers a wide variety of accessible outdoor diversions, with a decidedly western flavor. Amarillo Botanical Gardens (806-352-6513, www.amarillobotanicalgardens.org) tops the list, with a diverse collection of plants, plenty of accessible pathways and no admission charge. And don't miss the Palo Duro Garden for a look at some native Panhandle plants. It's a huge idea farm too, as it's hard not to come away with at least a few ideas for home.

For a look at more Panhandle plants, check out Libb's Trail at the Wildcat Bluff Nature Center (806-352-6007, www.wildcatbluff.org), located just a few minutes from downtown Amarillo. Although the center primarily serves as a research and educational facility, the trails are open to the public. Libb's Trail features wide paved pathways, barrier-free access and interpretive signs along the way.

And although it's not technically wheelchair-accessible, the Prairie Loop Trail might be doable for some slow walkers. The biggest obstacle is the 12-inch-wide entrance gate, which can't accommodate wheelchairs or scooters. Still, if you can squeeze past it, there's a 24-inch-wide hard-packed trail that leads through the adjacent grassland area.

For a full dose of the great outdoors, save a day for an excursion to nearby Palo Duro Canyon State Park (806-488-2227, www.paloduro canyon.com), located just a half-hour southeast of Amarillo. The most accessible way to enjoy the park is to pick up a map at the Visitors Center and drive to bottom of the canyon. It's a very scenic drive, with lots of great windshield views along the way.

And when you reach the bottom, save some time to explore the Paseo Del Rio trail. Although there are no accessible trails in the park, this riverside trail may be doable for some people. It's important to note that there are several access points for the Paseo Del Rio trail; however, the upper trailhead, just past the first river crossing, is the best way for wheelchair-users and slow walkers to access it.

The hard-packed dirt trail is doable for many wheelers and slow walkers, but don't even attempt it after a rain. After the trail passes the Chinaberry Day Use Area, it becomes very narrow and bumpy, and inaccessible for wheelchair-users and slow walkers. At this point, you can either take the same trail back, or roll along the roadway to your car. It's a very scenic trail if you can manage it, and a great way to explore Palo Duro Canyon.

Big Bend National Park

Big Bend National Park is truly the hidden gem of the Lone Star state. Named for the giant bend in the Rio Grande that carves out the southern border of the park, this Southwestern Texas attraction features two entry stations—one at Persimmon Gap and one at Study Butte. Best bet is to plan a road trip through the park, overnight in the Chisos Basin and exit through the opposite gate. You'll find everything you need in the Chisos Basin, including comfortable lodging, a top-notch restaurant, a well stocked camp store and one of the park's two accessible campgrounds.

If camping is just a bit too rustic for you, then check out the Chisos Mountains Lodge (877-386-4383, www.chisosmountainslodge.com). It's well away from the maddening crowds, yet boasts all the creature comforts of home. The accessible rooms feature wide doorways, lowered peepholes, tile floors and bathrooms with tub/shower combinations and portable shower benches. But by far the best feature of these rooms are the back decks, which

View on the Window View Trail at Big Bend National Park.

offer spectacular views of the Chisos Mountains. There's level access to the decks, and they offer the perfect place to relax and enjoy the sunset.

For another great view, head across the lodge parking lot and take a stroll along the Window View Trail. This .3-mile barrier-free trail features paved access, with a gradual descent to the window viewpoint. Benches are strategically placed along the trail, and it's just a very pleasant place to enjoy the view of the spectacular canyon walls and the Chisos Mountains.

Save a full day for a drive along the Ross Maxwell Scenic Loop, as it's the highlight of any Big Bend visit. This 30-mile scenic drive leads to the Castolon Historic District and Santa Elena Canyon, and passes through some historic and geologic treasures along the way.

There are several accessible overlooks along the route, including Homer Wilson Ranch Overlook, Mule Ears Viewpoint and Goat Mountain Viewpoint. Tuff Canyon Overlook is also worth a stop. Although the viewing platforms are not wheelchair-accessible, you can get a great windshield view of this volcanic canyon from your car.

Last but not least, don't miss the Santa Elena Overlook at the end of the road. From the overlook you can look down on the limestone canyon created by the Rio Grande, and gaze across into neighboring Mexico. Although there's no curb-cut access from the parking area to the overlook, you can wheel down to the end of the curb and roll out to the overlook. Although the ground is a bit bumpy in places, it's still doable for most people, and the spectacular view is well worth the effort.

Carlsbad Caverns National Park

Carlsbad Caverns is a must-see along this route, so pack a picnic lunch and plan for a full day at this world class natural attraction. Although the natural entrance is too steep for wheelers or slow walkers, there's elevator access to the Big Room, where a good portion of the self-guided tour is wheelchair-accessible. Granted there are a few narrow spots along the way, but the accessible route is clearly marked. An access map and brochure is also available. The one-mile paved trail leads to the major features in the massive cave, and the audio tour explains how the features were created.

And if you visit in the summer months, don't miss the daily exodus of bats from the natural entrance. July and August are the best bat viewing months, as that's when the baby bats begin to join the flights, and the colony grows dramatically. A park ranger presents a bat flight talk before each flight, and wheelchair seating is available near the top of the amphitheater. The starting time of the program varies, as the bats start to appear at dusk; so check at the Visitors Center for more information.

There's also a nice nature trail near the Visitors Center, part of which is wheelchair-accessible. The trailhead is located in the east parking lot, and maps are available at the front desk. And if you'd like an interesting tour of the Chihuahuan Desert, then pick up a brochure on the Desert Drive auto tour at the bookstore. This 9.5-mile gravel road begins near the Visitors Center, and is suitable for most vehicles, except motor home and cars pulling trailers. It takes about an hour to complete the drive; even longer if you make frequent stops along the way.

And if you're looking for an accessible place to enjoy a picnic lunch, then look no further than the Rattlesnake Springs Picnic Area. Located about 15 miles from the Visitors Center, it features an accessible picnic table shaded by a large cottonwood tree. Accessible restrooms are also available, and it's just a very pleasant place to stop.

TIMING

· ·

Thvs is one of the few drives that you can actually do in the winter, as you're unlikely to encounter weather related road closures during that time. Winter is also prime time in Big Bend National Park, as the summer months are dreadfully hot there. Additionally, some park facilities are only open from November to April. If you want to also catch the bat flights at Carlsbad Caverns National Park, plan for a fall getaway; but schedule your cavern visit before mid-October, as that's when the bat flights end.

GREAT EATS

· ·

The Big Texan Steak Ranch (806-372-6000, www.bigtexan.com) is a must-do while in Amarillo, even if you don't like steak. Opened in 1960 on Route 66, the original Big Texan Steak Ranch soon became famous for their "free 72-ounce steak dinner deal." Of course there was a catch—you had to eat the whole dinner in one hour to get it for free. This eat-till-you-bust deal continues today at the new Interstate 40 location; in fact, travelers from around the world flock to Amarillo to attempt the feat. And it's just downright fun to watch!

The food is good too, with Prime Rib, Top Sirloin and T-Bone steaks topping the menu. And if you're not a meat person, the fried chicken, broiled salmon and fried shrimp are also pretty tasty. Access is good, with plenty of accessible parking in front, level access to the restaurant, ample room to roll around, and clean accessible restrooms. And you can't miss it—just look for the famous giant cowboy sign in front.

The Big Texan Steak Ranch in Amarillo, Texas.

DON'T MISS IT

Save some time for a stop at Russell's Truck and Travel Center Car Museum (575-576-8700, www.russellsttc.com), especially if you're a Route 66 fan. This unique museum is located off Interstate 40 at exit 369, right after you cross the Texas–New Mexico border. It's filled with vintage cars and other memorabilia, including old coke machines, toys, signs, posters and old Route 66 photos. There's something for just about everyone, and if you're hungry there's also a diner and a Subway sandwich shop there.

Best of all, there's no admission charge, but donations are gladly accepted. Even better, all the funds collected are donated back to programs that help feed hungry families. So stop by, see some cool cars, gas up and pitch in to help fight hunger in America.

LINGER ON IN THE GATEWAY

∎∎∎

Although the Dallas and Fort Worth areas literally run into one another, save a few days to focus on some strictly Dallas attractions, and to explore a few suburban haunts. Most offer good wheelchair access, so there's certainly no shortage of accessible fun for wheelers and slow walkers in the Big D.

- Get a little culture at the Dallas Museum of Art (214-922-1200, www.dallasmuseumofart.org). There's barrier-free access throughout the galleries which are loaded with American masterpieces, European and impressionist art, and art of the Americas, Africa, Asia and the Pacific. Accessible parking is available in the museum garage, and there's a drop-off area for wheelers and slow walkers at the main entrance.

- Hop on a Segway and take a guided tour with Dallas Segway Tours (800-880-2336, www.dallassegwaytours.com). A good option for slow walkers, these fun tours include an orientation session, a helmet and bottled water. They depart from the Springhill Suites Marriott on Lamar Street in the West End Historic District.

- Check out aquatic exhibits from around the world at the Dallas World Aquarium (214-720-2224, www.dwazoo.com). There is good wheelchair access throughout the aquarium, which features a South American rain forest, as well as the Mundo Maya exhibit that includes animals that were important to the Mayan culture.

- Pack up the kids and enjoy the day at the Museum of Science and Nature (214-242-5100, www.natureandscience.org). There are barrier-free pathways throughout this interactive museum, and plenty of room to roll around in this fun and educational attraction. Wheelchairs are also available for loan at the front desk.

- Plan a visit to the Nasher Sculpture Center (214-242-5100, www.nashersculpturecenter.org), home to one of the finest collections of modern and contemporary sculpture in the world. There's barrier-free access throughout the museum and adjacent gardens, which are filled with masterpieces by Calder, de Kooning, Matisse, Picasso, Rodin and other prominent sculptors. Loaner wheelchairs are also available at the front desk.

■ Learn about the life, death and legacy of President John F. Kennedy at the Sixth Floor Museum at Dealey Plaza (214-747-6660, www.jfk.org). Housed on the sixth floor of the former Texas School Book Depository, the museum features photographs, artifacts and videos of the infamous president that was assassinated by Lee Harvey Oswald. The accessible entrance is located on the northwest corner of the museum, and there is barrier-free access to all of the exhibits. Loaner wheelchairs are also available on a first-come basis.

■ For a touch of nostalgia, head to the suburbs and visit the National Scouting Museum (972-580-2100, www.bsamuseum.org) in nearby Irving. The museum presents a comprehensive view of scouting history; and chances are you won't go more than a few display cases without saying, "I had one of those when I was a kid." The Pinewood Derby track, Fort Fun and the virtual reality adventures are just plain fun. Access throughout the museum is excellent, with good pathway access to all exhibits, accessible restrooms and plenty of accessible parking.

■ Continue on to Grapevine and stop in at Vetro Glassblowing (817-251-1668, www.vetroartglass.com) for a look at the art of glassblowing. This working studio features barrier-free access with front row seating for wheelchair-users, and level access to the adjacent gallery. It's a fun place to visit, and a great place to shop.

FLY-DRIVE OPTION

· ·

To make this a fly-drive vacation, fly to Dallas/ Fort Worth International Airport (972-973-8888, www.dfwairport.com), then rent an accessible van at United Access (877-503-9399, www.unitedaccess.com), Wheelchair Getaways (877-688-4695, www.wheelchairgetaways.com) or Wheelers Van Rentals (817-737-3355, www.wheelersvanrentals.com).

ALTERNATE ENTRY POINTS

- From Houston, take Interstate 45 north to Dallas.

- From Santa Fe, take Interstate 25 south and connect to Interstate 40.

- From Denver, take Interstate 70 east to Highway 287, and head south to Amarillo.

VARIATION ON A THEME

The Dallas and Fort Worth portion of this route makes a great four-day getaway from Oklahoma City. Likewise the Carlsbad Caverns and Big Bend portion can be easily done in five days from Las Cruces. And if you'd like an even longer road trip, then drive to Capitan from Roswell and connect with the Off the Beaten Path in the Land of Enchantment route.

- IF YOU GO
  - Fort Worth Convention & Visitors Bureau, (800) 433-5747, www.fortworth.com
  - Amarillo Convention & Visitors Council, (800) 692-1338, www.visitamarillotexas.com
  - Big Bend National Park, (432) 447-2251, www.nps.gov/bibe
  - Carlsbad Caverns National Park, (575) 785-2232 – General Park Information, (575) 785-3012 – Bat Flight Information, www.nps.gov/cave

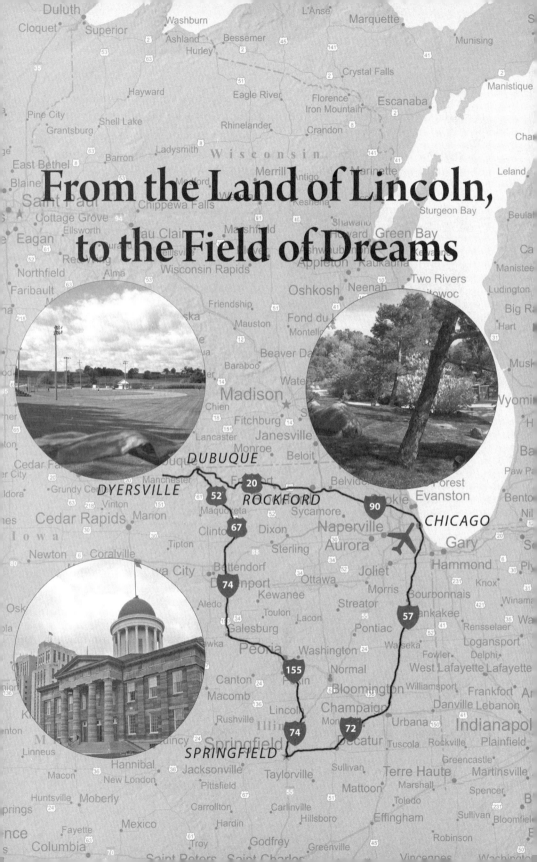

From the Land of Lincoln, to the Field of Dreams

DUBUQUE

DYERSVILLE

ROCKFORD

CHICAGO

SPRINGFIELD

This itinerary includes the full gamut of Midwestern delights; from a bit of small town culture in Rockford, to some spectacular architecture in the Windy City. Toss in a cozy B&B in Galena, a scenic drive along the Mississippi and some historic Lincoln sights in Springfield, and you have a fun-filled itinerary with enough variety to satisfy even the most finicky traveler. And with a short side trip to the filming location of *The Field of Dreams*, you'll have plenty of fond memories and some great stories to share when you return home.

ROUTE

This route begins in Chicago and heads west on Interstate 90 to Rockford; then continues along on Highway 20 to Galena and Dubuque. After a short side trip to Dyersville, it's time to head south on Highway 52 and Highway 67, following the Mississippi River to Interstate 74, to Springfield, Illinois. To complete the loop, take Interstate 72 east, then connect to Interstate 57 and follow Interstate 94 back in to Chicago.

ALONG THE WAY

Rockford

Located 90 miles west of Chicago, Rockford is a nice place to spend a few days. It's a little off the beaten path, and a good place to transition from high energy Chicago to sleepy little Galena.

Nicknamed, A City of Gardens, Rockford boasts over 7,000 acres of parkland, tree lined streets and magnificent public gardens; but by far the cream of the crop is Anderson Japanese Gardens (815-229-9390, www.anderson gardens.org). The twelve-acre garden is filled with pathways, pools, streams and pagodas; and includes a guesthouse, a gazebo and a traditional tea house. Access is good throughout the garden area with the accessible route clearly marked, and plenty of benches along the route.

If you'd prefer a cultural treat, then stop by Riverfront Museum Park, where you can park once and visit three museums—the Burpee Museum of Natural History, the Discovery Center Museum and the Rockford Art Museum. It's easy to spend a whole day there, as all of the museums feature barrier-free access, with accessible parking nearby.

The Burpee Museum of Natural History (815-965-3433, www.burpee.org) features four floors of interactive specimen-based exhibits, including Jane, a juvenile Tyrannosaurus rex skeleton. If you have kids in tow, then don't miss the Discovery Center Museum (815-963-6769, www.discoverycentermuseum.org), which features exhibits rooted in math and science, and includes everything from a robotics lab and a weather exhibit, to the Body Shop which focuses on genes and heredity. There's good pathway access to the exhibits, with wheelchair-access to Red Rock Discovery Park outside. And if you're an art lover, then don't miss the Rockford Museum of Art (815-968-2787, www.rockfordartmuseum.org), which boasts the largest art collection in Illinois, outside of Chicago.

Another work of art is located just down the street at the historic Coronado Theater (815-968-2722, www.coronadopac.org). Built in 1927, it was lovingly restored in 2000. Today it's once again in use as a performance venue; but it's also an attraction in itself. The Land of Lincoln Theater Organ Society conducts backstage tours once a month. This 1½-hour tour features wheelchair-access to the backstage area by ramp and freight elevator, with elevator access to all levels of the building.

Last but not least, if you'd like a good primer of Rockford history, then check out Midway Village Museum (815-397-9112, www.midwayvillage.com). Known as Rockford's living history museum, it features an inside gallery which chronicles the history of the town, plus an outside living history park with historical buildings set on 137 acres. There's plenty of accessible parking, with level access to the inside exhibits; and crushed gravel pathways to most of the historic buildings. All in all it's a fun place to get a little exercise and enjoy a bit of history; which in the end, will give you a better perspective on Rockford today.

The Coronado Theater in Rockford, Illinois.

Galena Retreat

There's certainly no shortage of quaint B&Bs in Galena, Illinois; in fact it's a popular weekend getaway spot for many Chicagoans. So if you really want to unwind for a few nights, then linger on at the Hawk Valley Retreat (815-777-4100, www.hawkvalleyretreat.com).

Set on 10 secluded acres, Hawk Valley Retreat is a bird watcher's paradise. And if you just want to sleep in and enjoy country life, it's a great place to do that too.

Located in the main house, the accessible Swan Lake room has a private entrance from the wrap around deck, as well as access through the house. There is ramp access to the B&B, and plenty of room to maneuver a wheelchair inside. The bathroom in the Swan Lake room features a roll-in shower, toilet and shower grab bars, a shower chair, a roll-under sink and a full five-foot turning radius. It's a comfortable room with plenty of room to navigate in a wheelchair.

If however you'd like a bit more privacy and a lot more room, then check out the nicely accessible Fox Glen cottage which features a king-size bed, a two person Jacuzzi tub, a fold-out sleeper sofa, a kitchenette, a private porch and a fireplace.

Access features include accessible parking directly in front of the cottage, wide doorways, level thresholds and an open floor plan with excellent pathway access. The bathroom has a roll-in shower with a fold-down shower seat and a hand-held shower head. Other access features include, grab bars, a pedestal sink and a full five-foot turning radius.

And although The Pines Cottage and Somerset Cottage are not technically wheelchair-accessible, they may work for many slow walkers. The Pines cottage offers the same access features as Fox Glen, except that it's located farther from the main house and parking area, while Somerset Cottage is located even further up the hill and has a double whirlpool tub in place of the roll-in shower.

Although the whole property is not accessible, there are many level areas to explore. Innkeepers Wendy and Hal also offer a number of special packages and extras, including a romantic dinner for two in your cabin, a cheese and cracker tray and even some fresh flowers to adorn your room. And if you're celebrating a special occasion, then just let Wendy know—she is full of creative ideas.

Dubuque

Located 175 miles west of Chicago, the Port of Dubuque offers a variety of fun diversions, along with some very affordable and comfortable lodging options. And thanks to a $188 million America's River development project, it's a very popular vacation spot for many Midwesterners.

The cornerstone of the America's River project is National Mississippi River Museum and Aquarium (563-557-9545, www.rivermuseum.com); an aquarium and natural history museum that focuses on the Mississippi River.

Access at the museum is excellent, with a level entry, accessible restrooms, spacious galleries and elevator access to the second floor. The first floor focuses on wildlife in and along the river, while the second floor features exhibits about the natural history of the area. And outside, the elevated Woodward Wetlands boardwalk is nicely accessible and offers visitors an opportunity to see some native flora and fauna and get a great view of the museum boatyard and the Mississippi River.

If you'd like a closer look at the river, then take a day cruise on the *Spirit of Dubuque* (563-583-8093, www.dubuqueriverrides.com), which is docked at the Port of Dubuque. There's ramp boarding to this paddle wheeler, and although there is a two-inch lip at the entrance, assistance is available. Once the *Spirit of Dubuque* sets sail, it's a calm and stable cruise experience along the Big Muddy. And although you have to be able to stand to use the on board restroom, the sightseeing cruise is only 1½ hours long, so it's very doable with some advance planning.

If you'd like to try your hand at lady luck, then stop by the new Diamond Jo Casino (563-690-4800, www.diamondjo.com), which features level access and plenty of room to navigate a wheelchair inside. And since it never closes, you can linger all night if you wish.

And for a breath of fresh air, check out the Mississippi Riverwalk. This quarter-mile paved trail connects all of America's River attractions. It's wide, level and very accessible.

For a good primer on Dubuque's history, book a city tour with Trolleys of Dubuque (563-552-2896, www.trolleys.thestevenscompany.com). Co-owner Charlene Nauman gives an excellent historical presentation, and this tour is a must-do for anyone who likes architecture. There are four steps up to the trolley; however, boarding assistance and a wheelchair stowage space is available. It's a good option for slow walkers.

Save one afternoon for a side trip out to the *Field of Dreams* movie site (563-875-8404, www.fodmoviesite.com) in Dyersville. Located 25 miles west of Dubuque on the 91-year-old Lansing family farm; it's a little out of the way, but to be honest, that's part of its charm.

Admission is free and the site is flat and fairly accessible. If you like movie locations, this is a good one to take in, as it hasn't changed since the filming. It should also be noted that at press time the home was being sold to a Chicago investment group, who hopes to add more baseball fields, but intends to keep the site open. Currently the site is only open from April to November.

The Grand Harbor Resort (866-690-4006, www.grandharborresort.com) is the ideal place to stay in Dubuque, as it's just steps away from America's River major attractions. It's also the home of Iowa's first indoor water park, and connected to the Grand River Center convention and conference facility by a skywalk.

Field of Dreams movie site in Dyersville, Iowa.

The 193-room resort features accessible parking, wide doorways, a level entrance, elevator access to the upper floors and barrier-free access to the resort facilities. The property has eight accessible guest rooms, two of which have roll-in showers. It's a great family resort, with good wheelchair access, and an excellent location.

Springfield

Although Abraham Lincoln was born in Kentucky, he spent some of the happiest years of his life in Springfield, which makes this Illinois capitol an excellent choice for folks who want to learn more about our sixteenth president.

Located in the heart of downtown Springfield, the Abraham Lincoln Presidential Museum (217-588-8844, www.alplm.org) is a must see on any historic tour. This cornerstone attraction features 40,000 square feet of gallery space devoted to the history, life and politics of Abraham Lincoln.

Access is excellent throughout the museum, with a level entrance, accessible restrooms and barrier-free access to all the exhibits. Don't miss the Treasures Gallery which includes Lincoln's stovepipe hat, his glasses and shaving mirror, and a handwritten copy of the Gettysburg Address.

The Abraham Lincoln Presidential Museum in Springfield, Illinois.

Save some time for a stroll down to the Old Capitol (217-785-7960, www.illinoishistory.gov/hs/old_capitol.htm), which is just a few blocks away from the museum. At first glance, the Old Capitol looks very inaccessible, with eight steps leading up to the front entrance; however, if you ring the bell for assistance you will be directed to the lift in the back of the building. Once inside, there is elevator access to both floors, as well as the lower parking garage.

The Old Capitol served as the seat of Illinois government from 1839 to 1876, and it was the site of Mr. Lincoln's famous "house divided" speech. Today the rooms are furnished as they were in Lincoln's time, and visitors can stroll through them at their leisure.

Operated by the National Park Service, The Lincoln Home (217-492-4241, www.nps.gov/liho) is a must-do on any Springfield visit. Although there are steps at the front entrance of the house, a lift has been installed in back. Wheelchair-users can tour the first floor, but the second floor is only accessible by stairway.

Outside, boardwalk sidewalks lead throughout the neighborhood with the Arnold House and the Dean House also open for self-guided tours.

Both homes have displays, models, interpretive exhibits and photographs inside. The Dean House features lift access up to the porch, while the Arnold House has ramp access through the side gate.

Last but not least, no Springfield visit would be complete without a stop at Lincoln's Tomb (217-782-2717, www.illinoishistory.gov/hs/lincoln tomb.htm). Located outside of the downtown area in Oak Ridge Cemetery, the tomb serves as a monument to the Great Emancipator. There is level access to the tomb, with accessible parking just a short walk away. Inside you'll find marble walls filled with Lincoln quotes, and hallways dotted with reproductions of important Lincoln statues. It's quite impressive.

And don't leave home without a look at the excellent access guide available at www.EasyAccessSpringfield.org. It's a great trip planning resource, as it has updated access information on hotels, attractions, restaurants and transportation in Springfield.

TIMING

Fall and spring are the best seasons to drive this route; preferably the late spring or the early fall. Winters are cold and icy in Chicago, and not very conducive to sightseeing; while the summers can be hot and very humid. Additionally, if you want to stop at New Salem, it's important to note that it's only open from April to November.

GREAT EATS

For a departure from typical Midwestern fare, be sure and stop by Kuma's Asian Bistro (815-490-1000, www.kumas.us) while you're in Rockford. Chef Kuma Kim is always adding new dishes to her menu, which features Korean, Japanese, Thai, Chinese and other Southeast Asian specialties. Her focus is on natural ingredients, homemade sauces and a contemporary taste. As an added bonus, she doesn't use MSG, so it's healthier than most other Asian fare. Access is excellent, with a level entrance and plenty of space to roll around inside. Accessible sidewalk dining is also available, which is a great option in the warmer months.

DON'T MISS IT

For a look at how Abraham Lincoln spent his early adulthood, plan a day trip out to Lincoln's New Salem State Historic Site (217-632-4000, www. LincolnsNewSalem.com), just 30 minutes from downtown Springfield. Here you'll find some permanent exhibits on Lincoln's life, along with the reconstructed town of New Salem, where Lincoln lived from 1831 to 1837. There is a level paved pathway through the town; however, some of the buildings have a step or two up into them. Still you can see into many of the buildings, and costumed interpreters are happy to bring items outside for you to see if you can't access a particular building. Additionally, the Second Lincoln Berry Store, the Blacksmith Shop and the Cooperage are wheelchair-accessible. Take along a picnic lunch as there's an accessible picnic area there. It's a fun departure from city life, and a good opportunity to learn more about our sixteenth president.

LINGER ON IN THE GATEWAY

Sporting a proactive attitude about access, Chicago is a great place to spend a few days before or after your road trip. Not only are there plenty of fun accessible sights to explore, but the Easy Access Chicago (www.easyaccesschicago.org) access guide makes planning your trip a snap.

■ Sign up for a Chicago Greeter Tour (312-744-8000, www.chicagogreeter. com). This volunteer-led free program offers over 40 free walking tours to visitors. Accessible tours are available with advance reservations.

■ Learn about the history, culture and architecture of Chicago on a Walk Chicago Tour (708-557-5400, www.walkchicagotours.com). These wheelchair-accessible tours include transportation from Loop hotels in a lift-equipped van. Loaner wheelchairs and assistance with pushing is also available. These customized tours are tailored to individual tastes and access needs.

■ Set out on your own, then download a free MP3 tour from the Chicago Loop Alliance website (www.chicagoloopalliance.com) or the City of Chicago Tourism website (www.explorechicago.org). These entertaining and informative audio tours all travel along accessible routes and can be done at your own pace.

■ Enjoy a lunch time lecture at the Chicago Architecture Foundation's (312-922-3432, www.architecture.org) Wednesday lecture series. Held in the barrier-free John Buck Lecture Hall Gallery, this free program runs from 12:15 P.M. to 1:00 P.M. Bring a sack lunch, and save time to browse through the adjacent Arcelor Mittal CitySpace Gallery after the program.

■ Get your art fix at the Art Institute of Chicago (312-443-3600, www. artic.edu) and the Museum of Contemporary Art Chicago (312-397-4000, www.mcachicago.org). Both museums have a barrier-free entrance, elevator access to all floors and plenty of space to roll around the galleries.

■ Go visit Sue the dinosaur—considered to be the best preserved Tyrannosaurus rex fossil ever discovered—at the Field Museum of Natural History (312-922-9410, www.fieldmuseum.org). The museum features barrier-free access to all exhibits, which focus on animals, plants, ecosystems, rocks and fossils from around the world.

■ Hit the beach and enjoy Lake Michigan. Accessible beach mats are available at 16 swimming beaches, from Leone Beach on the north to Calumet Beach on the south lakefront. Contact the Chicago Park District (312-742-7529, www.chicagoparkdistrict.com) for more information.

- Take a guided walking tour of Oak Park, home to the world's largest collection of Frank Lloyd Wright-designed buildings. The hour-long tour is presented by the Frank Lloyd Wright Preservation Trust (312-994-4000, www.gowright.org), and features a wide selection of Wright-designed structures along an accessible route of travel.

- Hop in an accessible taxi and strike out on your own. More than 20 taxi companies offer ramped minivans, which can be ordered through central dispatch at (800) 281-4466.

- Catch the Chicago Trolley (773-648-5000, www.chicagotrolley.com) and explore the Windy City. The lift-equipped trolley stops at key sites around Chicago, and the all day ticket includes reboarding privileges.

FLY-DRIVE OPTION

To make this a fly-drive vacation, fly to O'Hare International Airport (773-686-2200, www.flychicago.com) or Midway International Airport (773-686-2200, www.flychicago.com), then rent an accessible van at Wheelchair Getaways (847-987-2083, www.wheelchairgetaways.com), Mobility Works (877-275-4915, www.mobilityworks.com) or Wheelers Van Rentals (866-696-0138, www.wheelersvanrentals.com).

ALTERNATE ENTRY POINTS

- From Indianapolis, take Interstate 65 north to Gary, then connect to Interstate 90 east to Chicago.

- From Detroit, take Interstate 94 west to Chicago.

- From Minneapolis, take Interstate 35 south to Des Moines, then go east to Highway 20 to Dubuque.

VARIATION ON A THEME

. . . .

The Dubuque and Springfield portion of this itinerary makes a nice five- or six-night getaway from Des Moines; while the Chicago and Rockford segment can be easily done as a week-long trip from Milwaukee. If you'd like to extend your road trip, then head to St. Louis from Springfield, Illinois, and continue along on the Missouri's Mother Road and More route.

- IF YOU GO
    - Rockford Area Convention and Visitors Bureau, (800) 521-0849, www.gorockford.com
    - Dubuque Convention & Visitors Bureau, (800) 798-8844, www.traveldubuque.com
    - Springfield Convention & Visitors Bureau, (800) 545-7300, www.visit-springfieldillinois.com
    - Chicago Office of Tourism, (312) 744-2400, www.explorechicago.org

Beyond the Texas
Presidential Corridor

TEXAS HILL
COUNTRY

71 **79** **190**

35 **21** COLLEGE
AUSTIN STATION

SAN ANTONIO

77

281

MC ALLEN

SOUTH PADRE
ISLAND

This route is a fun choice for history lovers, as it includes a good primer on Texas history in Austin, a stop at two presidential museums along the way, and takes in LBJ's Western White House in Texas Hill Country. Add in some bird watching in McAllen and a little accessible beach time on South Padre Island, and you'll get a healthy dose of the great outdoors too. Top it off with a stay in multicultural San Antonio, for a generous sampling of the local cuisine and a stop at the Alamo, and you've all the makings of a five-star road trip.

ROUTE

This route begins in San Antonio and travels south on Highway 281 to McAllen. After a short detour out to South Padre Island, it's time to take Highway 77 north to Highway 21 to College Station. Next, head west on Highway 190 to Rockdale, where you'll pick up Highway 79 and continue west to Interstate 35. Then it's just a short drive south on the interstate to Austin. Next it's time to take Highway 71 west to Highway 281 and head south to Johnson City. To complete the loop, continue south along Highway 281 to San Antonio.

ALONG THE WAY

McAllen

Located 275 miles south of San Antonio, McAllen is a great place to base yourself for a birding tour of the Rio Grande Valley. Because of its unique location on the Central Flyway, the Rio Grande Valley has long been considered a premier birding site, with colorful migrants beginning to appear in November and peaking during the spring months.

It's also the home of the World Birding Center (956-584-9156, www.worldbirdingcenter.org), a network of nine birding sites dotted along 120 miles of South Texas river road. As the sites were developed, accessible trails, viewing platforms, blinds, boardwalks and interpretive centers were added, so it's a great choice for wheelers and slow walkers.

Located in McAllen, Quinta Mazatlan (956-681-3370, www.quinta mazatlan.com) is a good place to begin your visit. The centerpiece of this urban oasis is a 10,000-square-foot hacienda which has been lovingly restored to its former grandeur. Built in 1935, the mansion features adobe walls, beamed ceilings and tile murals.

Ramp access has been added to the front entrance, and level pathways wind around the property. Food and water stations that are placed along the paths attract more than 100 bird species. It's not uncommon to spot Red-crowned Parrots and Green Parakeets there either.

The official headquarters for the World Birding Center is located just seven miles northwest of McAllen at Bensten-Rio Grande Valley State Park (956-584-9156). Private vehicles are not allowed in the park, however a wheelchair-accessible tram makes a loop through the park every half-hour. Highlights of the park include the Green Jay Blind, which features wheelchair-height viewing slots; and the Hawk Observation Tower, which has ramped access to the top, level areas every 30 feet, and unobstructed wheelchair-height sight lines. They're both very nicely done.

Wrap up your Rio Grande Valley birding tour with a trip over to Edinburg Scenic Wetlands (956-381-9922, www.EdinburgWBC.org). The accessible interpretive center features floor-to-ceiling windows with wheelchair-height scopes aimed at the adjacent wetlands. Outside, there are level crushed gravel trails to the boardwalk overlook and Dragon Pond, both of which are only a short distance away. From the boardwalk overlook you can spot a variety of ducks out on the lake, and probably a few snakes and turtles too.

The 2½ miles of trails around the complex are doable for most wheelchair-users in dry weather; however, they can be problematic after a rain. If you'd like to tour the whole complex, but don't think you can manage the distance, call ahead and make arrangements for a golf cart tour. There's no charge for this service, and it's a very accessible way to get a look at the entire site.

George Bush Presidential Library and Museum on the Texas A&M campus.

College Station

Located about 100 miles east of Austin, College Station isn't your typical tourist hotspot. It is however worth inclusion in this presidential-themed itinerary because it's the site of the George Bush Presidential Library and Museum (979-691-4000, www.bushlibrary.tamu.edu). Located on the campus of Texas A&M University, the museum focuses on the life of the former president, George H. W. Bush, as well as memorable events of his presidency.

There's plenty of accessible parking near the museum, with level access through the plaza to the front lobby. Wheelchairs are available for loan at the front desk, and there's elevator access to all floors, with barrier-free pathways though the galleries.

The exhibits begin on the first floor, with the main gallery dedicated to "The Life and Times of George Bush." The gallery includes family memorabilia, photos, and some interesting reflections of Mr. Bush's time in the Navy. As one of the Navy's youngest pilots, he was shot down in the Pacific, and his rescue was recorded on a hand-held movie camera. Today that film clip is on display in the museum, and it puts an entirely different perspective on the man that held office when Desert Storm began. Other exhibits focus on

Mr. Bush's presidential campaigns, his oil business and his stint as a United Nations Ambassador.

Several exhibits focus on events that had an impact on the Bush presidency, with video screens playing back snippets of history. Then there's the replica of the Oval Office, the requisite collection of state gifts and even the president's reaction to Watergate. And of course there is a gallery dedicated to the First Lady, as well as one which focuses on the life of President and Mrs. Bush after leaving the White House.

It's very well done, and quite interesting, even if you don't agree with Mr. Bush's politics; as it gives visitors a very good idea of what the world was like back then. It's a bit nostalgic for older people, but definitely educational for the youngsters. You'll certainly leave with a sense of time and place for the Bush presidential years, and maybe even learn a thing or two about the era.

Austin

Although Austin is well known for its musical entertainment, it's also a great place to get a good primer on Texas history. A good way to get your Austin bearings is to take a historic walking tour of the downtown area, presented by the Austin Visitor Center. There's no charge for this 10-block tour, but advance reservations are required. Call (512) 478-0098, at least 48 hours in advance, to secure your space.

The 90-minute tours begin on the front steps of the Capitol, and the route is fairly level, with curb-cuts at every corner. The tours are conducted at a leisurely pace, and the guides stop often and talk about the historic buildings, architecture and sites of downtown Austin. Depending on the tour, you may also get a peek inside some of the more interesting buildings. No worries though, as the buildings all have level access; in fact the whole tour is billed as wheelchair-accessible.

The Bob Bullock Texas State History Museum (512-936-4649, www. thestoryoftexas.com), located on the other side of the Capitol at 1800 N. Congress Avenue, is also a must-see, as it presents a good overview of Texas history. There's ample accessible parking in the underground garage, with the accessible spaces located near the elevators. From there, it's just a short ride up to the museum entrance. Inside the museum you'll find barrier-free access throughout the galleries, with elevator access to all floors and accessible restrooms located near the first-floor lobby.

The Bob Bullock Texas State History Museum in Austin, Texas.

The Lyndon Baines Johnson Presidential Museum and Library (512-721-0200, www.lbjlibrary.org), located just a half-mile away, is also worth a visit. Access is excellent throughout the museum, with accessible parking near the entrance, level access across the plaza to the museum, elevator access to all floors and plenty of space to wheel around the galleries.

As with all presidential museums, a good chunk of the exhibits chronicle the life of the first family. And along the way you'll learn some interesting tidbits. For example, Lady Bird got her nickname from a nurse who declared that she was "as pretty as a lady bird."

Best of all, it's the only presidential museum that doesn't have an admission charge.

Last but not least, no visit to Austin is complete without a stop at the Lady Bird Johnson Wildflower Center (512-232-0100, www.wildflower.org). There's level access from the parking lot to the Visitor's Gallery, and good pathway access through most of the gardens.

Additionally, the Hill Country Trail System offers two wheelchair-accessible trails—the quarter-mile-long John Barr Trail, and the mile-long Restoration Research Trail. You can do each trail separately or connect them

The Johnson Settlement at LBJ National Historic Park, where President Johnson's grandparents lived.

together for a longer hike. No matter which route you take, you won't be disappointed, as the scenery is beautiful.

Texas Hill Country

Located in the heart of Texas Hill Country, LBJ National Historic Park (830-868-7128, ext. 244, www.nps.gov/lyjo) is a must-see on this Texas presidential itinerary. The park is located in two separate areas, some 14 miles apart. In Johnson City you can see President Johnson's boyhood homes as well as the Johnson Settlement, where the President's grandparents first settled in the 1860s. And over near Stonewall, you can tour the LBJ Ranch. Both sites feature good access, and it's a great way to spend the day.

There's plenty of accessible parking at the Visitors Center in Johnson City, with ramp access to President Johnson's boyhood home, and level access on a hard-packed dirt path to the Johnson Settlement. If you can't manage the half-mile walk, you can also park near the barn, just off of Highway 290.

The Johnson Settlement features level access to the event center, which contains exhibits on ranching history and the Johnson Settlement; while the

189

Johnson dog-trot cabin features ramp access, with enough room to get a peek inside. And if you'd like to get a look at some Texas Longhorns, then just roll on over to the barn, for an up-close-and-personal-experience with these massive creatures.

Located just 14 miles west of Johnson City on Highway 290, the LBJ Ranch features level access to the Visitors Center, where you can pick up a self-guided audio tour of the grounds. Along the way you'll pass by the Johnson School, the reconstructed Johnson birthplace and the family cemetery, where LBJ and Lady Bird are buried. Once you arrive at the ranch, you'll find plenty of accessible parking near the hangar—where the ranch tour starts.

From there, there's level access over to what became known as the Western White House, where LBJ entertained dignitaries and saw to state business. There's ramp access up to the front porch, with room to maneuver a wheelchair on the tour. And afterwards, you're free to wander the grounds and check out LBJ's Air Force One (a Lockheed JetStar which he jokingly referred to as Air Force One-Half), his collection of vintage cars and daughter Luci's 1964 corvette which she got as a graduation gift. It's an excellent tour, and very nostalgic.

If you'd like to overnight in the area, Runnymede Country Inn (830-990-2449, www.runnymedecountryinn.com) in rural Fredericksburg, features the wheelchair-accessible Chatsworth Garden Cottage. This oversize rooms includes good pathway access and a spacious bathroom with a roll-in shower. It's very luxurious and just what the doctor ordered after a long day of Texas Hill Country sightseeing.

TIMING

The optimal time to drive this route is in the early spring, when the migrant bird population peaks in the Rio Grande Valley, and the Blue Bonnets burst forth in a sea of color. Make sure to avoid spring break on South Padre Island though, as it's a favorite party spot for vacationing college students.

GREAT EATS

· ·

Although there's no shortage of good restaurants in San Antonio, Boudro's (210-224-8484, www. boudros.com) stands alone as an all time favorite. Located on the Riverwalk, there's level access to inside or outside seating, and good access through the restaurant. And the food is to die for. Texas and southwest specialties top the menu, with dishes like smoked shrimp enchiladas, grilled portobello tostados and blackened prime rib emerging from the kitchen. The desserts are equally delicious, including the incredibly tempting Louisiana bread pudding. And you just can't leave San Antonio without having some fresh Boudro's guacamole—made right at your table. I guarantee— you've never had better!

DON'T MISS IT

· ·

Save a day for some beach fun on South Padre Island, after your visit to McAllen. There are several accessible dune boardwalks on the island, and 11 of the city beaches are equipped with rubber beach mats that provide wheelchair access over the sand. Beach wheelchairs are available for loan from the South Padre Island Fire Department (956-761-3040). There's no charge for the beach wheelchairs, but advance reservations are advised, especially during peak times.

LINGER ON IN THE GATEWAY

· ·

For a good dose of Southwestern culture and history, linger on a few days in San Antonio. Thanks to a dedicated Disability Access Office, major modifications and access upgrades have been made over the years, so now it's more accessible than ever.

- Take a stroll on the River Walk (210-227-4262, www.thesanantonio riverwalk.com), where you'll find a wide variety of restaurants, bars, clubs and shops, on the banks of the San Antonio River. Although this historic structure was built in 1939, ramps were added in 1979, and a $3 million redevelopment program eliminated the remaining access obstacles in 2010.

- Soak up a little history at The Alamo (210-225-1391, www.thealamo. org), where Jim Bowie and Davy Crockett defended the city from Santa Anna's army. Level flagstone paths lead to the Long Barracks, while there's ramp access to the front entrance of the shrine itself.

- Take a stroll over to San Fernando Cathedral (210-227-1297, www. sfcathedral.org), where you'll find a marble coffin which contains the remains of some of the defenders of the Alamo. Although steps grace the front of the sanctuary, there's ramp access on the back left side.

- For a different perspective on local history, pay a visit to the Buckhorn Saloon and Museum (210-247-4000, www.buckhornmuseum.com). Grab a beer and stroll through this offbeat museum which features taxidermy, a wax museum and an interesting collection of beer bottles. There is level access to the building, with elevator access to the second floor, and plenty of room to wheel around.

- Hop on a streetcar and explore the city. Three different routes wind through the downtown area, and all streetcars are lift-equipped. Streetcar maps are available at www.viainfo.net or at the Visitors Information Center across from the Alamo.

- Hop on the Rio Taxi (210-244-5700, www.riosanantonio.com) river taxi and take a cruise on the San Antonio River. All boats are equipped with portable ramps, and there's room for two wheelchairs up front, near the driver.

- Visit the San Antonio Museum of Art (210-978-8100, www.samuseum. org) for a look at their extensive collection of pre-Columbian, Spanish Colonial and Latin American works. The museum features a ramped entrance, elevator access to all floors, accessible restrooms and good pathway access in all of the galleries. Plus it's right on the river taxi route, so it's easy to get to.

- Take a drive out to Mission Conception, and explore the sanctuary, as well as the new Mission Reach section of the Riverwalk. There is level access to most areas of the church. And although some doorways are a bit tight, most people can get a good look at the major areas of this beautiful 1755 church.

- Wet your whistle at the oldest VFW Post in Texas—VFW Post 76 (210-223-4581, www.vfwpost76.org). Housed in an old Victorian home, there's also ramp access to the front porch. Plus you don't even have to be a member to belly up to the bar.

- Spend the day at Morgan's Wonderland, (210-637-3434, www.morgans wonderland.com), a theme park designed especially for kids with disabilities. The 25-acre park is filled with low key rides such as the Wonderland Express Train, the Carousel and the Jeep Adventure Ride— all of which are 100% accessible, even for power wheelchair-users. Advance reservations are suggested, as the gate is capacity controlled in order to make it a more accessible experience for everyone.

FLY-DRIVE OPTION

To make this a fly-drive vacation, fly to San Antonio International Airport (210-207-3433, www.ci.sat. tx.us/aviation), then rent an accessible van at Premier Van Rental (866-755-8267, www.premiervanrental.com) or Alamo Mobility (888-442-5266, www.alamomobility.com).

ALTERNATE ENTRY POINTS

- From Oklahoma City, take Interstate 35 south to Austin.
- From Baton Rouge, take Interstate 10 west to San Antonio.

■ From Amarillo, take Highway 287 to Dallas, then head south on Interstate 35 to Austin.

VARIATION ON A THEME

. . . .

The McAllen and South Padre Island portion of this route make a good five-night getaway from Houston; while the Austin, San Antonio and Texas Hill Country segment can be done as a week-long trip from Dallas. If you fancy a longer road trip, then drive to Dallas from Austin and connect with the Cowboys, Indians and New Mexicans route.

• IF YOU GO

  • McAllen Convention & Visitors Bureau, (877) 622-5536, www.mcallencvb.com
  • Austin Visitor Center, (800) 926-2282, www.austintexas.org
  • Johnson City Chamber of Commerce, (423) 461-8000, www.johnsoncitytnchamber.com
  • San Antonio Convention & Visitors Bureau, (210) 207-6700, www.visitsanantonio.com

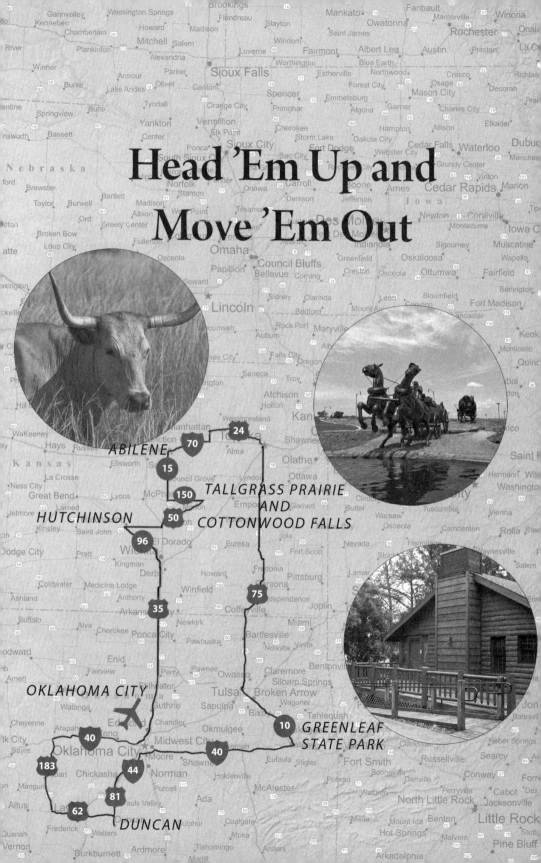

Head 'Em Up and Move 'Em Out

ABILENE

TALLGRASS PRAIRIE
AND
COTTONWOOD FALLS

HUTCHINSON

GREENLEAF
STATE PARK

OKLAHOMA CITY

DUNCAN

This is another ambitious route; however, it's one that really gives you the opportunity to get off the beaten track and explore some Kansas and Oklahoma back roads. It's definitely got a huge dose of the old West, with stops along the Chisholm Trail, at the Tallgrass Prairie National Preserve, and in the old cowboy town of Cottonwood Falls. It also includes a fun cowboy chuckwagon dinner just outside Wichita. Add if you tire of the old west theme, there's also a healthy dose of the great outdoors, a tour of a salt mine and even a stop at President Eisenhower's boyhood home. Take your time and meander along this route, and you'll be rewarded with offbeat sights and attractions, as well as a healthy smattering of interesting characters along the way.

ROUTE

This route begins in Oklahoma City and travels west on Interstate 40 to Clinton; then heads south on Highway 183 and east on Highway 62 to Lawton. Then it's east on Highway 7 and south on Highway 81 to Duncan. From there, head north on Highway 81, then connect to Interstate 44 and head back towards Oklahoma City. Before you reach the city center, take Interstate 240 east to Interstate 40 and continue east. Then take exit 291 and follow Highway 10 north to Greenleaf State Park. Next, continue north along Highway 10 to the Muskogee Turnpike and head north to Tulsa; then take Highway 75 north and cross the Kansas border. Continue along Highway 75 to Topeka, then head west on Highway 24 to Wamego, and then follow Highway 177 south and connect to Interstate 70. Next, follow Interstate 70 west to Abilene, then take Highway 15 south to Highway 150 East to Cottonwood Falls and the Tallgrass Prairie National Preserve. From there, take Highway 150 back west a few miles and connect to Highway 50 and continue west to Hutchinson. To complete the route, follow Highway 96 to Wichita, then head south on Interstate 35 to Oklahoma City.

ALONG THE WAY
· ·

The Chisholm Trail

Founded by Jesse Chisholm, the 800-mile-long Chisholm Trail stretches from South Texas to Abilene, Kansas. It's truly a slice of the old west, as wranglers drove as many as 10,000 cattle at a time from Texas ranches to the Kansas stockyards. And although those cattle drives only lasted from 1867 to 1871, they're responsible for the birth of the American cowboy.

And since the Chisholm Trail went right through central Oklahoma, there's no better place to soak up a little cowboy culture. So save at least a full day to explore the Chisholm Trail Heritage Center (580-252-6692, www. onthechisholmtrail.com), located in Duncan, Oklahoma, just 1½ hours west of Oklahoma City. To be honest, the museum is hard to miss as a massive Paul Moore bronze sculpture of a cattle drive graces the entrance.

Access is good throughout the facility, with plenty of accessible parking near the entrance and good pathway access throughout the galleries. The best place to begin your visit is in the Garis Gallery of the American West. The rotating exhibits in this gallery include pieces from the Center's large permanent collection of Western art. The works range from sculptures to paintings and include pieces by Charles Russell, Frederic Remington and Allan Houser.

The rest of the museum is devoted to interactive exhibits about life on the Chisholm Trail. They include a branding station, a chuckwagon and even a replica of the old Duncan General Store. And don't miss the Chisholm Trail Experience Theater, where you'll be surrounded by the sights, sounds and even the smells of the Chisholm Trail.

All in all, it's a fun, accessible and very educational way to spend the day. And in the end you'll take away a new appreciation for the cowhands that rode the Chisholm Trail.

If you'd like to overnight in Duncan, then head over to the Lindley House B&B (580-255-6700, www.lindleyhouse.com) for some real down home hospitality. Located in a quiet neighborhood, just off the main drag, this seven-room property includes the nicely accessible Rose Cottage.

The Garis Gallery of the American West at the Chisholm Trail Heritage Center.

This spacious cottage room features level access and is furnished with a king-sized bed. The bathroom is equipped with a large roll-in shower with a hand held-showerhead and a fold-down shower bench.

And although there are two steps up to the main house, innkeeper Debby Brewer is happy to deliver breakfast to your room if you can't manage them. Additionally, there's a very pleasant and accessible patio area where you can enjoy your meal. All in all, it's a very comfortable and accessible place to stay along the Chisholm Trail.

Greenleaf State Park

Located three miles south of Braggs, on Highway 10, Greenleaf State Park is a little off the beaten path, but it's definitely worth a visit. This 565-acre green space is touted as one of Oklahoma's most scenic parks, and it offers a number of accessible recreation opportunities, plus a purpose-built cabin that's great for wheelchair-users and slow walkers.

The best way to get your bearings in the park is to hike the 1½-mile Family Fun Trail. Although this paved trail technically begins near the park

Great Blue Heron Fishing Pond on the Family Fun Trail at Greenleaf State Park, Oklahoma.

office, there are several other access points throughout the park, so you can do a little bit at a time if endurance is a problem. Wheelchair-access is excellent along this wide level trail, which winds past the campgrounds and through a wooded area. Interpretive signs are located along the trail, and the trail also passes by the kids fishing pond, where children under 16 and disabled visitors can catch their limit for free.

If you'd prefer to fish on Greenleaf Lake, then head on down to the marina, where you'll find an accessible floating dock, which was built with a generous donation from the Paralyzed Veterans of America. Greenleaf Lake is known for its great fishing, with lots of largemouth bass, crappie and catfish to be had.

Make plans to spend at least a few nights in the park at the very accessible Cabin on the Lake. Built in 1994, by the Oklahoma Chapter of the Telephone Pioneers of America, the cabin offers a high degree of privacy, as it's located at the end of a secluded road, well away from the other cabins.

There is a paved parking area in front of the cabin, with ramped access to the screened-in porch that overlooks the lake. The oversized bedroom is furnished with a queen-sized bed and a twin hospital bed, while the bathroom is equipped with a roll-in shower with a fold-down shower seat.

As an added bonus, the cabin comes stocked with a wide variety of adaptive equipment, including a commode chair, a trapeze, a ceiling track lift in the bedroom and bathroom, and a manual wheelchair. Best of all, there is level access down to a private dock, where you can fish, enjoy the lake view or even tie up your own boat.

As you can imagine, this cabin is very popular, so advance planning is essential in order to secure a reservation. First priority is given to disabled visitors, but the cabin is also available to able-bodied visitors on a space available basis. Call (918) 487-5196 for more information or to request an application to reserve the Cabin on the Lake.

Abilene

Located at the terminus of the Chisholm Trail, Abilene is a must-see on this itinerary. Although the stockyards are long gone, the downtown area is filled with historic mansions—some of which date back over 100 years.

The best way to get a good look at these gems is on an Abilene Trolley Tour (785-263-2231). Priced at just $5, the hour-long tour gives visitors a real feel for the colorful history of this prairie town. Access is good on the trolley too, with lift access to the trolley and two wheelchair spaces aboard. It's a good way to get a primer on Abilene history.

And while you're in the historic district, be sure and stop at the Dwight D. Eisenhower Presidential Library and Museum (785-263-6700, www. eisenhower.archives.gov). The museum complex consists of the Visitors Center, the Place of Meditation, Ike's boyhood home, the museum and the library.

There is level access to the Visitors Center, where you can pick up a free loaner wheelchair. The campus is quite extensive; however, it's level with paved pathways to all of the buildings. Still, if you have trouble with distances, it's best to take advantage of the loaner wheelchair.

Just to the left of the Visitors Center you'll find Ike's boyhood home. Although there are three steps at the front, there is also a wheelchair lift on the side. The first floor of the house is open to the public and it features the original furnishings, photographs and personal items of the Eisenhower family. There's room enough to take a peek inside all of the rooms, which are roped off to protect the furnishings.

The museum, which is just a short walk from the home, features barrier-free access and a wheelchair-lift at the front entrance. It's really a must-see for anyone interested in World War II history, as the excellent Military Gallery features documents, photographs and artifacts from the war. It also includes a gallery devoted to Mamie Eisenhower, and one that presents a comprehensive overview of President Eisenhower's life and achievements.

Last but not least, save some time to visit the Place of Meditation, where President Eisenhower was buried on April 2, 1969. There is level access to the chapel and good pathway access inside. The stained glass windows, which were designed by Odell Prather, are particularly striking.

And if all this sightseeing has worked up your appetite, then stop by the historic Brookville Hotel (785-263-2244, www.brookvillehotel.com) for a finger-licking-good chicken lunch or dinner. This local favorite was origi-nally located in nearby Brookville, but was relocated to Abilene in 1999. Today the whitewashed front facade and the interior furnishings replicate the original structure; however, the new incarnation features wheelchair-access, with a level entry and good pathway access inside.

And the food—which is billed as a Kansas tradition since the 1870s—is wholesome, hearty and served family style. They only serve one entree—fried chicken—and it's accompanied by mashed potatoes, gravy, biscuits, creamed corn, cole slaw, cottage cheese and relishes. And if you have room, there's also ice cream for desert. It's a very nostalgic—and yummy—way to top off your Abilene visit.

Tallgrass Prairie National Preserve

There's no better way to get a feel for the cattle drive days in Kansas than to visit the Tallgrass Prairie National Preserve. Located just north of Strong City on the Flint Hills Scenic Byway, the bulk of this 10,000-acre preserve occupies the land of the former Spring Hill Farm and Stock Ranch, which dates back to the late 1800s.

There is accessible parking in front of the limestone barn, and although the terrain is level it's also a bit bumpy. Still it's doable for many people. There is level access to the limestone barn, where you will find a number of inter-pretive exhibits on early farming methods.

The ranch house is located at the top of a gravel driveway, so your best bet is to drive up and park near the back door. A portable ramp is available at the back door of the 1881 ranch house. Once you access the house, you can

Prairie grass at the Tallgrass Prairie National Preserve.

get a look at the second floor bedroom and the dining room. The main floor of the house is only accessible by a flight of stairs, but there is a photo album available in the visitor center.

And if you'd like to get a closer look at the tallgrass prairie, then take a ranger-led bus tour, which travels to parts of the preserve where private vehicles are prohibited. Although there aren't any accessible trails through the tallgrass, you can still get a great view from the bus.

Save some time to explore nearby Cottonwood Falls, a town that residents proudly proclaim boasts 3,000 people and 250,000 cattle. It's a quaint little burg with a number of shops, small businesses and restaurants. Access varies throughout town, and the brick streets may be difficult for some folks, but there are curb-cuts at some corners and many businesses have level access. Don't miss the historic Chase County Courthouse, which was built in 1873.

If you'd like to overnight in town, then head on over to the Grand Central Hotel (620-273-6763, www.grandcentralhotel.com), where you'll find the accessible Crocker Ranch Room. This ground floor room has good pathway access and includes a bathroom with a roll-in shower. The hotel only has 10 rooms, but it's a fun place to stay as there is a definite ranch and cowboy feel to this 1884 property.

Hutchinson

Located in Central Kansas, Hutchinson is worth a stop, as it has a few unique attractions. At the top of the list is the Kansas Cosmosphere and Space Center (800-397-0330, www.cosmo.org). There is level access to the front entrance of the museum, elevator access to all floors and barrier-free pathways to all areas of the museum. Wheelchairs are available for loan at the front desk.

You can't miss the SR-71 Black bird in the lobby; however, the highlight of this museum is the permanent collection of US and Russian space artifacts. Don't miss the Apollo 13 command module, the Liberty Bell 7 Mercury capsule, and the Vostok spacecraft. And for fun, be sure and check out the replica Bell X-1 Rocket Plane that was used in the movie *The Right Stuff*.

The Kansas Underground Salt Museum (620-662-1425, www. undergroundmuseum.org) is also worth a visit while you're in town. Billed as the eighth wonder of Kansas, the museum is located 650 feet underground, in what was once the ancient Permian Sea. There is elevator access down to the museum, with a barrier-free path through the galleries, which are filled with exhibits about salt mining.

Visitors have the opportunity to see the exhibits and touch a 6,000 pound crystal salt block, before they climb on the tram and experience the dark ride through the mine. It's pretty much what it sounds like—a dark and eerie ride through the cavern—but it's actually a fun experience. And with roll-in access to the tram, everyone can enjoy it. It's truly a unique museum, and a great opportunity to learn how salt gets from the cavern walls to your dinner table.

TIMING

· ·

Spring and fall are pleasant along this route, but it can get very hot and humid in the summer. It's also best to avoid it in the winter, as snowstorms have closed even the major roads in past years.

GREAT EATS

L ocated on a working cattle ranch in Benton, Kansas, just 15 miles east of Wichita, the Prairie Rose Chuckwagon Supper (316-778-2121, www. prairierosechuckwagon.com) is a required stop on any Kansas cowboy itinerary. Not only do you get a yummy all-you-can-eat dinner of smoked brisket and sausage, cowboy baked beans, rosemary baby yukon gold potatoes and homemade biscuits; but you also get a rousing set of live entertainment.

There is level access to the Opera House, where dinner is served family style. Although the seating is composed of tables and benches, accommodations can also be made for folks who can't transfer. After dinner, guests are treated to the cowboy music (not to be confused with county western music) of the Prairie Rose Wranglers. It's a fun evening filled with family entertainment, good food and a hearty dose of cowboy culture.

DON'T MISS IT

S ince you just can't visit Kansas without thoughts of Dorothy and Toto popping to mind, make sure and stop at Oz Museum (866-458-8686, www.ozmuseum. com) in Wamego. Dedicated to "all things Oz," the museum houses a substantial collection of Oz memorabilia, photographs and collectibles; along with some of L. Frank Baum's earlier books. There is level access to the museum and plenty of room to wheel around the exhibits. It's just a fun place.

Another fun museum—the Oklahoma Route 66 Museum (580-323-7866, www.route66.org)—is located in Clinton, just 85 miles west of Oklahoma City. There's plenty of accessible parking in front, with level access to the entrance. Inside there's good pathway access to the gallery space, which houses the world's largest curio cabinet filled with Route 66 souvenirs; from kachina dolls and signs to salt shakers and ash trays. The museum also presents a good overview of Route 66 history and even contains a piece of the mother road, complete with the curb. It's all very nostalgic, and the gift shop is a real hoot too.

LINGER ON IN THE GATEWAY

B est described as an eclectic mix of contemporary culture and Western history, Oklahoma City is a great place to spend a few days, pre or post road trip. Not only is it a great walking city, but there's no shortage of wheelchair-accessible attractions, restaurants and entertainment venues in this cowtown capital.

- Check out the most comprehensive collection of Chihuly glass in the world at the Oklahoma City Museum of Art (405-236-3100, www. okcmoa.com). The recently renovated museum features an accessible entrance with good pathway access to all of the galleries.

- Hop on the Bricktown Water Taxi (405-234-8263, www.bricktownwa tertaxi.com) for a 35-minute tour of the Bricktown Canal. There's ramp access down to the canal near the Biting Sow Blues on California Street, and elevator access near the water taxi ticket booth across from Brick-town Ballpark. All of the water taxis have portable ramps, with room for wheelchairs in the front.

- Linger on in the Bricktown Entertainment District (405-236-4143, www.bricktownokc.com) and enjoy some good food and live music. Level walkways and curb-cuts are ubiquitous throughout the area, and most of the restaurants and clubs have level access.

- Get a good dose of cowboy culture at the National Cowboy & Western Heritage Museum (405-478-2250, www.nationalcowboymuseum.org). There's good wheelchair-access to all areas of this museum, which features an internationally renowned collection of Western art and artifacts.

- Hop on the Oklahoma Spirit Trolley (405-235-7433, www.gometro.org) and explore the downtown area. It runs every 15 minutes and stops at popular downtown attractions. And with lift access, everyone can ride it.

- Learn a little more about the Sooner State at the Oklahoma History Center (405-522-5248, www.okhistorycenter.org). This interactive museum features barrier-free access and houses over 200 audio, video and computer exhibits, which illustrates Oklahoma's unique history of geology, transportation, commerce and culture.

- Save time for a visit to the Oklahoma City National Memorial & Museum (405-235-3313, www.oklahomacitynationalmemorial.org), which tells the story of the bombing and pays tribute to the victims of this horrible tragedy. Access is excellent throughout the museum, with wheelchairs available for loan at the front desk, elevator access to all levels and barrier-free pathways through the galleries.

FLY-DRIVE OPTION

To make this a fly-drive vacation, fly to Will Rogers World Airport (405-316-3200, www.flyokc.com) in Oklahoma City, then rent an accessible van at Wheelchair Getaways (405-285-5380, www.wheelchairgetaways.com) or Handi-cap Aids (800-689-0511, www.handicapaids.net).

ALTERNATE ENTRY POINTS

- From Kansas City, take Interstate 70 west, then connect to Highway 24 and continue west to Wamego.

- From the Dallas/Fort Worth area, take Interstate 35 north to Oklahoma City.

- From Little Rock, take Interstate 40 west to Oklahoma City.

VARIATION ON A THEME

· ·

The Wamego, Abilene and Tallgrass Prairie National Preserve portion of this route can be done as a five-night trip from Kansas City; while the Clinton and Duncan segment makes a nice two-night side trip from Oklahoma City. For an extended road trip, continue on to Amarillo from Oklahoma City and connect with the Cowboys, Indians and New Mexicans route.

- IF YOU GO
    - Greenleaf State Park, (918) 487-5406, www.oklahomaparks.com
    - Abilene Convention & Visitors Bureau, (781) 263-2231, www.abilenecityhall.com
    - Tallgrass Prairie National Preserve, (620) 273-8494, www.nps.gov/tapr
    - Oklahoma City Convention & Visitors Bureau, (405) 297-8912, www.visitokc.com

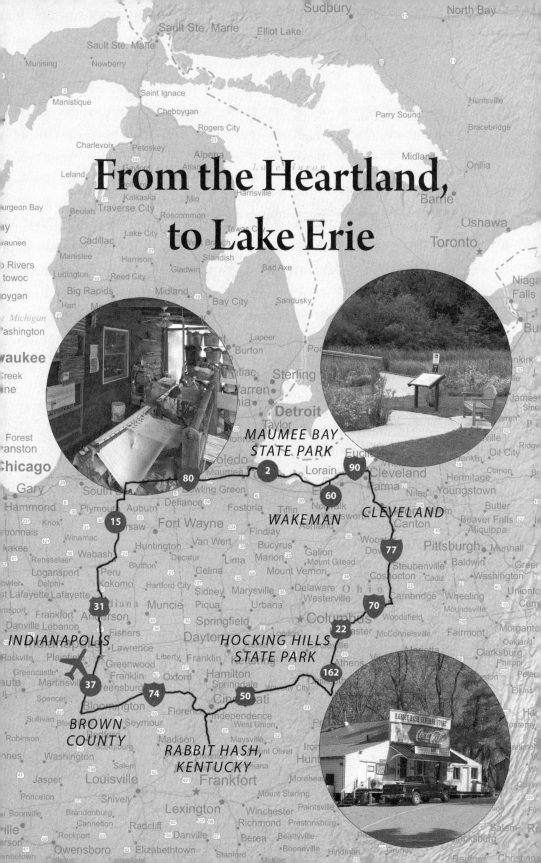

From the Heartland, to Lake Erie

MAUMEE BAY STATE PARK

WAKEMAN

CLEVELAND

INDIANAPOLIS

HOCKING HILLS STATE PARK

BROWN COUNTY

RABBIT HASH KENTUCKY

There's certainly no shortage of great scenery along this route, from the covered bridges of Brown County to the scenic shore of Lake Erie. Add in the fall colors in Hocking Hills State Park and a little Amish Culture in Northern Indiana, and you've got a full spectrum of sights, sounds and activities. And for a little variety there's the lively arts and culture scene in Cleveland and Indianapolis. This route is truly a little bit country and a little bit city; and one that's filled with diverse experiences that complement one another.

ROUTE

· ·

This route begins in Indianapolis and follows Highway 37 south to Highway 46 east to Nashville, Indiana and Brown County. From there it continues east on Highway 46 to Highway 74, crosses into Ohio and skirts Cincinnati on Highway 275. Next it follows Highway 50 east to McArthur, then takes Highway 93 north to Highway 56 west to Hocking Hills State Park. It then continues north along on Highway 374 to Highway 664 North, and connects to scenic Highway 22 East to Interstate 70. Next it follows Interstate 70 east to Interstate 77 North to Cleveland. Then it's time to skirt the shore of Lake Erie and head west on Interstate 90, then continue west on Highway 2 and take a short detour on Highway 60 south to Wakeman. Next head back north on Highway 60, and rejoin Highway 2 and continue west along the lakeshore, until you spot the turn off for Maumee Bay State Park, just outside of Toledo. From there head back to Highway 2 and continue west, then take Highway 280 south and connect to Interstate 90 and cross back into Indiana. For an Amish country detour, take Highway 9 south to Highway 120 west, then follow Highway 5 south to Shipshewana; then continue along Highway 5 south to Highway 6 west, and take Highway 15 north to Goshen. For the final leg, take Highway 15 south and connect to Highway 24 west, then follow Highway 31 back to Indianapolis.

Artists Colony Inn in Nashville, Indiana.

ALONG THE WAY

Brown County

Located just an hour south of Indianapolis, Brown County is dotted with country lanes and secluded back roads. It's a great place to decompress, kick back and just enjoy the local flavor. The best place to begin your Brown County visit is in Nashville, as it's the largest city in the county and it boasts the widest selection of shops, restaurants, entertainment venues and lodging options.

Make sure and stop in at the Brown County Visitors Center, located on the corner of Main and Van Buren Streets. They have detailed maps of the area, a very helpful staff and free wifi access. And if you find that walking is a bit more tiring than you anticipated, they also rent wheelchairs there.

Save at least one day to explore Brown County State Park (812-988-6406, www.browncountystatepark.com), located just south of Nashville. Make your first stop the Friends Trail, located in the middle of the park, near the park office. Constructed by the Friends of Brown County State Park, this barrier-free trail winds though a hardwood forest and features a wide paved pathway, with a short boardwalk section.

When you tire of hiking, hop in your car and take a driving tour of the park. It's especially scenic in the fall and spring. And on your way out, take the north exit so you can drive over the very scenic Henry Wolfe Covered Bridge. It's a little larger than the Bean Blossom Covered Bridge, which is located north of Nashville, but it's just as scenic.

Of course no visit to Brown county is complete without a stop at an artist's studio, and Chris Gustin's Homestead Weaving Studio (812-988-8622, www.homesteadweaver.com) tops the list for both creativity and inclusion. Located in Columbus, there's level access to the studio with plenty of room to wheel around inside. And if you want a closer look at something that's out of reach, Chris is happy to get it for you. The great thing about Chris's work is that it's created from recycled materials—everything from fabric mill by-products to plastic bags and even surplus neckties. Her studio is a treat to the senses.

Chris also teaches one-day weaving classes, where you can learn the craft and take home a finished project at the end of the day. Everybody is welcome in these classes, and Chris has experience teaching wheelchair-users. "I just work with my students to find the appropriate project and loom for them," says Chris. And she heartily encourages everyone to give it a try.

Hocking Hills State Park

Located just an hour from Columbus in Southeast Ohio, Hocking Hills State Park is noted for it's natural beauty. Indeed, it's an ideal chunk of the Buckeye State to leisurely explore.

Ash Cave tops the list of natural attractions in the park as it's the largest recess cave in Ohio. Named for the huge pile of ashes found by early settlers, it's not a cave in the traditional cavern sense, but rather a massive horseshoe-shaped recess. And today it's accessible to all, as a barrier-free trail leads to the recess.

There is accessible parking at the trailhead and the quarter-mile paved trail that winds alongside the river. The surrounding trees provide a nice shade cover and the level trail is easily navigable in a wheelchair or a scooter. It's a very pleasant stroll and the trail is well maintained.

As an added bonus there's a misty waterfall at the end of the trail right next to the cave. There are also a number of picnic tables at the trailhead, and it's a very pleasant spot for a midday break.

Another place worth a visit in the park is Conkles Hollow State Nature Preserve. Located approximately 12 miles south of Logan on State Route 664, this sandstone gorge features some spectacular vistas.

Although previously not wheelchair-accessible, today the half-mile Gorge Trail features a 6-foot-wide concrete path along most of the trail. There are no railings along the trail so there are some small drop offs on the sides. Although it's not technically billed as "totally ADA compliant" it's just as accessible as the Ash Cave trail. There are no steps at all along the trail, and although parts are a bit rustic, this improved trail affords wheelers and slow walkers a glimpse of some spectacular scenery.

For the perfect place to overnight, try the Inn & Spa at Cedar Falls (740-385-7489, www.innatcedarfalls.com), located about halfway between Ash Cave and Conkles Hollow. This rural inn is surrounded on three-sides by Hocking Hills State Park, and offers a variety of cabins and cottages, including two that are wheelchair-accessible.

The two-bedroom Redbud Cabin features ramp access to the front door and good pathway access inside. It has one bedroom and a bathroom with a roll-in shower on the ground floor, and one bedroom upstairs. Because of the size and layout it's more suited for a family, or for someone traveling with an attendant.

The smaller one-bedroom Sumac Cottage also features a level entry and good pathway access inside; however, the bed is in a large living area instead of a separate bedroom. The bathroom has a roll-in shower, and there's level access to the back porch, where you can relax and enjoy the scenery.

No matter which option you pick, the Inn & Spa at Cedar Falls is a very peaceful, relaxing and accessible place to stay. And since it's just down the road from Hocking Hills State Park, the location is perfect too.

Cleveland

After you've have a good dose of the great outdoors, plan to spend a few nights in Cleveland and immerse yourself in the local arts and culture scene. The best way to get a feel for the city is to take a walking tour and enjoy the public art and interesting architecture in the downtown area. With wide sidewalks and curb-cuts at nearly every corner it's very accessible; and with two free tour options it's also quite affordable.

If you'd like to piece together your own tour, then download the *Walk Cleveland* map and brochure, from the Positively Cleveland website (www.positivelycleveland.com). This well-done guide contains several walking tours and includes brief snippets about the architecture and public art along the routes.

If you'd prefer an audio walking tour, then cruise on over to City Prowl (www.cityprowl.com) and download one of their free tours to play on your MP3 player. The tours can be done at your own pace and they include information about the city's culture, architecture and history. Best of all, they really focus on the character of the individual neighborhoods.

There's no shortage of cultural attractions in Cleveland, but if you'd like to make a day out of museum hopping, then head over to University Circle and hop on the wheelchair-accessible Circle Link bus. This free shuttle runs every 15 minutes and stops at all the major attractions. Best of all, it's free.

Best bet is to hit the Cleveland Museum of Natural History (216-231-4600, www.cmnh.org) in the morning and the Cleveland Botanical Garden (216-721-1600, www.cbgarden.org) in the afternoon. The former features natural history exhibits inside, and the Ralph Perkins II Wildlife Center and Woods Garden out back. There is barrier-free access throughout the entire museum, including level pathways in the outdoor section.

The Cleveland Botanical Garden is equally impressive, with 10 acres of outdoor gardens and the Eleanor Smith Glasshouse. There is ramp access to the entrance, level access to the glasshouse and level pathways throughout the outdoor areas. And although there are a few uneven surfaces outside, a number of alternate accessible routes allow visitors to fully enjoy most areas of the gardens.

Plan on attending at least one live theater performance while you're in Cleveland, as there's certainly no shortage of choices. Billed as the second largest performing arts venue in America, Playhouse Square Center (216-641-6000, www.playhousesquare.org) features five stages; the State, Ohio, Palace, Allen and Hannah theaters. All of the theaters feature wheelchair-accessible seats next to companion seats, however access varies depending on the theater.

The State and Ohio theaters feature accessible seating on the main level; while the Palace (where most Broadway shows are presented) offers the broadest range of accessible seating choices. The historic Allen Theater has stair-lift access to the main level, and the cabaret style Hannah features accessible seating at almost every table. There is an accessible drop-off location in front of the theaters, and they have approximately 30 wheelchairs on hand to accommodate slow walkers. Just let the ticket agent know about your access needs when you make your reservation, and they will do their best to accommodate you.

Cleveland is also home to Dancing Wheels (216-432-0308, www. dancingwheels.org) an integrated dance company that features wheelchair-users and able-bodied dancers. Although the company spends a lot of time on the road, they also have a few local performances each year. They really put on a good show, so check their performance calendar on-line to see if you can catch one while you're in town.

Of course no visit to Cleveland is complete without a stop at the Rock and Roll Hall of Fame and Museum (216-781-7625, www.rockhall.com). Known as the "Rock Hall" to the locals, this massive museum features excellent access, with a level entrance, elevator access to all floors and plenty of room to wheel around the spacious galleries. Throughout the museum you'll find interactive listening exhibits, films, memorabilia, guitars and stage clothing from all the great rock legends. Die-hard fans will want to purchase a two-day pass, as there's really a lot to see.

Wakeman Cabin

Although it's a little off the main route, Peggy Pleban's Cabin in the Woods (440-965-5525, www.cabininthewoods.net) is definitely worth the slight detour. Located in Wakeman, Ohio, this family-run B&B is an eclectic cross between a rustic lodge and an upscale inn. It's located in a rural subdivision, so it's not like you're miles away from civilization; yet it's set back enough from the road so you still get a real feeling of privacy.

Prior to building the B&B, Peggy worked for Invacare, so she understands the importance of access. She also understands it on a personal level, as one of her friends is a C-4 quadriplegic. So it comes as no surprise that Peggy and husband Walt designed their property to be accessible.

There's ramp access from the parking area up to the large wraparound porch; and level access to the B&B through the wide front door. The most accessible room in the house is Rosie's Room—named for Peggy's friend—but it's also called the USA Room.

Access features include wide doorways, barrier-free pathways and wood floors. It's furnished with a 25-inch-high double bed and a twin hospital bed. A wide double door leads out to the wraparound porch, so you can access the room without going through the front entrance.

The bathroom is equipped with a roll-in shower with a hand-held showerhead and a fold-down shower bench. Other access features include grab bars in the shower and on the left side (as seated) of the toilet, a roll-under sink, wheelchair-height soap and shampoo dispensers and a portable shower chair. Truly, Walt and Peggy thought of just about everything in this well equipped room.

The Luxury Suite—located across the hall—may also work for some slow walkers. This room features a 35-inch bed with a step stool, grab bars on the right side of the toilet (as seated), a low step shower and sliding door access out to the wraparound porch. It's ideal for someone who needs a little more room, and can't do stairs.

There is barrier-free access to the great room, where a full breakfast is served daily. Peggy can also accommodate dietary restrictions, and she's got a great collection of gluten-free recipes. No matter what she whips up, you definitely won't go away hungry.

Maumee Bay State Park

Bordering Lake Erie, Maumee Bay State Park features 1,850 acres and hosts a diverse collection of wildlife. And as one of Ohio's newest state parks, it also offers a wide range of wheelchair-accessible recreation opportunities.

Bicycling and hiking tops the list at Maumee Bay, as there are a number of accessible bicycle trails throughout the park. Although they weren't specifically designed to be accessible, most of the trails are level and very doable for wheelers and slow walkers. So bring along your handcycle, or just enjoy them on foot or in your wheelchair.

Avid anglers are also in luck, as Lake Erie is known as the walleye capital of the world. And with two wheelchair-accessible piers in the park, you'll have ample opportunity to catch your limit.

Finally, if you want to learn a little about the native flora and fauna, head over to the Trautman Nature Center. There is barrier-free access to the building, which houses a number of interpretive exhibits detailing the nature and history of the area.

Afterwards, save some time to get a first-hand look at the local wildlife, on the two-mile boardwalk out back. There is barrier-free access to this excellent loop trail, with interpretive signs along the way. Best of all, one side of the boardwalk is pleasantly devoid of railings, so wheelers can enjoy unobstructed views of the surrounding wetlands.

And if you still haven't had your fill of birding, head down the road to the Ottawa National Wildlife Refuge (419-898-0014, www.fws.gov/miwest/ottawa). Located just east of Maumee Bay on State Route 2, this birding hotspot features plenty of accessible parking at the Visitor Center and barrier-free access to the building. Inside you'll find a variety of interpretive exhibits, an information desk and a book store. There's also a nice viewing deck in back and wheelchair-accessible picnic tables located in a nearby shelter.

Out back, there's a wheelchair-accessible boardwalk which winds out over the marshlands. The refuge also opens its roads to vehicle traffic once a month for a special auto tour. Maps for these self-drive tours are available at the Visitor Center, and the tour can be done at your own pace. It's a leisurely and very accessible way to enjoy the refuge.

If you'd like to overnight in Maumee Bay State Park, the Maumee Bay Resort & Conference Center (419-836-1466, www.maumeebaystatepark lodge.com) has 12 accessible lodge rooms as well as several accessible family cottages. The accessible lodge rooms are very spacious and have wide doorways, level thresholds and barrier-free pathway access. They include an accessible bathroom with a tub/shower combination, a hand-held showerhead, a roll-under sink and shower and toilet grab bars.

The cottages, which are equally spacious, are located just a short drive from the main lodge. They feature accessible parking and level access to the front door, and have at least one accessible bedroom and a bathroom with a roll-in shower. It's a great option for a family or small group, and since the cabins overlook the surrounding marsh, you don't even have to leave your deck to enjoy the wildlife show.

Accessible cabin at Maumee Bay Resort & Conference Center.

TIMING

F all is prime time to drive this route, as the fall colors are absolutely beautiful in Brown County and the Hocking Hills area. Additionally the annual Mennonite Relief Quilt Auction (888-503-8559, www.mennonitesale.org) is held at the Elkhart County Fairgrounds in Goshen on the fourth Saturday of September. It's a fun event, with accessible parking, restrooms and level access to the buildings. And you just might come away with a great deal on an Amish quilt.

GREAT EATS

F or a real treat, make dinner plans at the Artists Colony Inn (812-988-0600, www.artistscolonyinn. com) while you're in Brown County. Although steps grace the front of this Nashville restaurant, there's an accessible entrance from the side courtyard, with plenty of room to navigate a wheelchair inside. This local favorite is known for creative dishes crafted from fresh ingredients. Jack's Chicken is a good choice if you're watching calories, while Lucie's Pot Pie is the way to go if you just want to throw caution to the wind. Save room for dessert too, as the home made blueberry cobbler is to die for.

DON'T MISS IT

Make sure and schedule your itinerary so you'll be in Shipshewana, Indiana on Wednesday morning, as that's when the lively Shipshewana Antique Auction (260-768-4129, www.tradingplaceamerica.com) is held. Inside the auction house you'll find as many as 11 auctions going on simultaneously, with vintage glassware, furniture, dishes and toys all up for grabs. There's level access to the auction building, and although it can get crowded it's fun to watch—even if you don't bid.

Also, save time for a little detour down to Rabbit Hash, Kentucky, when you head through Cincinnati. Just take Interstate 71 south to Highway 338 and follow the signs. Admittedly there's not much to do in this Boone County burg, but it's a lovely fall drive. And if you're lucky you can play fetch with the mayor—he's a dog. Literally.

LINGER ON IN THE GATEWAY

Although Indianapolis is well know for its famous race track, it also it boasts a treasure trove of cultural attractions. Access wise it's also a very progressive city, so much so, that it earned the 2009 Accessible America Award from the National Organization on Disability. So save a few days to linger on and enjoy these cultural attractions before or after your road trip.

The general store in Rabbit Hash, Kentucky.

- Visit the Indianapolis Zoo (317-630-2001, www.indianapoliszoo.com), located in the western corner of White River State Park (317-233-2434, www.in.gov/whiteriver). There's plenty of accessible parking available near the entrance, with level access to the ticket kiosk and entrance, and paved level pathways leading to most areas of the zoo. They even have a wheelchair-accessible playground with a ramped slide.

- Save some time to wheel along the accessible 1½-mile pathway skirting the Central Canal in White River State Park. It's a pleasant place to stroll, kick back and enjoy the scenery, or even nosh on a picnic lunch.

- Learn a little bit about the history of the area at the Indiana State Museum (317-232-1637, www.indianamuseum.org). What started out as a small mineral collection in 1862 has evolved into a massive 12,000-square-foot exhibition. Accessible parking is available in the White River State Park underground parking garage, with elevator access up to the lobby and barrier-free access throughout the museum.

- Visit the Eiteljorg Museum of American Indians & Western Art (317-636-9378, www.eiteljorg.org), located just across the street. Featuring am impressive collection of Western art, including works by Victor Higgins, Georgia O'Keefe, Frederic Remington and Charles M. Russell, the museum has barrier-free access to all galleries and loaner wheelchairs at the front desk.

- Get your art fix at the Indianapolis Museum of Art (317-923-1331, www.ima-art.org). Graced by Robert Indiana's famous LOVE sculpture on the front lawn, it's one of the largest general interest museums in the country. Access is first-rate too with good pathway access to the galleries and loaner wheelchairs and rollators available at the front desk. Visit as often as you like, as there's no admission charge.

- For a hands-on cultural experience, check out the sampler class schedule at the Indianapolis Arts Center (317-255-2464, www.indplsartcenter.org). The classrooms go above and beyond in access, with features like a wheelchair-accessible dark room and two potter's wheels designed for wheelchair-users. It's a fun way to learn some new skills.

- Save some time for a stroll though the Artspark at the Indianapolis Arts Center, which features 12 acres of interactive sculptures in an open-air setting. From the whimsical Twisted House to the interesting shapes in Still Life With Sticks, there's a broad range of mediums and styles represented, with wheelchair-accessible pathways throughout the park.

FLY-DRIVE OPTION

To make this a fly-drive vacation, fly to the Indianapolis International Airport (317-487-7243, www.indianapolisairport.com), then rent an accessible van at Wheelchair Getaways (317-781-6900, www.wheelchairgetaways.com) or Superior Van & Mobility (317-781-6900, www.superiorvan.com).

ALTERNATE ENTRY POINTS

- From Pittsburgh, take Interstate 76 west, then connect to Interstate 80 West and take Interstate 77 north to Cleveland.

- From Detroit, take Interstate 75 south to Toledo.

- From St. Louis, take Interstate 70 east to Indianapolis.

VARIATION ON A THEME

The Brown County section of this itinerary makes an excellent three-night trip from Indianapolis; while the Maumee Bay and Wakeman portion can be easily done as a five-night getaway from Cleveland. If you fancy a longer trip, then head over to Urbana from Indianapolis, and connect to the From the Land of Lincoln to the Field of Dreams route.

- IF YOU GO
  - Brown County Convention & Visitors Bureau, (812) 988-7303, www.browncounty.com
  - Hocking Hills Tourism Association, (740) 385-9706, www.1800hocking.com
  - Hocking Hills State Park, (740) 385-6842
  - Positively Cleveland Convention & Visitors Bureau, (800) 321-1001, www.positivelycleveland.com
  - Maumee Bay State Park, (419) 836-7758
  - Indianapolis Convention & Visitors Association, (800) 323-4639, www.visitindy.com

Eastern States

Left: Sponge diver in Tarpon Springs, Florida.
Upper right: Franklin Delano Roosevelt's Little White House Historic Site in Warm Springs, Georgia.
Lower right: Historic train station in Manassas, Virginia.

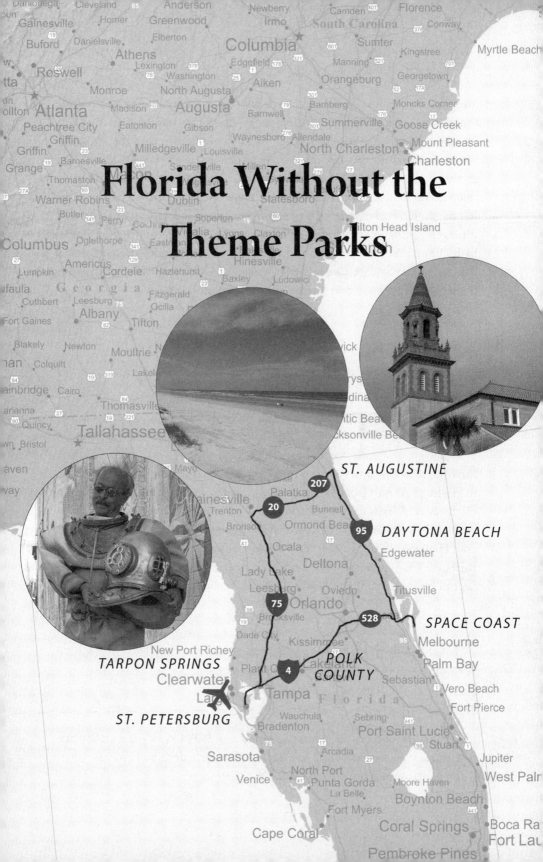

Florida Without the Theme Parks

ST. AUGUSTINE

DAYTONA BEACH

SPACE COAST

TARPON SPRINGS

POLK COUNTY

ST. PETERSBURG

You just can't think of Florida without theme parks popping to mind. Granted, you can have a very nice holiday at a theme park; however, if you just don't like them, you're not going to suddenly take to them just because you happen to use a wheelchair. Unfortunately, many people think that theme parks are the only vacation option for people with disabilities; however, that stereotype just couldn't be further from the truth. Truth be told, Florida has much to offer besides thrill rides and costumed rodents, and this diverse itinerary highlights some of the other accessible attractions of the Sunshine State. From accessible beaches and world class museums, to historic forts, a lighthouse, the Space Coast and even a piece of Greek culture along the way, there's a whole other world outside the theme park gates.

ROUTE

T his route begins in St. Petersburg and follows Interstate 275 to Tampa, then connects to Interstate 4 and heads east to Lakeland and Polk County. From there, it continues east on Interstate 4, then follows Highway 528 east to Highway A1A to Cocoa Beach and the Space Coast. Next it's time to take Highway A1A back to Interstate 95 and head north to Daytona Beach; then head to the coast and take Highway A1A north to St. Augustine. From there take Highway 207 west, then connect to Highway 20 and continue west to Interstate 75. To complete the loop, take Interstate 75 south to Tampa, connect to Interstate 275, and head back to St. Petersburg.

ALONG THE WAY

Polk County

Located halfway between Tampa and Orlando, Polk County is a great place to kick back and wander for a few days, as it's nicely devoid of crowds, yet it still boasts some cool off-the-beaten-path attractions.

The best place to begin your visit is at the Polk County Historical Museum (863-534-4386) in Bartow. Housed in the former courthouse at 100 E. Main Street, this small town museum features ramp access, with loaner wheelchairs available at the front desk. It includes a nice collection of interpretive exhibits about the early Indian inhabitants, pioneers, political history and early town life, as well as a large Genealogical Library. There's no admission charge, but plan accordingly as the museum is closed on Sundays and Mondays.

Located just 12 miles north of Bartow on Highway 98, Lakeland is also worth a stop on your Polk County itinerary, especially if you're a Frank Lloyd Wright fan. Unknown to many people, Florida Southern College (www.flsouthern.edu) features the largest one-site collection of Frank Lloyd Wright architecture in the world. There is good pathway access throughout the campus, with wide sidewalks, curb-cuts, and ramped or level entrances to the buildings. Even better—there's no charge for a self-guided tour of the campus.

There's plenty of accessible parking for visitors in the VB lot, on the corner of McDonald and Johnson Streets, with free walking tour maps located under the esplanades. Don't miss the Annie Pfeiffer Chapel (known affectionately as the bicycle rack in the sky), the William Danforth Chapel (which has some beautiful cypress woodwork) and the 1½ miles of esplanades which line the west campus. And if you work up an appetite, then stop in at Tu Tu's Café, which features level access and offers a variety of reasonably priced sandwiches, salads and snacks.

While you're in Lakeland, make sure and stop at Hollis Gardens (863-834-2280). This 1¼-acre formal garden is located within Lake Mirror Park and features more than 10,000 flowers and ornamental shrubs. There are six steps at the front entry; however, there is level access from the promenade on the shores of Lake Mirror. Accessible parking is located at the far end of the lot, near the Parks and Recreation building. There is good pathway access throughout the park, and an accessible route to every plot. It's a great place to spend a quiet afternoon.

If you're an aviation junkie, you'll definitely want to visit Fantasy of Flight (863-984-3500, www.fantasyofflight.com), located in Polk City, just 15 miles northeast of Lakeland. The brainchild of Kermit Weeks, this unique museum features interpretive exhibits which illustrate the history of flight and includes a large collection of vintage aircraft. Access features include accessible parking and restrooms, a level entry and ramped access to most exhibit areas. The vintage aircraft are displayed in a large hangar with cement floors and level access, and although the inside of the B-17 bomber is not accessible, you can still get a good look at this beauty from the outside.

To round out your Polk County itinerary, head south to Lake Wales and spend the day at Bok Tower Gardens (863-676-1408, www.boktower gardens.org). This 200-acre garden site features an Olmstead-designed woodland garden, a centerpiece bell tower with a carillon, and a number of nature trails. There is good access to most of the garden pathways; however, the route to the carillon has a steady incline and may be difficult for manual wheelchair-users. Mobility carts (which look like heavy duty manual wheelchairs) are available for rent at the entrance, and they are a good option if you can't do distances or tire easily. Still, Bok Tower Gardens is a great place to relax and enjoy a piece of nature, with most of it being doable for wheelers.

Space Coast

Stretching from Titusville to well past Melbourne, Florida's Space Coast offers a number of diverse attractions. It garners it's name from the Kennedy Space Center (866-737-5235, www.KennedySpaceCenter.com), the anchor attraction in the area. Access is excellent throughout the complex with level walkways, wide doorways, accessible restrooms and ample space to maneuver in all the exhibition areas. Additionally, an access brochure is available at the ticket booth. A lift equipped bus runs from the main visitors complex to Launch Complex 39 and the Apollo/Saturn V Center. Don't miss the 3-D presentation at the IMAX theater; and save some time to walk (or roll) aboard the Space Shuttle Explorer.

One of the Space Coast's newer attractions focuses on a different type of aviation—historic warbirds. Located west of Kennedy Space Center at the Space Center Executive Airport in Titusville, the Valiant Air Command Warbird Museum (321-268-1941, www.vacwarbirds.org) includes a comprehensive display of military aircraft dating back to WWI. Access is good throughout the museum; with accessible parking near the entrance and level access to the main building and the restoration shed.

And if you'd like to do a little star gazing, then head on over to the Astronaut Memorial Planetarium & Observatory (321-433-7373, www. brevardcc.edu/planet), located on the campus of Brevard Community College

Rocket Garden at the Kennedy Space Center.

in Cocoa, Florida. There's no admission charge to the rooftop observatory, which is accessible by elevator. Be forewarned though, the observatory is only open on Friday and Saturday nights, so plan ahead.

There's no shortage of outdoor spaces along the Space Coast; in fact Merritt Island National Wildlife Reserve (321-867-0668, www.fws.gov/merrittisland) shares its property with Kennedy Space Center. This 35-mile-long barrier-island features an abundance of wildlife, and a quarter-mile accessible boardwalk behind the visitors center. Just up the road, the Black Point Wildlife Drive is also a must-see, with several viewing platforms and turnouts along the road.

Another great outdoor area—Lori Wilson Park (321-633-1874, www.brevardparks.com)—is located in Cocoa Beach on Atlantic Avenue. This beachside park includes a 1,000-foot beach boardwalk, the Johnnie Johnson Nature Center and an excellent marine hammock boardwalk trail. There is ramp access to the nature center, which contains a number of interpretive exhibits about local wildlife and marine ecology; and level access to the six-foot-wide boardwalk trail. If you like nature, it's a great way to top off your Space Coast visit.

Daytona Beach

Known as the birthplace of speed, Daytona Beach is a familiar haunt of NASCAR fans. And although racing dominates the local scene, there's also plenty of beaches and outdoor areas to enjoy. Still it's hard to visit the area without a stop at the famous Daytona International Speedway (877-306-7223, www.daytonainternationalspeedway.com). Even if there isn't a race in progress, you can still tour the facility.

The speedway tour lasts approximately 30 minutes and it's conducted in a ramp-equipped tram. The tour guides provide a good history of the speedway, and offer visitors a look at the infield, the high banks of the race track and pit row. It's a fun tour, and if you're not a NASCAR fan, you'll probably learn a thing or two. Tour capacity is limited and no advance sales are made, so it's best to be there for the first tour at 11:30 A.M.

Daytona's racing history also served to make their public beaches a bit more accessible. The hard packed sand has long attracted races to the area beaches; in fact Major Henry Segrave broke the 200-mile-per-hour speed record on the sands of Daytona Beach in 1927. Today the tradition of driving on the beach continues, and for $5 you can get a day pass to motor along the hard packed sand, from February 1 to November 30. And if you have a disabled placard or plate, there's no charge for beach access. For the most part, the sand is easy to walk or wheel on, but if you can't manage that, the driving option still lets you get closer to the surf.

And if you'd like to explore the beach, beach wheelchairs are available for loan at lifeguard stations in Ormond Beach. Daytona Beach, Daytona Beach Shores, Ponce Inlet, New Smyrna Beach and Ormond-by-the Sea. You can usually check them out for the day, but you must bring them back at the appointed time. This is a great option for wheelers who want to roll into the ocean surf or for slow walkers who just can't manage the sand.

And if you'd like to park the car for the day, then just hop on the A1A Trolley (386-761-7700, www.volusia.org/votran/trolley.htm), which runs up and down Atlantic Avenue and stops at the major attractions and beach hot spots along the way. Fares are just $1.25 and there is lift access to all vehicles. The trolleys run from mid-January through Labor Day and you can also purchase a money saving day pass for $3. It's the easy way to get around Daytona Beach.

North Turn of the historic 1948 beach racing course at Ponce Inlet.

Another way to enjoy the beach is to head down to the Ponce Inlet Lighthouse (386-761-1821, www.ponceinlet.org), located just south of Daytona Beach. Built in 1887, the lighthouse and the surrounding buildings have been lovingly preserved. Today, costumed docents offer tours which give visitors a glimpse into the past of Florida's tallest lighthouse.

There is level access from the parking area to the gift shop and ramp access to all of the outbuildings. And although the lighthouse itself is not wheelchair-accessible, there are plenty of other accessible exhibits to enjoy there. Don't miss the lens museum, which houses the original Fresnel lens or the historic boats in back of the keeper's quarters. It's all very well done.

St. Augustine

For a good dose of Florida history, plan to spend a few days in St. Augustine, America's oldest city. Make the St. Augustine Visitors Information Center your first stop. Located on San Marco Avenue, between Orange Street and

Historic buildings on St. George Street in St. Augustine, Florida.

East Castillo Drive, there is ramp access to the building which has brochures and guidebooks for area attractions. It also has a nice accessible restroom. And although there is a charge for parking in the adjacent lot, parking is free for people with a disabled placard or plates.

From the Visitors Information Center, make a right when you go out the front door, cross the street at the light, and follow the accessible pathway to Castillo de San Marcos National Park (904-829-6506, www.nps.gov/casa). Alternatively, if you have problems with distance it's probably best to drive over and park in the accessible parking area near the entrance.

Originally constructed by the Spanish between 1672–1695, the fort has pretty good access for a historic structure. There's level access to the fort, but only stair access up to the second level. Most of the rooms off the ground floor courtyard have cement ramps leading into them, so you can get a pretty good look at most of the exhibits. The stone and brick pathways can get a little bumpy in places, but it's doable for most people.

The St. Augustine History Museum (www.historictours.com/staugus tine)—just down San Marco Avenue next to the Old Jail—is also worth a stop. There's plenty of accessible parking in front, with level access to the museum. Inside there's barrier-free access through the galleries which feature artifacts, audio programs, photographs and models that illustrate the history of Florida. Granted, it's not as historically enriching as a tour of the Old Jail; however the Old Jail is only accessible by a flight of stairs. There's also some clean accessible restrooms at the museum, as well as a substantial gift shop.

Truly the best way to soak up a little history in St. Augustine is to just walk through the streets. Today the town is laid out as it was in colonial times, with an number of original buildings remaining. Cobblestone streets and the lack of curb-cuts make navigation difficult in some areas; however, St. George Street is a better choice for wheelers and slow walkers.

If you'd like to overnight in St. Augustine, then head on over to the Centennial House B&B (904-810-2218, www.centennialhouse.com), located on the corner of Saragosa and Cordova Streets. There's ramp access to this historic property, which features eight rooms, including the accessible Fleur de Lis Room.

This first-floor room is furnished with a queen bed and includes a bathroom equipped with a roll-in shower, a pedestal sink, a hand-held showerhead and grab bars in the shower and around the toilet. It's a very comfortable room, and you just can't beat the location—right in the middle of the historic district.

TIMING

· ·

Winter is prime time for a Florida visit, and indeed many snow birds flee the cold icy north to bask in the warm Florida sun. That said, it's also peak season, with more crowds and higher prices. And although summer is dreadfully hot in Florida, early spring and late fall still offer fair weather, but they're minus the winter crowds. Whatever you do, steer clear of Christmas, Thanksgiving and Easter weeks, as it can be a real zoo then.

GREAT EATS

. . . .

For a look at Daytona racing history and a tasty bite to eat, make sure and stop in at Racing's North Turn Beach Bar and Grille (386-322-3258, www.racings northturn.com) in Ponce Inlet. Built near the North Turn of the historic 1948 beach racing course, this casual restaurant serves up generous portions and features a wide selection of sandwiches, steaks, seafood and pasta. House favorites include the Vicki Wood cheesesteak wrap, the Wes Truelove prime rib sandwich, and an excellent lobster ravioli in whiskey sauce. There is level access to the restaurant, and not only is it a nice place to tie on the old feed bag, but it's also filled with old photos and other racing memorabilia. It's a fun stop and a great place to enjoy a casual meal on the beach.

DON'T MISS IT

. . . .

Located just 30 miles north of St. Petersburg, Tarpon Springs makes a great side trip, as it's a piece of Greece of Florida's Gulf Coast. Known as the sponge capital of the world, Tarpon Springs first attracted large numbers of Greek sponge divers at the turn of the century. Today their descendants continue this old world trade.

The sponge docks are the real heart and soul of Tarpon Springs. Stop by and see the sponge diver's suit (complete with lead booties) on display in front of the Billiris Sponge Market. The area is nicely accessible, as it's fairly level with lots of curb-cuts. And for some authentic Greek food, roll on over to Mama's Greek Cuisine (727-944-2888, www.mamasgreekcuisine.net), which has a ramped entrance, accessible restrooms and an extensive menu of Greek specialties. Try the dolmades (stuffed grape leaves) or pastitso (Greek style lasagna)—they're both delicious.

Last but not least, don't miss the historic St. Nicholas Greek Orthodox Cathedral, which features ramp access on the left side. Patterned after Istanbul's St. Sophia, the copper rotunda is particularly striking.

LINGER ON IN THE GATEWAY

S ave a few days to enjoy the cultural attractions and scenic beauty of the St. Petersburg area. Not only are there a wide variety of accessible options, but you'll also find some affordable and accessible public transportation in this Gulf Coast hotspot.

■ Hop aboard the lift-equipped Looper Trolley (727-781-5166, www.looper trolley.com) and explore the downtown area. The fare is just 50 cents and it stops at all of the major attractions.

■ Learn a little about St. Petersburg's past at the St. Petersburg Museum of History (727-894-1052, www.spmoh.org). Access is good throughout the museum, which features a canoe of the Tocobaga Indians from the 1500s, a replica of the world's first commercial airliner and a 3,500-year-old mummy.

■ Enjoy some art at the Museum of Fine Arts (727-896-2667, www.fine-arts.org), which features works of the masters, plus special traveling exhibitions. There's barrier-free access throughout the museum, with wheelchairs available for loan at the front desk.

■ Visit the Florida Holocaust Museum (727-820-0100, www.flholocaust museum.org), which features barrier-free pathways through all of the galleries and free loaner wheelchairs at the front desk. The centerpiece exhibit is a box car from the Poland death camps. Although there are no graphic images portrayed in the museum, it's not recommended for children younger than 10 years old.

■ Visit the Salvador Dali Museum (727-823-3767, www.salvadordali museum.org) for a comprehensive collection of the artist's work, including many pieces from his early and transitional periods. There is level access to the entrance, with plenty of room to roll around the galleries.

■ Head on over to Pier 60 in Clearwater and enjoy the beach. Surf wheelchairs are available at the life guard station, near the parking lot exit, so you can roll right along the beach. There's no charge for the beach wheelchairs, but a picture identification is required as a deposit.

■ Stick around Pier 60 as the sun goes down for the nightly sunset celebration. The pier features barrier-free access; and it attracts a variety of local vendors, artists and entertainers, as locals and visitors alike gather to watch the sun slip below the horizon.

FLY-DRIVE OPTION

To make this a fly-drive vacation, fly to St. Petersburg -Clearwater International Airport (727-453-7800, www.fly2pie.com) or Tampa International Airport (813-870-8700, www.tampaairport.com), then rent an accessible van at Vacation Mobility (877-744-0744, www.vacationmobility.com), Wheelchair Getaways (800-242-4990, www.wheelchairgetaways.com) or Wheelers Van Rentals (800-456-1371, www.wheelersvanrentals.com).

ALTERNATE ENTRY POINTS

■ From Miami, take Interstate 95 north to Highway A1A, and start the route on the Space Coast.

■ From Mobile, take Interstate 10 east to Interstate 75, then head south to Tampa.

■ From Atlanta, take Interstate 75 south to Tampa.

VARIATION ON A THEME

T he Polk County and St. Petersburg part of this itinerary can easily be done as a four-night side trip from Orlando; while the St. Augustine and Daytona Beach segment makes a nice five-night getaway from Savannah. It you want to extend your trip even longer, then head to Jacksonville from St. Augustine and connect with The Gulf Coast and More route.

- IF YOU GO
  - Central Florida Visitors & Convention Bureau (Polk County), (800) 828-7655, www.visitcentralflorida.org
  - Space Coast Office of Tourism, (800) 692-1338, www.space-coast.com
  - Daytona Beach Convention & Visitors Bureau, (386) 255-0415, www.daytonabeach.com
  - St. Augustine Convention & Visitors Bureau, (800) 653-2489, www.floridashistoriccoast.com
  - St. Petersburg Clearwater Convention & Visitors Bureau, (727) 464-7200, www.FloridasBeach.com

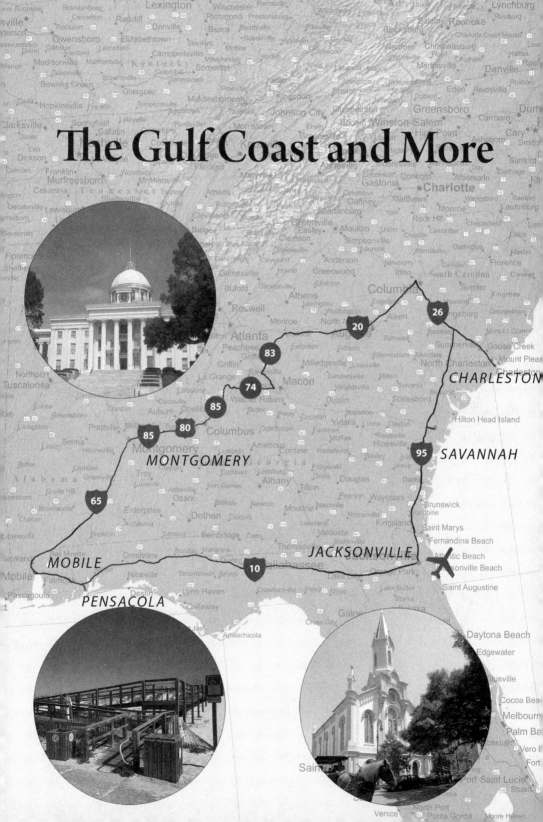

The Gulf Coast and More

Although this route has a healthy dose of Gulf Coast attractions, with stops in Mobile Bay and Pensacola; it travels well beyond the confines of the gulf shores. From the lively cultural scene in Jacksonville, to the historic attractions of Savannah and Charleston, there's a little something for everyone along the way. Add in a Georgia back road adventure, an overnight in a secluded cabin, and a visit to President Roosevelt's Warm Springs retreat; then top it off with a tour of the Hyundai factory in Montgomery, and you've got all the makings for a true southern adventure.

ROUTE

T his route begins in Jacksonville and follows Interstate 95 north to Georgia, then connects with Interstate 16 and heads east to Savannah. It then follows Interstate 16 back west, continues along Interstate 95 North, then takes Interstate 26 east to Charleston. Next, head back west on Interstate 26, then take Interstate 20 west into Georgia, then take Highway 83 and go south to Interstate 75. After a short jog south on the interstate it's time to hit the Georgia back roads. Take Highway 74 west through Thomaston, then continue on to Highway 85 and follow the signs to Warm Springs. After your Warm Springs visit, continue south on Highway 85 to Highway 27 ALT through Columbus, cross the Alabama state line and connect to Highway 80 West to Interstate 85 West, to Montgomery. Then it's time to head south on Interstate 65 to Mobile. To complete the loop, follow Interstate 10 east to Pensacola, then continue across the Florida Panhandle to Jacksonville.

ALONG THE WAY

Savannah

Spend a few days in Savannah and soak up a little history. Get an early start and make your first stop the Savannah Visitors Center, located in the old

Central of Georgia Railway Passenger Station. There's plenty of accessible parking near the entrance, and you can park all day for just $7. There's level access to the depot building, with lift-access up the Savannah Visitors Center, where you'll find lots of maps, brochures and information about the city.

The Savannah History Museum (912-651-6825)—located in the same building—is also worth a visit. There's barrier-free access to most parts of the museum, which showcases Savannah's history. Highlights include a Johnny Mercer exhibit, the Forrest Gump bench and an old Ford Model A.

And if you'd like a bit to eat, then stop in at the Whistle Stop Cafe next door. They offer a great lunch special—meat and two sides—for a very reasonable price. There's ramp access to the train car in the middle of the restaurant; however, it's a bit tight for wheelchairs and scooters. Still, there's plenty of accessible seating at the tables near the car.

Take a few minutes to explore Battlefield Park, located just across the street. Take the back entrance out the Whistle Stop Cafe and cross the street to see this memorial to the more than 800 men who died in the Revolutionary War's Siege of Savannah October 9, 1779.

After you've explored the attractions in the old depot, then hop on the free DOT Express Shuttle (912-447-4026, www.connectonthedot.com) and take a short tour around the historic district. All buses feature lift access, and they run every 20 minutes and stop at 11 attractions in the historic district. You can just stay on the bus for a tour of the area, or hop off and explore the sights along the way.

Make sure and save some time for a tour of the Juliet Gordon Low Birthplace (912-233-4501, www.juliettegordonlowbirthplace.org), as it's the only historic home in Savannah with an elevator. There's ramped access to the street level entrance of the 1821 home, where the founder of the Girl Scouts was born. The home contains most of the original furnishings, and all areas of the tour are wheelchair-accessible.

If you'd like to explore the local art scene, be sure and stop at the Art Center of City Market (912-232-4903, www.savannahcitymarket.com). Patterned after the Torpedo Factory project in Alexandria, Virginia, this gallery and studio space occupies 19,000 square feet. There's level access to the building, with elevator access to the second floor. Stop in and see the artists at work, and take home a piece for your own collection.

Savannah's historic waterfront.

No visit to Savannah is complete with a stroll along the historic riverfront. There's elevator access down to the river behind City Hall, on the Corner of Bay and Bull Streets. Alternatively, the DOT Express Shuttle also stops down there. The riverfront features level access and it's just fun to stroll along or stop in at one of the many great seafood restaurants. Try and hit the area on the first Saturday of the month, as First Saturday on the River runs all day and attracts a nice selection of arts and craft vendors, and features fun and entertainment for the whole family.

And for a fun cruise on the Savannah River, hop on the Savannah River Queen at City Hall Landing. There's ramped access to the boat, and plenty of room for wheelchairs aboard. The ferry stops at the Westin dock and the Waving Girl Statue before it returns to City Hall Landing. Best of all, there's no charge for the ferry, which is operated by the same folks who run the DOT Express Shuttle.

Easy boarding on the Fort Sumter ferry.

Charleston

For a good dose of military history, stay on a few days in Charleston and explore the historic sites in Charleston Harbor. Fort Sumter (843-883-3123, www.nps.gov/fosu) tops the list as it's where the first shots of the Civil War were fired.

There's no charge for entrance to the historic site; however, there is a charge for the ferry, which is operated by Fort Sumter Tours (843-722-2628, www.FortSumterTours.com). The boats depart from Patriots Point and down-town Charleston, and they feature ramped access and ample wheelchair seating.

Once you dock, there's barrier-free access over to the fort, and level access to the parade grounds, through the Sally Port entrance. There are dirt and brick pathways around the interior of the fort, and it's easy to follow the self-guided tour. There is lift access to the Visitors Center, which features interpretive exhibits about the fort and its restoration.

Another must-see in Charleston is the USS *Yorktown* (843-884-2727, www.patriotspoint.org), which is docked at Patriots Point. Steeped in military history, the battleship was commissioned in 1943 and played a major role in the Pacific offensive in World War II. Her last mission was in 1968, when she recovered the Apollo 8 astronauts.

Today, there is lift access to the hangar deck, with elevator access up to the flight deck. All other areas are only accessible by stairs, but there's still plenty to see on those two decks including a great collection of military aircraft.

Last but not least, save some time to visit Fort Moultrie (843-883-3123, www.nps.gov/fosu) on your Charleston Harbor tour. Also known as the Palmetto Fort—because it was originally constructed from Palmetto logs—it's just 15 minutes south of Patriots Point, and easily reachable by bridge.

Access is good at the fort, with plenty of accessible parking near the Visitors Center. Inside, there's barrier-free access to a number of interpretive exhibits, with level access to the fort across the street. The self-guided tour is certainly wheelchair-accessible; however, the ranger-led tour has a few steps, as it goes inside some of the structures.

Admittedly, some manual wheelchair-users may need a little help on parts of the trail, but it's still doable for most people. All in all, Fort Moultrie is an excellent place to get primer on Charleston Harbor history.

Montgomery

Filled with historical buildings, Montgomery is well worth a stop on this itinerary; but make sure and time your visit accordingly, so you can also work in a tour of the local Hyundai factory.

The best place to begin your Montgomery visit is at the Union Station Visitors Center on Water Street. There's accessible parking in back near the accessible entrance, and plenty of room to navigate a wheelchair through the building. Inside, you'll find interpretive exhibits about Montgomery, as well as a gaggle of helpful volunteers.

You can also buy a ticket for the lift-equipped trolley here. The trolley runs a circuit through downtown Montgomery and stops at most of the popular attractions. You can just ride the whole route and listen to the narrated tour, or use the trolley as transportation between attractions.

Alternatively, you can walk to many areas in town. Most of the streets are level, with curb-cuts at every corner. The exception is the area around the capitol, which has a steady incline and might be difficult for manual wheelchair-users and slow walkers.

Those interested in civil rights history should download the free Civil Rights Walking Tour from the Montgomery Convention & Visitors Bureau website. The audio program includes information on 21 sites, with details about the people and places that were instrumental in the civil rights movement. Many of the sites are within walking distance of the Visitors Center, and you can do the self-guided walk at your own pace.

Make sure and include the capitol on your Montgomery itinerary, as visitors are welcome to wander through the old governor's office, the old state supreme court, and the old house of representatives and senate chambers. The rotunda is also worth a look, as it's quite striking. The accessible entrance is located on Union Street, and there's good pathway access throughout this historic building, as well as elevator access to all floors.

Save some time for a stop at the First White House of the Confederacy (334-242-1861, www.firstwhitehouse.org), just up Union street. Although it's pretty close to the capitol, it's on an incline, so slow walkers and manual wheelchair-users might want to drive.

Although steps grace the front entrance, there's an accessible entrance on Union Street, near the accessible parking space. As an added bonus, wheelchair-users get a close look at Jefferson Davis's study, as it's on the accessible path of travel. Although you can only see the main floor of the house, it's definitely worth a visit as it houses the largest collection of Jefferson Davis's artifacts in the world.

And for a look at modern Montgomery, make sure and take a tour of the Hyundai Factory (334-387-8019, www.hmmausa.com), where Sonatas and Elantras are built. There's plenty of accessible parking in the visitors lot, with level access to the visitors center building.

After a short orientation session, visitors are taken by a wheelchair-accessible tram through the stamping shop, welding shop, general assembly shop, engine shop and out to the test track. It's a very interesting tour, and although it's free, advance reservations are required. The tours are offered during the day on Monday, Wednesday and Friday, as well as Thursday evenings. Truly the only bad thing about this tour is that they don't give out free samples.

Bellingrath Gardens offers paved pathways throughout.

Mobile Bay

To get a really good feel for the gulf coast area, spend a few days in Mobile and take a driving tour around Mobile Bay.

From downtown Mobile, head west on Interstate 10, then take Highway 59 south to Bellingrath Gardens (251-973-2217, www.Bellingrath.org). Dating back to 1932, this 65-acre estate is alive with blooms all year long. There's plenty of accessible parking near the entrance, paved pathways throughout the gardens and level access to the conservatory. Morning is the best time to visit, as it's very peaceful and nicely devoid of people.

After you've had your fill of the gardens, continue south on Highway 59, then take Highway 188 to Heron Bay and follow Highway 193 to Dauphin Island. This leg of the drive is particularly scenic; in fact, it's part of the Alabama Scenic Byway system.

Make sure and stop at the Dauphin Island Sea Lab (251-861-7500, www.sealabestuarium.org), located on the eastern tip of Dauphin Island. This estuarium and public aquarium highlights the four key habitats of coastal Alabama and showcases the plants and animals that live there.

Access is good throughout the facility with accessible parking near the entrance and level access over a boardwalk to the estuarium. Outside, a nicely accessible boardwalk trail leads out to the bay, and gives visitors a first-hand look at some of the local inhabitants.

Fort Gaines (251-861-6992)—one of the most historic points on Dauphin Island—is located just down the road. The site of the battle of Mobile Bay, it's where the phrase "Damn the torpedoes—full speed ahead" was first uttered. There is accessible parking near the entrance, but there's a steep incline up to the gift shop. Still, you can get a nice view of the massive structure from the parking lot.

As you continue along on Mobile Bay, you'll then have to take the Mobile Bay Ferry (251-861-3000, www.mobilebayferry.com) to continue the journey onward to Fort Morgan.

After you dock, continue along Highway 80, then take Highway 59 north to Alligator Alley (251-946-2483, www.gatoralleyfarm.com) in Summerdale. Opened in 2004 as a refuge for rescued and nuisance alligators, it's a great place to get a closer look at these massive beasts.

There's accessible parking with ramp access up to the ticket office; however, there are two steps down to the hard-packed dirt trail at the refuge entrance. Not to worry though; if you can't manage it, you can always go back out to the parking lot, where there's level access to the trail. At the end of the trail there's an accessible boardwalk over a swamp that's teeming with gators. It's a nice place to get a look at some large specimens; and although there's a good deal of walking involved, it's a good choice for wheelchair- and scooter-users.

To complete the drive, continue on Highway 59, take Interstate 10 west back to Mobile and stop in at the USS *Alabama* Battleship Memorial Park (251-433-2703, www.ussalabama.com). The park is home to a nice collection of vintage aircraft, the USS *Drum* submarine and the USS *Alabama*.

There's good access to the aircraft pavilion and to the main deck of the USS *Alabama*; however, the submarine is not accessible. Still, it's worth a stop, as it's very nicely preserved.

Pensacola

Pensacola is also worth a two- or three-night stopover, as it boasts a number of accessible and affordable Gulf Coast attractions. At the top of the list is the excellent National Naval Aviation Museum (850-452-3604, www.naval aviationmuseum.org). Billed as the world's largest naval aviation museum, this free attraction boasts more than 4,000 artifacts and over 150 beautifully restored aircraft.

There's plenty of accessible parking in front, with level access to the entrance, and elevator access to the upper floors. It should be noted that even though there's no admission charge to the museum, you'll need a valid ID to visit it, as it's located on a naval base.

Try to time your visit so you can catch a practice run of Blue Angels Navy Flight Demonstration Squadron (www.blueangels.navy.mil). There's no charge for this excellent air show, which can be viewed from the National Naval Aviation Museum. Plan accordingly though, as the Blue Angels only practice there from March to November on Tuesday and Wednesday mornings. The show starts at starts at 9 A.M., but plan to get there a half-hour early.

For a glimpse into the Pensacola of yesteryear, be sure and stop in at Historic Pensacola Village (850-595-5993, www.historicpensacola.org). This popular Gulf Coast attraction features 27 properties in the Pensacola National Register Historic District. Although many of the historic buildings have steps up into them, there are level brick pathways throughout the neighborhood, with level access to the Museum of Commerce and the Museum of Industry. It's a pleasant place to wander and explore, and because it's not 100% accessible, it's free for wheelers.

Another good place to learn about Pensacola's past is over at Fort Pickens (850-934-2600, www.nps.gov/guis) in the Gulf Islands National Seashore. There's plenty of accessible parking near the Visitors Center, with level access to the building, and wheelchairs available for loan inside. This massive pre–Civil War fort features level access and cement walkways through many areas of the fort. Best of all, there's no admission charge for America the Beautiful Access Pass Holders.

Located just down the street from Historic Pensacola Village, the Lee House Bed & Breakfast (850-912-8770, www.leehousepensacola.com) is a great place to overnight. Suite 1 features wide doorways and is equipped with a roll-in shower. There's also level access to the wraparound porch—a great place to enjoy a glass of wine in the evening or a cup of morning coffee.

TIMING

Summer can be dreadfully hot and humid along this route, so it's best to avoid it at that time. Fall and spring are nice, but the optimal timing would be to hit Warm Springs on Labor Day (so you can have a soak in the historic pool) then continue along the rest of the route in early September. If you want to forgo the soak, then October is a better choice as the weather is even cooler then.

GREAT EATS

Make sure and stop for lunch at Mary's Place (251-873-4514, www.theoriginalmarysplace.com), while you're exploring Mobile Bay. Located just south of Bellingrath Gardens at the intersection of Highway 59 and Highway 188, this Coden eatery has been around since 1922. The menu features a good selection of po-boys, salads and entrees, but the best deal on the menu is the lunch buffet. It's priced at just $8.99 and includes a drink. Buffet selections include black-eyed peas, stuffed pork chops, hamburger steaks, turkey pot pie, chicken and dumplings, greens, fried okra, green beans, rice and a well stocked salad bar. Access is good too, with ramp access to the front entrance, good pathway access inside, and very clean accessible restrooms. It's a winning combination with good home cooking, great service and very reasonable prices.

DON'T MISS IT

lthough it's a bit off the beaten path, Roosevelt's Little White House (www.gastateparks.org/Little WhiteHouse) is definitely worth a stop as you travel through West Central Georgia. There's plenty of accessible parking near the entrance to this Warm Springs site, with barrier-free access throughout the small presidential museum.

Out back there's a paved pathway over to the Little White House, where President Franklin D. Roosevelt conducted business while he was in town. The building is accessible to manual wheelchairs, but because of walkway weight restrictions, power wheelchairs and scooters are prohibited. Alternatively, there's a loaner manual wheelchair available for self-guided tours of the house.

Don't forget to stop at the historic pools, where the president soaked in the healing waters to alleviate his painful polio symptoms. They're located just a short drive away and they feature level access with a cement ramp leading down into the main pool. The pools remain empty most of the year, but they turn on the water for Memorial Day and Labor Day weekends. Be forewarned though, the public swim sessions fill up fast, so make your reservations early. Call (706) 655-5870 for more information.

And if you'd like to overnight in the area, check out Still Meadows Cabins (706-741-5012, www.stillmeadowscabins.com) in neighboring Thomaston. Cabin 2 is nicely accessible with a boardwalk entrance, wide doorways and a bathroom with a roll-in shower. As an added bonus, innkeeper Mary Pat Jones thoughtfully stocks the cabin refrigerator with fresh eggs from the resident chickens.

LINGER ON IN THE GATEWAY

ave a few days to wander around Jacksonville and take in some of the very accessible cultural attractions.

■ Hop on the SS Marine Taxi (904-733-7782, www.jaxwatertaxi.com) and see the sights on both sides of the St. Johns River. The water taxi runs about every 20 minutes, and all boats carry portable ramps.

■ Take a walk or roll around the downtown area. There's paved walkways on both sides of the river, with wide sidewalks and plentiful curb-cuts throughout the downtown area. It's really a pleasant walking city.

■ Stop in at Jacksonville Landing (904-353-1188, www.jacksonville landing.com) for a little shopping and a bite to eat. Access is good throughout this riverside complex, with elevator access to all levels and level access to most shops and restaurants.

■ Check out the Jacksonville Maritime Heritage Center (904-355-9011, www.jacksonvillemaritimeheritagecenter.org) located on the ground floor of Jacksonville Landing. This unique museum features photos, artifacts, models and documents that interpret the maritime history of Jacksonville and the Florida coast. Access is good too, with level access to the entrance and plenty of room to wheel around the galleries.

■ Visit the Museum of Contemporary Art (904-366-6911, www.moca jacksonville.org). This north bank mainstay boasts the largest contemporary art collection in the Southeast, with over 700 pieces in their permanent collection. It features good pathway access throughout the galleries, lift access to the mezzanine level, and elevator access to all other floors. The museum's Nola restaurant also makes a good lunch stop.

■ If you're in town on Friday, visit the Hemming Plaza Market, where you'll find fresh produce, handmade jewelry, baked goods and live entertainment from 10 A.M. to 2 P.M. Located across the street from the Museum of Contemporary Art, there's level access to most areas of the plaza, and it's just a fun place to take a break, have a bite to eat and enjoy some music.

■ Visit the Museum of Science and History (904-396-6674, www.the mosh.org), located on the south side of the river. There is level access to the front entrance, and plenty of room to roll around in all the galleries. Although this museum is a favorite for kids, there's lots for adults to see and do as well. Don't miss the Hixon Native Courtyard, which features a short boardwalk over a pond filled with native vegetation, turtles and fish. It's just a pleasant place to take a break, sit down and relax.

■ Stop in at the River City Brewing Company (904-398-2299, www. RiverCityBrew.com) for a bite to eat. Located just west of the Friendship Fountain on the south side of the river, there's ramp access to the restaurant from the Riverwalk and level access at the entrance. The casual menu offers everything from fish and steaks to sandwiches, pasta and salads, and the river view is fantastic.

■ Save a day for a visit to the Cummer Museum of Art & Gardens (904-356-6857, www.cummer.org). Located in the Riverside Avondale district, just minutes from downtown; the museum features a large permanent collection of porcelain, paintings, sculpture and tapestries, plus over 2½ acres of formal gardens. Parking is available in the gravel lot across the street, and the museum features a ramped entrance and barrier-free access throughout all of the galleries, as well as good access to the gardens.

FLY-DRIVE OPTION

To make this a fly-drive vacation, fly to the Jacksonville International Airport (904-741-2000, www.jia.aero), then rent an accessible van at Wheelers Van Rentals (800-456-1371, www.wheelersvanrentals.com) or Wheelchair Getaways (301-699-2238, www.wheelchairgetaways.com).

ALTERNATE ENTRY POINTS

■ From Nashville, take Interstate 65 south to Montgomery.

■ From Miami, take Interstate 95 north to Jacksonville.

■ From Chattanooga, take Interstate 59 south and connect to Interstate 65, then head south to Montgomery.

VARIATION ON A THEME

. . . .

The Mobile Bay and Pensacola portion of this itinerary makes a nice five-night getaway from Jacksonville; while the Warms Springs and Montgomery segment can be easily done as a three-night side trip from Atlanta. If you'd like a longer road trip, then head west along the Gulf Cost to New Orleans from Mobile, and connect to the Down on the Bayou route.

• IF YOU GO
  • Savannah Convention & Visitors Bureau, (912) 944-0455, www.savannahvisit.com
  • Charleston Convention & Visitors Bureau, (843) 853-8000, www.charlestoncvb.com
  • Montgomery Convention & Visitors Bureau, (334) 261-1100, www.visitingmontgomery.com
  • Mobile Bay Convention & Visitors Bureau, (800) 566-2453, www.mobilebay.org
  • Pensacola Convention & Visitors Bureau, (800) 874-1234, www.visitpensacola.com
  • Jacksonville Convention & Visitors Association, (904) 798-9111, www.visitjacksonville.com

Springtime in New England

LAKE PLACID

STOWE

JOHN DILLON PARK

WOODSTOCK

GREENFIELD

RUSSELL

BOSTON

This itinerary is packed full of accessible outdoor sites in New England, and it's the perfect trip to enjoy after a long cold winter. There's no shortage of accessible lodging options along the way either, with an Adirondack lean-to, a Berkshire cabin and a cozy Stowe B&B topping the list. You'll also be treated to some great scenery on this route, including magnificent views from Whiteface Mountain, a secluded covered bridge and some sleepy country lanes in Vermont. Take your time to discover the back roads along the way too, as getting lost is all part of the adventure.

ROUTE

This route begins in Boston and follows Highway 2 west to Highway 13, then heads north to New Hampshire. Next it takes Highway 136 west to Greenfield, then continues west to Highway 123, heads north to Highway 12 North, and crosses the Connecticut River at Charleston. Next it's time to follow Interstate 91 north and connect to Interstate 89 North, then take Highway 100 to Stowe. It then follows Highway 100 back to Interstate 89 and continues west to Burlington. After crossing Lake Champlain on the ferry from Burlington, the route follows Highway 373, then connects to scenic Highway 9N, and takes Highway 86 to Lake Placid. Next it follows Highway 73 to Interstate 87 and heads south to Interstate 90. Finally, it follows Interstate 90 to Highway 23 to Russell, then connects back to the interstate via Highway 20, and loops back to Boston.

ALONG THE WAY

Crotched Mountain

Located about two hours north of Boston in Greenfield, the Crotched Mountain Foundation (603-547-3311, www.crotchedmountain.org) campus is worth a stop while you're in Southern New Hampshire. In keeping with their mission to support people with disabilities through education, rehabilitation and residential services, they've added two nicely accessible hiking trails to their facility. Best of all, there's no charge to use the trails, which are open to the general public.

The Dutton Brook Trail—the longer of the two trails—features a hard-packed dirt surface and a series of wheelchair-accessible boardwalks. It travels through a variety of forest habitats before it winds around a beaver pond and through some wetland areas. Interpretive signs are located along the way, and the two-mile round-trip hike is a great way to get a good overview of the Monadnock Region. And if you'd like to cut the hike in half, just turn around at the first overlook and return to the trailhead.

Named for the founding family of the Crotched Mountain Foundation, the Gregg Trail is just under a mile in length and features a hard-packed dirt surface, and an elevation change of 200 feet. It travels over a series of switchbacks, through blueberry fields and open grasslands to a highland knoll, where there's a wheelchair-accessible observation deck. From there you'll get a panoramic view of the Contoocook River and the Monadnocks. It's also a great place to get a good view of the migratory hawks that frequent the area.

The trails are open from 30 minutes after sunrise to 30 minutes before sunset. And although they're usually open by June, a late snowfall could easily delay the season opening. So plan your visit accordingly, as it's a great opportunity for wheelchair-users and slow walkers to get out and enjoy the great outdoors.

Woodstock

The Woodstock area is well worth exploring for a few days, as it's the quintessential Vermont experience, filled with country lanes, covered bridges, lots of farm land and some great scenery. Make sure and stop at the Billings Farm & Museum (802-457-2355, www.billingsfarm.org) in Woodstock, for a good primer on the state's rural heritage.

This working farm and museum features plenty of accessible parking with good wheelchair access to the visitors center, livestock barns and farm exhibits. And if you tire easily, they also have a loaner wheelchair available. There's ramp access up to the historic farm house and level pathways throughout the campus.

1885 Queen Anne Victorian mansion at the Marsh-Billings-Rockefeller Historic Park.

And don't miss the Marsh-Billings-Rockefeller Historic Park (802-457-3368, www.nps.gov/mabi), located just across the street. Although you can walk over to this 550-acre park, the approach is a bit long and steep for wheelchair-users. That said, if you can't manage it, then just ask the folks at the Billings Farm & Museum for a special pass so you can park near the mansion.

There's ramp access to the 1885 Queen Anne Victorian mansion, which was home to the Marsh, Billings and Rockefeller clan. Today it contains some of the original furnishings and artwork, with guided tours available throughout the day. Best bet is to make advance arrangements, as the tours fill up fast, and are limited in size. There's ramp access to the house, with elevator access to the second floor. Loaner wheelchairs are also available, and there's even places to sit down if you get tired. All in all it's a great tour, with a personal focus on the former residents.

And although the Vermont Institute of Natural Science (802-359-5000, www.vinsweb.org) is located 12 miles east of Woodstock in Quechee, it's definitely worth the short side trip. As an added bonus, you'll pass by the Taftsville and Quechee covered bridges along the way.

Best bet is to drive all the way down to the maintenance area if you have trouble with distances, as the upper parking lot presents a few access obstacles. Just ask the folks in the gift shop and they'll tell you where to park. The pathway to the main exhibits features good wheelchair-access, and you can get a good look at the raptor shows, songbird exhibits and the raptor enclosures. Take the trail all the way to the Vernal Pool, then just kick back and enjoy the wildlife. It's a great place to experience the natural side of Vermont.

Stowe

Located in Northern Vermont, Stowe is one of the most scenic areas in the state. Although the big winter attraction is skiing, when the snow melts, the countryside comes to life. Access varies throughout Stowe Village, but in some places there are sidewalks with curb-cuts, while in others there aren't even any sidewalks. Don't be discouraged though, as many of the shops and restaurants feature level access; however, it's best to park as close as possible to the business you plan to patronize.

The Vermont Ski and Snowboard Museum (802-253-9911, www. vtssm.com), located in the heart of the Stowe Village at the intersection of Route 100 and Route 108, is also worth a stop. Housed in the old Town Hall built in 1818, the museum focuses on the history of skiing in Vermont. The building, which is listed on the National Register of Historic Places, features ramp access from the parking lot and elevator access to all floors.

When you're done exploring Stowe Village, continue south on Route 100 and turn left on Gold Brook Road. Veer left after you cross the cement bridge, and continue along until you spot the covered bridge on your left. Known locally as Emily's Bridge, legend has it that Emily died there broken-hearted, and it's said that her spirit haunts the bridge. There's no official parking place, but it's all fairly level so just park alongside the road and wheel on over to the bridge. And watch out for Emily!

Back out on the main road, continue south on Route 100, turn right on Moscow Road and head over to 593 Moscow Road, where you'll find Little River Hotglass (802-253-0889, www.littleriverhotglass.com), the studio and gallery of glass blower, Michael Trimpol. There is a dirt parking lot

Emily's Bridge spanning Gold Brook in Stowe, Vermont.

in front of the studio and a small lip at the doorway, but the driveway is pretty level. Inside there is plenty of room to wheel around and observe the artist at work. Even if Michael isn't there, it's worth the trip to just to see his work, which features vibrant colors, original designs and unique shapes.

And for a nicely accessible place to overnight in Stowe, check out The Stone Hill Inn (802-253-6282, www.stonehillinn.com). Nestled on a secluded hilltop, this nine-room inn is built on one level, and includes The Notch, a wheelchair-accessible room with a roll-in shower. Other access features include a hand-held showerhead, a fold-down shower seat, grab bars in the shower and around the toilet and a roll-under sink.

The inn has a definite romantic ambiance, and it's a great place to get away from it all and enjoy the beautiful Vermont countryside.

Lake Placid

Save some time to take in the Adirondacks in the Lake Placid area. Downtown Lake Placid is a nice walking city—in the non-snow months, that is! Shops and restaurants line this quaint village and former Olympic venue, and there are curb-cuts, level sidewalks and benches throughout the business district. Additionally, most of the businesses have level access. Accessible parking is available in the public lots, and the lift-equipped Lake Placid XPRSS Trolley (518-232-2002) runs through the village and stops at many of the major hotels and the visitors center. Best of all, the trolley is free.

For a good primer of Adirondack wildlife, check out the Wild Center (518-359-7800, www.wildcenter.org) in nearby Tupper Lake. This natural history museum of the Adirondacks features interpretive exhibits, live animals and educational programs about the flora and fauna of the region. There is excellent access throughout the museum with a level entry, accessible restrooms and barrier-free access to all exhibits.

Outside, you can experience a real slice of Adirondack life on the wheelchair-accessible Pond Lake Loop Trail. This interpretive trail features boardwalks and bridges which lead out to the shores of Blue Pond. It makes for a very pleasant stroll, and you never know what you'll see along the way.

And for a very scenic view of the whole area, take a drive up the Veterans Memorial Highway (www.whiteface.com) to the top of Whiteface Mountain. This five-mile drive offers some spectacular views of the Adirondack peaks with several scenic viewpoints along the way.

At the top you can take the elevator up to Whiteface Castle. Just follow the tunnel from the parking area and wait for the attendant to operate the platform lift up the five steps to the elevator. Up on the top, there are viewing platforms located around the perimeter of the castle.

And for a nicely accessible place to overnight in the Adirondacks, check out the Hotel Saranac (800-937-0211, www.hotelsaranac.com). Located in Lake Saranac, this 88-room property was built in 1924; however, today it features one accessible room with a roll-in shower (317) and one accessible room (612) with a tub/shower combination.

Both rooms have good pathway access and wide doorways. Access features in the bathrooms include a hand-held showerhead, a transfer bench, grab bars in the shower and around the toilet and a roll-under sink. Room 317 even includes a removable lip on the roll-in shower, so the water actually stays in the shower pan. It's very nicely done.

Berkshire Retreat

Last but not least, save some time for a stop at the Noble View Outdoor Center (413-572-4501, nobleviewoutdoorcenter.org) in Russell, before you head back to Boston. It's a great place to spend a few nights and take in the beautiful Berkshires. A project of the Appalachian Mountain Club, this complex features two accessible lodging options—Double Cottage and North Cottage.

Double Cottage and North Cottage each include wide doorways, an accessible veranda and one wheelchair-accessible bedroom. The cabins have shared public areas—including kitchen and dining areas—and an accessible pathway to the nearby bath house. Access features in the bath house include wide doorways, an accessible family restroom, and a roll-in shower with a hand-held showerhead, grab bars and a shower seat.

North Cottage can accommodate groups of up to 10 people, while the eight bedrooms in Double Cottage can be booked on an individual basis. Nightly room rates at Double Cottage start at just $40, while the entire North Cottage can be rented for $175 per night. Weekly rates are also available, and a two-night minimum is required.

And although there are technically no accessible trails at the Noble View Outdoor Center, many are relatively flat and less than a half-mile in length. The good news is, the Appalachian Mountain Club is currently adding a wheelchair-accessible nature trail there, which should be on-line by late 2012.

TIMING

A lthough this is a spring itinerary, it's important to note that late spring is the best time to drive it; as it's not unlikely to run into snow in early and even mid-spring. Truly, just before Memorial Day and into the first weeks of June is the perfect time for this route, as after school lets out the summer crowds descend upon the area. It should be noted that you also need to watch your timing for the Lake Chaplain Ferry (802-864-5293, www.ferries.com) from Burlington to Port Kent, as it usually opens in early June and has a limited number of runs each day. If you have to travel earlier, the route from Charlotte to Essex is usually open all year.

GREAT EATS

· ·

Although it's not exactly a restaurant, make sure and stop by the Cabot Cheese Factory (800-837-4261, www.cabotcheese.coop) for some tasty treats, on the way to Stowe. Just take exit 8 off of Interstate 89 in Montpelier and continue until you hit Highway 2 East to Marshfield. Take a left on Route 215 and continue on for 5 miles to Cabot Village, where you'll find the Cabot Cheese Factory, on the right. There's plenty of accessible parking near the entrance, with level access to the building. The factory tour is just $2, and afterwards you can nibble on the cheese to your heart's content. It's so tasty, you'll probably take some home too.

DON'T MISS IT

· ·

While you're in the Adirondacks, make sure and plan a day—and maybe even an overnight— at John Dillon Park (518-524-6226, www. johndillonpark.org). Located just 15 miles from Tupper Lake, this barrier-free park features nine Adirondack lean-tos, over three miles of hiking trails, and several docks on Grampus Lake.

Best of all, it's about a mile off the main road, so it's a great place to get away from the crowds. All of the lean-tos are either ramped or built at the appropriate wheelchair-transfer height, and they come equipped with a fold-down bed, a fireplace and a picnic table. Bear Cub is the closest one to the welcome center, and it's the only one you can drive to.

Accessible composting toilets and potable water are available at each lean-to, and the welcome center has a flush toilet and a refrigerator. And they even have a portable solar powered battery charger, which can be wheeled to the lean-tos upon request. Best of all, there's no charge to overnight in the park, but it's only open to people with disabilities and their companions. It's also open for day use during the summer months.

One of nine accessible Adirondack lean-tos at John Dillon Park.

LINGER ON IN THE GATEWAY

After you've had your fill of the country, save a few days to linger on and explore the accessible attractions in Boston. Even though this East Coast capital is filled with historic attractions, many of them are wheelchair-accessible.

■ Explore all or part of the Freedom Trail (617-357-8300, www.the freedomtrail.org). This 2½-mile wheelchair-accessible pathway winds through downtown and passes 16 historic sites. Set out on your own or book a tour through the Freedom Trail Foundation.

■ Stop in at the Paul Revere House (671-523-2338, www.paulreverehouse. org) and the Old North Church (671-523-6676, www.oldnorth.com). There's portable ramp access to the house, and although the doorway is narrow it's doable for most folks. There is ramp access to the church with a barrier-free access to the sanctuary.

■ Visit the Old South Meeting House (617-482-6439, www.oldsouth meetinghouse.org), where the 1773 mass protest meetings that led to the Boston Tea Party were held. Today the 1801 Paul Revere Bell hangs in the steeple of this wheelchair-accessible building.

■ Stop in for a bite to eat at Faneuil Hall Marketplace (www.faneuilhall boston.org). This restored market building features good wheelchair access and it's now home to a variety of restaurants, specialty shops and street vendors.

■ Learn a little bit about the Revolutionary War at the Battle of Bunker Hill Museum (www.nps.gov/bost/historyculture/bhmuseum.htm). There's no admission charge to this wheelchair-accessible museum, which features exhibits about the historic battle.

■ Hop on a Boston Duck Tour (617-267-3825, www.bostonducktours. com) for a tour of Boston's historic sites, followed by an exciting splash-down in the Charles River. A portable lift makes this fun tour accessible to everyone.

■ Visit the USS Constitution Museum (617-426-1812, www.ussconstitu tionmuseum.org). There's good wheelchair access throughout the museum which features interpretive exhibits about the Old Ironsides.

FLY-DRIVE OPTION

To make this a fly-drive vacation, fly to the Logan International Airport (800-235-6426, www.mass port.com) in Boston, then rent an accessible van at AMS Vans (888-880-8267, www.aavans.com) or Wheelchair Getaways (800-727-1656, www.wheelchairgetaways.com).

ALTERNATE ENTRY POINTS

- From New York City and Providence, take Interstate 95 north to Interstate 93 North, to Boston.

- From Hartford, take Interstate 91 north to Interstate 90, then follow the route east or west along the interstate.

- From Syracuse, take Interstate 90 east to Albany, then go north on Interstate 87 or continue along to Boston on Interstate 90.

VARIATION ON A THEME

The Greenfield, Woodstock and Stowe portion of this itinerary makes a nice five-night trip from Hartford; while the Berkshire retreat in Russell can be done as a two-night side trip from Boston. If you want to extend your road trip, then drive down to Baltimore from Albany and connect to the Mid-Atlantic History and Mystery route.

- IF YOU GO
  - Woodstock Vermont Area Chamber of Commerce, 888-496-6378, www.woodstockvt.com
  - Stowe Area Association, (802) 253-7321, www.gostowe.com
  - Lake Placid Convention & Visitors Bureau, (800) 692-1338, www.lakeplacid.com
  - Greater Boston Convention & Visitors Bureau, (888) 733-2678, www.bostonusa.com

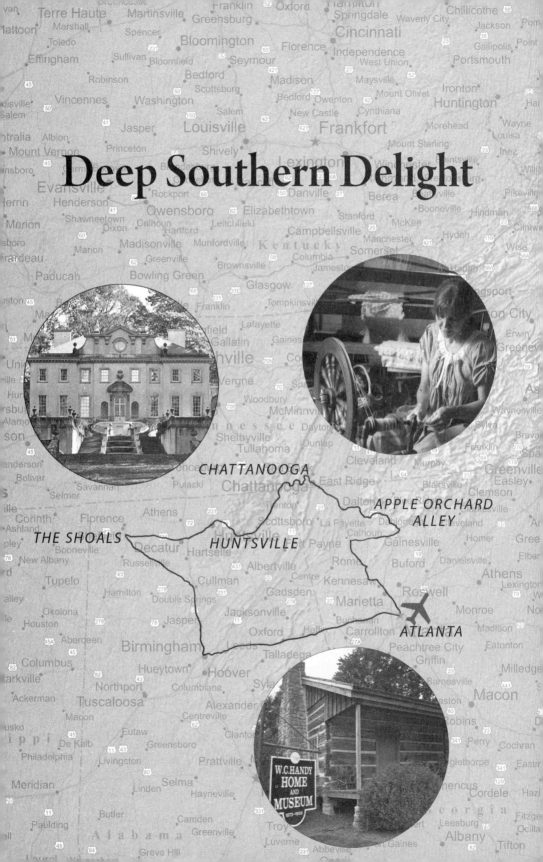

Deep Southern Delight

CHATTANOOGA

APPLE ORCHARD
ALLEY

THE SHOALS

HUNTSVILLE

ATLANTA

This route boasts some gorgeous drives; from the historic Natchez Trace Parkway in Northwestern Alabama, to scenic Apple Orchard Alley in rural Georgia. Along the way you'll experience small town Southern hospitality at its best in The Shoals, Ellijay and Jasper. And don't forget the big cities of Atlanta and Chattanooga, where you'll find a bevy of wheelchair-accessible anchor attractions. Best summed up as a slice of the true South, this itinerary is a true cultural treat for all your senses.

ROUTE

This route begins in Atlanta and follows Interstate 75 north, then connects with Highway 53 east to Jasper. From there it continues east on Highway 53, to Highway 183 West, then west on Highway 52 through Apple Orchard Alley to Ellijay. It then takes Highway 76 west and connects back with Interstate 75, and heads north to Chattanooga. From there it follows Interstate 24 west, then takes Highway 72 west to Huntsville. Next it continues west along Highway 72 and connects with Highway 43 North to The Shoals. To complete the loop, it follows Highway 43 south, and takes Highway 157 east to Interstate 65 South, then connects with Interstate 20 and heads back to Atlanta.

ALONG THE WAY

Apple Orchard Alley

Located north of Atlanta, Apple Orchard Alley is one of the most scenic drives in the state. This two-lane country road—better known as Highway 52—runs between Highway 183 and Ellijay, and is flanked by orchards and dotted with apple houses along the way.

Fall is prime time for the apple houses; however, their seasons vary, depending on the variety of apples grown. That said, it's even worth a drive out of season, as it's a very pleasant ramble. The apple houses are great places to stop and buy fruit or even try some homemade goodies.

Mack Aaron's Apple House (706-273-3600) is open from mid-July to December, and features a level entrance and plenty of room to roll around on the cement floor inside. They have a wide variety of apples for sale, and they're also known for their fried fruit pies. And if you're watching your diet, they even have some sugar free fruit pies.

BJ Reece's Apple House (706-276-3048) also has a level entry and barrier-free access inside. This is one of the larger apple houses and you can even pick your own apples there during the fall. They also have a bakery and a wide selection of jellies and jams. And don't forget to try their apple cider— it's delicious.

Located at the western end of Apple Orchard Alley, Ellijay is a fun place to stop for lunch. Accessible street parking is located at the end of River Street, and there are several accessible restaurants within rolling distance. The Cantaberry Restaurant (706-636-4663), The Blue Door Cafe (706-635-2233) and Jilly's Pub (706-635-6166) are located on River Street, and they all feature level access. 28 Main (706-698-2828)—which is named for its address—is a little further away, and features barrier-free access and a nice accessible restroom. All of these eateries serve up sandwiches, salads and lunch specials at very reasonable prices. Plan for an early lunch stop though, as many of them close up early.

If you're in the area for the second and third weekends in October, then head on over to the Ellijay Lions Club Fairgrounds for the Georgia Apple Festival (www.georgiaapplefestival.org). This annual event features over 300 vendors, crafting demonstrations and lots of homemade apple products. There's also a parade and an antique car show, and of course lots of apples.

And if you'd like to overnight in the area, just take Highway 53 back to Jasper and check out the Seventy-Four Ranch B&B (706-692-0123, www.seventyfourranch.com). The Porch Cabin is a great choice for slow walkers. It features a 26-inch-high bed with good access on both sides; and a shared bathroom with a low-step shower, shower grab bars, a handheld showerhead and a free-standing sink. Best of all, it has its own private porch, where you can kick back and watch all the animals. It's a very relaxing place to stay.

Chattanooga

Park the car for a few days and take some time to explore Chattanooga. It's a great walking city for wheelers and slow walkers, with wide sidewalks and plentiful curb-cuts throughout the downtown area. And with free accessible transportation to most of the major attractions, it's easy to get out and enjoy Chattanooga.

Start your visit at the Tennessee Aquarium (800-262-0695, www. tnaqua.org), the cornerstone attraction of the riverfront redevelopment plan. Located in two buildings on the banks of the Tennessee River, the aquarium features elevator and escalator access to all levels, with barrier-free pathways through the galleries. The River Journey building is filled with river otters, turtles, alligators and giant catfish; while the Ocean Journey building boasts penguins, sharks, butterflies and even scuba divers. And don't forget your cell phone, as they have an excellent audio tour.

After you've had your fill of the undersea world, head on over to the Hunter Museum (423-267-0968, www.huntermuseum.org), located in the Bluff View Art District (www.bluffviewartdistrict.com) on the North Shore. Just walk up 1st Street and take the wheelchair-accessible funicular to the top of the hill. From there, follow the brick path and cross over the glass bridge to the museum's front entrance. The museum is actually located in two buildings—a historic mansion and a sleek contemporary building—and features an excellent collection of American art, from colonial times to the present day. There's level access to both buildings, with elevator access to all floors, and plenty of room to roll around the galleries.

Save some time to browse around the Bluff View Art District (www. bluffviewartdistrict.com), which boasts a definite European flavor and includes shops, restaurants, galleries and a nice sculpture garden. Be sure and stop in at the River Gallery (423-265-5033 ext. 5, www.river-gallery.com), which is housed in a turn-of-the-century home on 2nd Street. Although steps grace the main entrance there's a level entrance a little farther up the street. The gallery features a great collection of regional and national art work, and the owners also operate the River Gallery Sculpture Garden at the end of the street. The garden includes a nice variety of pieces, many of which are for sale; and it also boasts level pathways and good wheelchair access.

Of course you just can't leave Chattanooga without a look at the famous Chattanooga Choo Choo. You'll find the iconic engine in the garden area behind the Chattanooga Choo Choo Hotel (www.choochoo. com), and there's no charge to see it. There's level access throughout the garden area, which also features a number of other historic train cars. The best way to get there is to take the free CARTA (423-629-1411, www. gocarta.org) electric shuttle, which has ramp access and a wheelchair space with tie downs.

And don't miss the beautiful rotunda in the hotel lobby. Formerly the Terminal Station, this historic building has level access and there's barrier-free pathways throughout the lobby area. And if you'd like to overnight at the hotel, they also have wheelchair-accessible rooms with roll-in showers. It's a nice property and a definite must-see for train buffs.

Huntsville

Huntsville is well worth a visit, especially if you're a space junkie, as it's home to the US Space and Rocket Center (800-637-7223, www.rocket center.com). From a Saturn V rocket and a moon rock, to a historical display of Dr. von Braun's work and even the Apollo 16 Command Module, you'll want to save a full day for this interesting museum.

Access features include a ramped entry, accessible restrooms and level pathways to most of the inside exhibits and the outside rocket garden. If you encounter a few steps, just ask an employee to point out the accessible path of travel. They are very knowledgeable and happy to help. Loaner wheelchairs are also available at the guest services desk.

And for a more historical take on Huntsville, head on over to Constitution Village (256-564-8100, www.earlyworks.com). This recreated 1819 village is billed as the birthplace of Alabama, as it's located on the site where the Alabama Territory leaders met to petition congress for statehood.

Conveniently located just a block from the downtown courthouse, Constitution Village features costumed docents who interpret early 1800s history. You'll find the docents throughout the village doing a variety of chores; spinning wool, making baskets, tending the garden and even doing the laundry the old fashioned way.

There is ramp or level access to most buildings, and wide level pathways around the village. A few of the buildings have narrow doorways or a few steps, but you can still see inside them. All in all, it's a great glimpse into the past.

A docent spins wool at the Constitution Village in Huntsville.

Getting around Huntsville is easy, as the lift-equipped Tourist Trolley departs from the train station and stops at most of the top attractions. The fare very reasonable too—$1 per trip, or $2 for an all day pass.

And although it's located 45 miles from Huntsville in nearby Scottsboro, the Unclaimed Baggage Center (256-259-1525, www.unclaimed baggage.com) is worth the slight detour. This 40,000 square foot outlet is the final resting place of unclaimed and misdirected luggage.

There is level access to the store, with accessible restrooms located near the main entrance. The whole store is nicely laid out, with wide aisles and plenty of room to navigate between the racks. Depending on when you go, you'll find everything from clothing and jewelry to sports equipment and camera accessories. Best buys include sunglasses, books, CDs and DVDs. Even if you don't purchase anything, it's a fun place to browse.

The Shoals

Named for the rocky shoals area on the nearby Tennessee River, the cities of Sheffield, Florence, Muscle Shoals and Tuscumbia are collectively known as

W.C. Handy Home, Museum and Library in Florence, Alabama.

The Shoals. It's a very rural area, filled with unique attractions, main street shopping and scenic country roads. It's a very relaxing place to linger on and explore. And there's no better place to base yourself than at the very accessible Marriott Shoals Hotel & Spa (256-246-3600, www.shoalshotel.com) in Florence.

Perched on the banks of the Tennessee River, this 200-room property features six accessible rooms, including two with roll-in showers and four with tub/shower combinations. The accessible rooms all have wide doorways, lowered closet rods, spacious sleeping areas and a full five-foot turnaround space in the oversized bathrooms. All rooms have a private balcony with a river view; and if you want to go for a swim, no worries, as the zero entry pool makes that possible too.

While you're in town, make sure and stop at the W.C. Handy Home, Museum and Library (256-760-6434). Known as the Father of the Blues, Mr. Handy hailed from Florence, and today his boyhood cabin sits on the museum's grounds. Other museum exhibits include pages of hand-written sheet music, Mr. Handy's trumpet and piano, and a number of photographs and artifacts that chronicle his life. There is level access to the museum, a free wheelchair available for loan at the front desk and good pathway access throughout the property, including the cabin.

Mr. Handy wasn't the only famous musician who lived in Alabama; in fact the Alabama Music Hall of Fame (800-239-2643, www.alamhof.org)—located just up the road in Tuscumbia—honors all music achievers who had some connection to the state. Some honorees, like Hank Williams and Sam Phillips are natives, while others lived in Alabama or had some other connection to the state.

There is level access to the building, with good pathway access to most of the exhibits. Throughout the museum you'll find guitars, clothing, records, cars, personal items, photographs and other memorabilia from some of the biggest names in the music industry. And if you're so inclined, you can even record a song in the recording studio.

Another Tuscumbia attraction worth a visit is Ivy Green (256-383-4066, www.helenkellerbirthplace.org), better known as Helen Keller's birthplace. There is ramped access to this 1820s house, with level access to the first-floor rooms. Outside, visitors can have a peek at the cottage, the pump and the cook house.

During the summer months, the *Miracle Worker* is performed in the outdoor theater at Ivy Green on Friday and Saturday evenings. And if you are in the area during the last week of June, don't miss the annual Helen Keller Festival (www.helenkellerfestival.com), which celebrates the achievements of Helen Keller. The events are held at venues throughout Tuscumbia, and some of them are even free.

TIMING

F all is a beautiful time to drive this route, as the colors are stunning along Apple Orchard Alley. And although the summers are hot and humid in this neck of the woods, if you can tolerate the July heat, you'll be treated to an excellent outdoor production of *The Miracle Worker*—complete with a backdrop of summer fireflies—at the Helen Keller Birthplace.

GREAT EATS

For a fun lunch in Atlanta, stop by Mary Mac's Tea Room (404-876-1800, www.marymacs.com), where the atmosphere is casual and the portions are generous. House favorites include fried chicken, roast pork, turkey and gravy and chicken and dumplings. Pair your entree with a choice of two sides—from fried green tomatoes and macaroni and cheese, to okra and tomatoes, turnip greens and squash soufflé—for a true southern delight. Access is good too, with a level entrance and plenty of room to wheel around inside.

DON'T MISS IT

If you love good music, then time your visit so you can attend the W.C. Handy Music Festival (256-766-7642, www.wchandymusicfestival.org) in The Shoals. The 10-day festival is held at the end of July and features 300 events throughout the area. From live music to art exhibits, theater productions and educational programs, there's something for just about everyone. Wheelchair-access at the venues is good, and you just can't beat the experience. And while you're there, save some time for a drive on the scenic Natchez Trace Parkway (662-680-4025, www.scenictrace.com).

LINGER ON IN THE GATEWAY

Save a few days to explore Atlanta, as it boasts a diverse menu of historic and cultural attractions. And thanks to the 1996 Olympic and Paralympic Games, it's also a very accessible city. From the world's largest aquarium to Ted Tuner's CNN broadcasting empire, there's no shortage of accessible fun in the Athens of the South.

■ Purchase an Atlanta CityPASS (888-330-5008, www.citypass.com) for discounted admission to some of Atlanta's top attractions. This money-saving ticket book is valid for nine days, and in many cases CityPASS ticket holders can bypass the long ticket lines and gain express admission to popular attractions.

■ Watch news being made on a CNN tour (404-827-2300, www.cnn.com/studiotour). Although the standard tour descends eight flights of stairs, an elevator assisted tour is available three times a day. Reservations must be made at least 72 hours in advance, but it's best to plan further ahead as this popular tour sells out fast.

■ Buy a MARTA (404-848-5000, www.itsmarta.com) day pass and explore the city. There is roll-on access to the MARTA trains, and 100% of the MARTA bus routes feature lift-equipped or kneeling buses. There's even a MARTA rail station inside the Hartsfield-Jackson Atlanta International Airport.

■ Visit the High Museum (404-733-4400, www.high.org), one of the leading art museums in the Southeastern US. Access is excellent, with elevator access to all floors and barrier-free access throughout the galleries. Wheelchairs are also available for loan at the front desk.

■ Explore Atlanta's past at the Atlanta History Center (404-814-4000, www.atlantahistorycenter.com). Located on 33 wooded acres, this history museum features two historic homes and exhibits on everything from the Civil War to the Centennial Olympic Games. There's barrier-free access to the main building and level access to the first floor of the historic Swan House. The Tullie Smith Farm has eight steps at the entrance, but you can still get a good look at things from the outside.

■ Save some time for a leisurely lunch at the Swan Coach House (404-261-0636, www.swancoachhouse.com). This teahouse-style restaurant features valet parking and ramp access at the front door. Menu items range from a very tasty chicken salad to curried chicken, sandwiches, salads and even crab cakes.

The historic Swan House at the Atlanta History Center.

- Explore the undersea world at the Georgia Aquarium (404-581-4000, www.georgiaaquarium.org). There's ramped access to the entrance and barrier-free access throughout all of the exhibit spaces. Don't miss the Beluga Whales in the Cold Water Quest gallery, or the 4-D film in the theater.

- See where *Gone With the Wind* was written at the Margaret Mitchell House and Museum (404-249-7015, www.gwtw.org). There is barrier-free access throughout the visitors center and museum, and elevator access up to Margaret's second floor apartment.

FLY-DRIVE OPTION

To make this a fly-drive vacation, fly to Hartsfield-Jackson Atlanta International Airport (800-897-1910, www.atlanta-airport.com), then rent an accessible van at AMS Vans (800-775-8267, www.amsvans.com), Wheelchair Getaways (800-544-6893, www.wheelchairgetaways.com) or Wheelers Van Rentals (877-569-0780, www.wheelersvanrentals.com).

ALTERNATE ENTRY POINTS

- From Nashville, take the Natchez Trace Parkway south to Florence, then drive the route after exploring The Shoals.

- From Savannah, take Interstate 16 west, then follow interstate 75 north to Atlanta.

- From Charleston, follow Interstate 26 west, then take Interstate 20 west to Atlanta.

VARIATION ON A THEME

The Jasper, Apple Orchard Alley and Ellijay portion of this route makes a nice weekend getaway from Atlanta; while you can easily visit Huntsville and The Shoals on a five-night trip from Nashville. For a longer road trip, head over to Macon from Atlanta and connect with The Gulf Coast and More route.

- IF YOU GO
  - Gilmer Chamber of Commerce (Apple Orchard Alley), (706) 635-7400, www.gilmerchamber.com
  - Chattanooga Convention & Visitors Bureau, (423) 756-8687, www.chattanoogafun.com
  - Huntsville Convention & Visitors Bureau, (256) 551-2230, www.huntsville.org
  - Colbert County Tourism & Convention Bureau (The Shoals), (800) 344-0783, www.colbertcountytourism.org
  - Atlanta Convention & Visitors Bureau, (404) 521-6600, www.atlanta.net

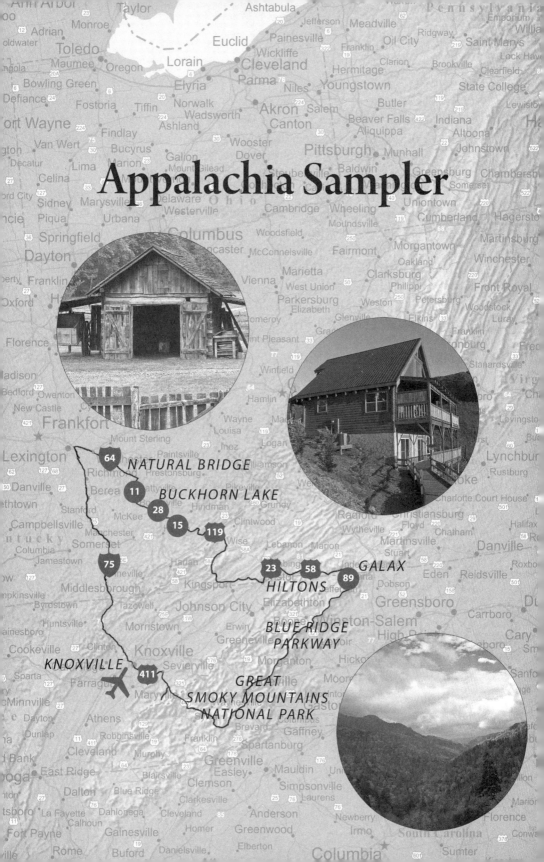

Appalachia Sampler

NATURAL BRIDGE

BUCKHORN LAKE

GALAX

HILTONS

BLUE RIDGE
PARKWAY

KNOXVILLE

GREAT
SMOKY MOUNTAINS
NATIONAL PARK

To be honest, this is one of the most challenging itineraries in the book, mostly because of the small country roads and highways that it includes. Make no mistake, there are a lot of them. Many just aren't adequately marked, and it's very easy to miss a turn, especially in Western Virginia. Additionally, it's not a good idea to rely on your GPS on this drive, as it will take you to some very unexpected places. That said, you just can't beat the scenic beauty along the Blue Ridge Parkway, the grandeur of the Smoky Mountains, or the vibrant colors along the Red River Gorge Scenic Byway. Add in some real Appalachian culture along Virginia's Crooked Road, with a chance to enjoy some mountain music in Galax and Hiltons, and you have all the makings of a very memorable road trip. So take the time to meander along this route, and don't get stressed when you get lost, as sometimes an unexpected turn may reveal an undiscovered gem. Keep your eyes open!

ROUTE

This route begins in Knoxville and follows Highway 411 east to Sevierville; then connects to Highway 321 and enters Great Smoky Mountains National Park near Townsend. Next it's time to take the scenic Newfound Gap Road through the park and hop on the Blue Ridge Parkway in North Carolina. After you enter Virginia take Highway 89 north to Galax, then follow Highway 58 west to Abington, and get on Interstate 81 and head south. Now it's time to take Exit 1 and connect to Highway 58 and continue west to Hiltons. From there, continue along Highway 58, then connect to Highway 23, cross over into Kentucky and follow Highway 119 to Highway 15; then take Highway 28 west to Buckhorn Lake State Resort Park. Next, continue along Highway 28 and take Highway 11 north to Natural Bridge State Resort Park. To complete the loop, get on the scenic Bert Combs Parkway and head west, then take Interstate 64 west to Lexington, and connect with Interstate 75 and head back down to Knoxville.

ALONG THE WAY

· ·

Sevierville Cabin

Staying in a Smoky Mountain log cabin is an absolute must-do on this route; and the good news is, Awesome Mountain Vacations (866-907-1747, <u>www.awesomemountainvacations.com</u>) offers two nicely accessible models. Not only is the accessibility of these cabins top drawer, but you just can't beat their ridge-top location.

The one-bedroom Eagles View cabin features ramp access to the wrap-around porch from the adjacent parking area, and barrier-free access to the front and back doors. Both entrances feature level thresholds and wide doorways.

Inside, there's barrier-free access to all the first floor areas, including the spacious bedroom. Access features in the adjacent bathroom include a roll-in shower, shower grab bars, a hand-held showerhead, a fold-down shower bench and a roll-under sink. The toilet is located in a 42-inch-wide alcove, with grab bars on both walls, and ample room for most transfers.

The living area is furnished with a sofa bed, an easy chair, a dining table and a washer and dryer; while the fully equipped kitchen features a refrigerator, stove and microwave. Truly there's everything you need to make yourself at home.

Just down the road, the Above the Clouds cabin is a good choice for a larger party, as it can accommodate up to 11 guests, There's ramp access to the first and second floor decks; and a wheelchair-accessible bedroom on the second floor. The adjacent bathroom has a roll-in shower with a fold-down shower bench, a hand-held showerhead, shower and toilet grab bars and a roll-under sink.

The cabin features the same amenities as Eagles View; and it's filled with homey touches, so you never feel like you're in a rental. The view from the deck is simply awesome. And you just can't beat the location, as these Sevierville cabins are just minutes away from Great Smoky Mountains National Park.

Awesome Mountain Vacations' accessible Above the Clouds cabin.

Great Smoky Mountains National Park

Great Smoky Mountains National Park is an excellent choice for wheelers and slow walkers, as you can see a good deal of it on scenic drives through the park. If you'd like to get out and stretch your legs a bit though, take the Cades Cove Driving Loop, as it features a number of historic buildings to explore along the way.

Although you can get a good view of most of the historic buildings from the road, the Primitive Baptist Church is definitely worth a stop. There's no accessible parking and there are three steps up to the 1827 church; however, the graveyard behind the church is well worth a visit. Here you'll find the graves of some of the earliest settlers. A level crushed gravel path leads around back, and even if you can't manage the whole graveyard, you can still get a good taste of history from an abbreviated visit.

Another required stop on the drive is the John P. Cable Grist Mill and Visitors Center, located midway along the 11-mile loop. There is accessible

The Primitive Baptist Church on the Cades Cove Driving Loop in Great Smoky Mountains National Park.

parking in the lot, with ramp access to the Visitors Center and gift shop. Built in 1870, the water-powered grist mill features ramp access, so feel free to roll on in and watch grain being milled into flour.

A number of other historical buildings are located nearby, with level pathways leading past several cabins, the cantilever barn, the smokehouse, the sorghum mill and the corn crib. There is also level access to the newly constructed blacksmith shop. It's all very nicely done, and when you add in the sounds from nearby Mill Creek, it's almost like stepping back in time.

One word of warning about the Cades Cove Driving Loop—you never know what Mother Nature will throw at you. Sometimes it's a flock of turkeys waddling across the road or maybe a few bears harvesting black cherries in the nearby woods. It could even be a resident deer bounding unexpectedly in front of you. So keep your speed down and be on the lookout for wildlife. It's a different show every day!

White Top Mountain entertains at the Carter Family Fold.

Hiltons

Located just 20 minutes from Bristol, Hiltons is definitely off-the-beaten-track. It's just a sleepy little Appalachian burg, and if not for the presence of the Carter Family Fold, it wouldn't even be worth a visit. This local theater is located on the AP and Sara Carter homestead, and it's the place to go for live entertainment on Saturday nights.

The shows change from week to week, but musicians are only allowed to play acoustic instruments, No two shows are ever alike, and the energy is simply amazing. It's a great opportunity to enjoy some good old fashioned mountain music, mingle with the locals and soak up some Appalachian culture.

Shows usually begin at 7:30, but allow yourself plenty of travel time, because you will probably get lost. Once you're in Hiltons, turn right on Highway 709, and make another right on Highway 614 (also known as the A.P. Carter Highway). The Carter Family Fold is located on the left side, just three miles up the road. And if you get lost, the locals are pretty friendly, so don't be afraid to stop and ask for directions.

There's also a nice snack bar in the theater, so make plans to have dinner there. The food is reasonably priced and homemade; and in keeping with tradition no alcohol is served.

Accessible parking is located near the theater with level access to the entrance. Wheelchair-accessible seats with adjacent companion seats are located up front. Indeed the front seats are the ones with a close up look at all the action, because once the music begins, the area in front of the stage turns into a massive dance floor. But again, that's all part of the show.

Buckhorn Lake State Resort Park

Located in Southeastern Kentucky, Buckhorn Lake State Resort Park is a good place to kick back and enjoy Mother Nature. Surrounded by tree-lined hills, Buckhorn Lodge overlooks the 10,000-acre lake; and features two accessible lodge rooms and an accessible cottage.

Each accessible unit includes a tub/shower combination with a hand-held showerhead, grab bars in the shower and around the toilet, a roll-under sink and a portable shower chair. The accessible lodge rooms also have level access to a spacious balcony, which offers a great view of Buckhorn Lake. Access is also good to all of the lodge public areas; including the lobby, gift shop, swimming pool and dining room.

There is accessible parking down at the marina, and the afternoon pontoon boat rides are doable with a little assistance. Although there are no accessible trails near the lodge, the paved road is a good alternative for folks who can't manage the moderate uphill grades of the hiking trails in the park.

Save some time for a day trip to rural Hindman, for a good dose of Appalachian arts and crafts. It's about an hour drive but it's well worth it. Make your first stop the Kentucky Appalachian Artisan Center (606-785-9855, www.artisancenter.net), which features an excellent selection of regional folk art. Although some of the pieces are for sale, the center primarily serves as an introduction to the local arts scene. Don't let the steps at the front entrance deter you, as a level entrance is located on the right side of the building.

For some serious shopping, head down to the Marie Stewart Craft Shop (606-785-9844), which has a good selection of traditional mountain crafts. Although space is tight in a few places, this fun shop has a ramped entry and accessible parking. It's definitely worth a stop, especially if you're in the market for high quality locally crafted wares.

Natural Bridge State Resort Park

Last but not least, save some time to explore the very scenic Natural Bridge State Resort Park, located just an hour from Lexington in the heart of the Daniel Boone National Forest. Located in the park, the 35-room Hemlock Lodge is a great place to base yourself for a few days, as the property has two wheelchair-accessible rooms.

Access features include wide doorways, level thresholds and good pathway access. Each room has a spacious private balcony which overlooks a scenic forested area, plus a large picture window which runs half the width of the room. The accessible bathrooms each have a tub/shower combination with a hand-held showerhead, grab bars in the shower and around the toilet, a roll-under sink and a portable shower chair. The lodge also offers one accessible cottage (209) with a tub/shower combination.

There is good access to the lodge public areas, including the lobby, gift shop and restaurant. The pool is quite a downhill hike from the main lodge, but it's beautiful and features a very accessible zero step entry. Best bet is to drive down as there is plenty of accessible parking. There is also a pleasant boardwalk trail to the right of the main lodge. Although the whole length is not accessible, there is a level 200-yard section which leads from the lodge to a waterfall.

The Sky Lift (606-663-2922, www.naturalbridgekyskylift-and-gift shop.com), which is operated by a private concessionaire, is also located on the lodge grounds. This chair lift ride transports guests to the top of the mountain and back. The caveat is that you have to be able to walk a few steps and transfer to the chair lift. It's a pleasant ride but realistically it's only an option for slow walkers.

Truly the most accessible way to see the area, is to hop in your car and explore the Red River Gorge Scenic Byway. This scenic route follows the Red River on Highway 715 and features stone arches, waterfalls and some great fall foliage.

This loop drive begins just north of Hemlock Lodge at the one-lane Nada Tunnel on Highway 77, and follows the Red River to Gladie Creek Bridge. The Gladie Cultural Environmental Learning Center, which is located here, is also worth a visit.

The visitors center houses a number of interpretive exhibits and has accessible parking, a level entry and good pathway access throughout the building. Nearby Gladie Cabin—a recreation of an 1800s log cabin—is just a short drive away. There is one very large step up to the cabin, but it's still worth a stop, as you can get a good view of the cabin and the resident bison from the parking area.

From the Gladie Cabin the byway meanders south towards the Bert Coombs Parkway, and then loops back to Hemlock lodge. Make sure and stop along the way at the Sky Bridge, the largest arch in Red River Gorge. There is a level dirt trail to the top of the arch, which is doable for many wheelchair-users. It's a very scenic stop.

TIMING

F all is the best time to take this trip, as the scenery along the Blue Ridge Parkway and in Great Smoky Mountains National Park is simply beautiful then. October is the optimal month, as it's after the summer tourists are gone, yet before the winter rains set in. Summer, although popular for families, can be rather humid.

GREAT EATS

W hile you're visiting Natural Bridge State Resort Park, make sure and stop in at Mark's Mountain Barbecue (606-668-6441, www.torrentfalls. com), located on Highway 11 in Campton, Kentucky. You can't miss it, as it's surrounded by a large natural amphitheater that boasts a series of vertical climbing routes. Called the via ferrata, this assisted climbing system is not accessible, but it's great fun to watch the climbers as you enjoy Mark's yummy barbeque. Access to the upper deck area is only by stairway, but there are a few accessible tables below.

DON'T MISS IT

Try to time your visit so you hit Galax, Virginia on a Friday, so you can enjoy the live broadcast of the Blue Ridge Backroads radio show at the historic Rex Theater (276-238-8130, www.rextheatergalax.com). This weekly production features a variety of fiddle, mandolin, acoustic guitar, autoharp and banjo music, along with some colorful local dancers. Access at the Rex Theater is good, with level access, an accessible unisex family restroom in the lobby, and plenty of wheelchair seating.

LINGER ON IN THE GATEWAY

Save some time to wander around Knoxville for a few days. There's no shortage of cultural attractions and fun things to do there, and all of the major attractions feature good access.

- Explore the Frank H. McClung Museum (865-974-2144, mcclung museum.utk.edu), which features exhibits on archaeology, natural history, geology and the decorative arts. Admission is free and there's barrier-free access throughout the museum.

- Get your art fix at the Knoxville Museum of Art (865-525-6101, www. knoxart.org). There's good wheelchair access throughout this museum, which features works from the 20th and 21st century. Wheelchairs are available for loan at the front desk.

- Spend the day at the Knoxville Zoo (865-637-5331, www.knoxville-zoo.org), which features level pathways to the enclosures, and rental wheelchairs available at the entrance. Don't miss the red pandas and the meerkats.

- Drop in at Ashley Nicole's Dream Playground (865-403-1194, www. dreamplayground.org), Knoxville's first fully accessible playground. Located in Caswell Park, it includes a fort, a ship and a playhouse; as well as accessible playground equipment.

- Cruise the Tennessee River on the Star of Knoxville (865-525-7827, www.tnriverboat.com). Although there are three steps down to the dock, ramp access and assistance is available upon advance request.

- Go for a stroll in World's Fair Park (www.worldsfairpark.org). Built for the 1982 World's Fair, this urban oasis features a number of paved, level walkways, and it makes for a very pleasant retreat.

- Visit the Women's Basketball Hall of Fame (865-633-9000, www.wbhof. com), which features exhibits about the history of the sport, as well as photographs and achievements of inductees. There's barrier-free access throughout this museum, which is a must-see for sports fans.

FLY-DRIVE OPTION

To make this a fly-drive vacation, fly to McGhee Tyson Airport (865-342-3000, www.tys.org) in Knoxville; then rent an accessible van at Wheelchair Getaways (865-622-6550, www.wheelchairgetaways.com).

ALTERNATE ENTRY POINTS

- From Louisville, take Interstate 64 east to Lexington.

- From Cincinnati, take Interstate 75 south to Lexington.

- From Atlanta, take interstate 75 north to Knoxville.

VARIATION ON A THEME

The Sevierville and Great Smoky Mountains National Park portion of the itinerary makes a good three-night getaway from Knoxville; while Buckhorn Lake State Resort Park and Natural Bridge State Resort Park can easily be done as a four-night excursion from Lexington. And if you'd like an even longer road trip, then just drive to Nashville from Knoxville and connect to the Rockin' and Rollin' Through the Mid-South route.

- IF YOU GO
    - Great Smoky Mountains National Park, (865) 436-1200, www.nps.gov/gram
    - Buckhorn Lake State Resort Park, (606) 398-7510, www.parks.ky.gov/parks/resortparks/buckhorn-lake
    - Natural Bridge State Resort Park, (606) 663-2214, www.parks.ky.gov/parks/resortparks/natural-bridge
    - Knoxville Convention & Visitors Bureau, (800) 727-8245, www.knoxville.org

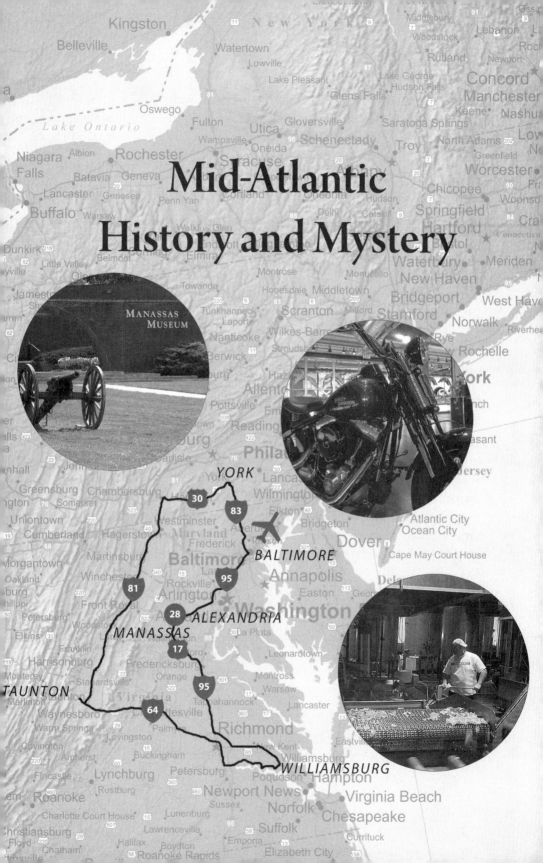

Mid-Atlantic
History and Mystery

You'll get a good dose of history on this itinerary, with stops at Civil War battlefields in Manassas, as well as historic sites in Colonial Williamsburg. Add in a stroll through Old Town Alexandria, a ride on an 1870s canal boat in Potomac, some factory tours in York, and a little ghost hunting in Fell's Point, and you've got a very interesting and well balanced trip. And don't forget your camera, as the fall foliage in rural Virginia is a photographer's delight.

ROUTE

This route begins in Baltimore and follows Interstate 95 south, then takes Interstate 495 to Highway 190 to Potomac. Then it follows Highway 190 back to Interstate 495, skirts Washington DC and continues on to Alexandria, Virginia. Next it travels west on Interstate 495 and connects to Interstate 66 West, then takes Highway 28 south to Manassas. From there, it follows Highway 28 south, then connects to Highway 17 and takes Interstate 95 South. Then it's time to circle Richmond on Interstate 295 and take Interstate 64 east, to Highway 199 to Williamsburg. Next, it's time to hop on scenic Highway 5 and go west, then take Highway 895 to Highway 190 and go west on Interstate 64 to Staunton. From there, follow Interstate 81 north, cross over into Pennsylvania and take Highway 30 to York. To complete the loop, just follow Interstate 83 south to Baltimore.

ALONG THE WAY

Alexandria

Founded in 1749, Alexandria was a Civil War supply center for the Union Army as well as home to George Washington and Robert E. Lee. There's certainly no shortage of accessible sites in town, but truth be told you can get a good dose of history by just wandering through the streets of Old Town. The main thoroughfare is King Street, where you'll find a bevy of shops, restaurants, bars and galleries.

The Visitors Center, which is located on the corner King and Fairfax Streets, is a good place to start your visit. There's level access to the building, where you can pick up a free Visitors Guide and a map of Old Town before you hit the streets.

Getting around in Old Town Alexandria is pretty easy. The brick side-walks on the main streets are well maintained and fairly smooth. Parking is limited; however, accessible spaces are available on the streets. It's a good idea to get there early though, as the accessible spaces tend to go fast. The good news is, there's no charge for parking, as long as you get a free all-day parking pass at the Visitors Center.

One of the top sites in Old Town is Gadsby's Tavern Museum (703-838-4242, www.gadsbystavern.org), which was the center of political, business and social life in colonial Alexandria. Prominent local patrons included George Washington, John Adams, Thomas Jefferson and James Madison.

Today the museum depicts a working tavern of the 1700s. The accessible entrance is on the left and there is barrier-free access throughout the first floor. The second floor, which includes the tavern's sleeping accommodations, is only accessible by stairs; however, a video is available for folks who can't manage the stairs.

Another don't-miss site is Christ Church (703-549-1450, www.historicchristchurch.org)—better known as George Washington's church. Washington purchased a pew during the construction of the church, and today that pew is the only one preserved in the original three-sided seating configuration. Although there are steps at the main entrance, the accessible entrance is located on Columbia Street. Docents are available to give visitors a brief overview of the history of the church. And don't miss the graveyard, for an interesting glimpse into Alexandria's past.

Another must-see is the Alexandria Archaeology Museum (703-838-4399, www.alexandriaarchaeology.org), located on the third floor of the Torpedo Factory Art Center. The museum features objects that were excavated at the corner of Lee and Queen Streets, and includes a number of table top exhibits. And if you're lucky, you'll be able to chat with the volunteers in the public lab, where artifacts from the latest dig are washed, marked and catalogued. There's good access throughout this small museum, and elevator access from the ground floor.

Last but not least, save some time for a lunch or dinner cruise on *Nina's Dandy* (703-683-6076, www.dandydinnerboat.com). Docked in Alexandria, the boat features roll-on access, barrier-free pathways and an accessible restroom. The night cruise is a great opportunity to see the Washington DC monuments all lit up; however, the lunch cruise is equally enjoyable. Not only is it a very accessible cruise, but it's also a pleasant way to enjoy Washington DC.

Manassas

Located just 20 miles south of Washington DC, Manassas was the sight of two major battles of the Civil War. Today, many remnants of the past remain; however, access features have been added over the years to make things accessible to wheelchair-users and slow walkers.

A good way to get an overview of the old part of the city is to hit the bricks and explore it on foot. Best bet is to park at the Manassas Train Depot and set out from there. There's plenty of accessible parking at the depot, with wheelchair access to the 1914 building. Inside, you'll find the Manassas Visitors Center and the James and Marion Payne Railroad Heritage Gallery. The visitors center is located in the former "colored" waiting room, while the former "white" waiting room serves modern day passengers. The gallery, which contains exhibits about the history of the railroad, is located between the two, in the original ticket room.

To explore Old Town, simply cross over the railroad tracks and follow the paved path past the historical markers. Along the way, stop at the City Square Cafe (703-369-6022, www.citysquarecafe.com) for a bite to eat. There is level access to the sidewalk dining area, and it's a very pleasant place to take a break.

The whole Old Town area is nicely accessible and a pleasant place to walk, with level sidewalks, curb-cuts at every corner and level access to most businesses. Save some time to step inside the old candy factory, located across the street from the City Square Cafe. Built in 1908, the Hopkins Candy Factory building is now home to the Center for the Arts (703-330-2787, www.center-for-the-arts.org), but the building itself is an architectural treasure. There is level access to the entrance and elevator access to the gallery.

The Manassas Museum focuses on Civil War times in the Northern Virginia Piedmont area.

Don't miss the old photos of the factory in operation, which are on permanent exhibition in the gallery lobby.

Save some time for a stop at the Manassas Museum (703-368-1873, www.manassasmuseum.org) located just behind the train depot. There is plenty of accessible parking in front, with level access to the entrance.

This 7,000-square-foot building boasts barrier-free access throughout all the galleries, with plenty of room to maneuver in a wheelchair. The exhibits focus on Civil War times in the Northern Virginia Piedmont area, with a heavy emphasis on the history of the railroad and the importance of Manassas in the war. Artifacts include tools, household items, weapons, clothing, furniture and everyday objects from that era. Also featured are some unique Civil War photos along with an excellent video.

No Manassas visit is complete without a stop at the two historic battlefields. The Henry Hill Visitors Center (703-361-1339, www.nps.gov/mana), which is adjacent to the first battlefield, features accessible parking and ramped access to the front door. Inside, there is barrier-free access to the museum and bookstore, and level access out to the battlefield. The battlefield itself is a bit bumpy, but doable for most wheelchair-users in dry weather. A ranger-led walk is also available.

The sites of the second battlefield are more spread out and better seen on a short driving tour. You can pick up a free National Park Service map or buy a CD driving tour at the visitors center. The driving tour is a great option for slow walkers and wheelchair-users, as you don't have to get out of your car to enjoy it; however, there are wheelchair accessible paths at the Stone House, Chin Ridge and the Stone Bridge.

Williamsburg

For a good primer on colonial history, a visit to Colonial Williamsburg is a must. This open-air living history museum features 301 acres filled with historic buildings, gardens and public greens; and is staffed by costumed docents who interact with visitors.

There is level access to the Visitors Center, where you can buy tickets, pick up maps and find out about the accessibility of Colonial Williamsburg. A limited number of wheelchairs are also available for rent on a first-come basis.

Although most of Colonial Williamsburg is fairly level, some of the uneven brick sidewalks make for a rough ride. Your best bet is to just roll down the middle of the street, which is fairly safe because vehicle traffic is not permitted in the park.

Access to the buildings in Colonial Williamsburg varies greatly. The capitol building has a unique concealed lift, while there's level access to some buildings like the blacksmith's shop. Other buildings, like the Governor's Palace, the Raleigh Tavern and the Randolph House have lift or ramp access to the first floor, but only stair access to the top floors. Photo albums of the top floors are available for visitors who are unable to navigate the stairs. And if you'd like to sit down for a tasty lunch or dinner, try the Shields Tavern, which has ramp access around the back.

York

For a change of pace, round out your Mid-Atlantic adventure by spending a few days in York County Pennsylvania. Located in the heart of Pennsylvania Dutch country, there's a good selection of interesting and accessible factory tours throughout the county.

Martin's Potato Chips (800-272-4477, www.martinschips.com)—which offers a 45-minute tour, with no steps or obstructions along the route — is a great place to begin your York County visit. The tour begins at the back of the plant, where the potatoes are delivered; and follows the production process through the washing, peeling and slicing stations, and on to the kettle cookers and the packaging department. You even get to taste the warm chips fresh off the line, and you leave with a free snack size bag for the road. Plan ahead though, as this popular tour is only available on Tuesdays, and advance reservations are required.

For a historic look at manufacturing in York County, be sure and check out the YCHT Agricultural & Industrial Museum (717-848-1587, www.yorkheritage.org). Think of it as a gigantic factory tour of the past.

Located in the old George Motter & Sons factory in downtown York, the museum features level access to the entrance, good pathway access throughout the exhibit areas and elevator access to all floors. Parking is a bit limited in the area, so it's best to try and grab a spot on the street.

Inside the museum, you'll find an amazing collection of items that were at one time manufactured in York County. The list is extensive and includes everything form vehicles, animal crackers and wallpaper; to cigars, coffins and even dentures. Highlights include a working grist mill and a 23-foot-tall ammonia compressor. Many of the exhibits feature an interactive component, and nearly everyone will recognize something from their childhood.

Last but not least, don't miss the Harley-Davidson (877-746-7937, www.harley-davidson.com) factory tour, which features a behind-the-scenes look at how the Harley touring bikes are made. The custom vehicle division is also located at this facility; and even though it's not on the tour, you can still catch a glimpse of the custom bikes as they are brought over to the main building for testing.

Access is good throughout the plant with lots of accessible parking, level access to the Visitors Center and barrier-free access along the tour route. A loaner wheelchair is also available. The Visitors Center features a number of Harleys on display, and they're fun to look at and even hop on for a photo op.

The tour begins with a short video. Then it's over to the plant for a look at the parts production area, followed by a walk along the production line and ending with a stop at the testing chamber. The production line is indeed

Get a behind-the-scenes look at how the Harley touring bikes are made at the Harley Davidson factory in York, Pennsylvania.

the highlight of the tour, so make sure it's open to tours before you make your plans. During the summer, the whole production line is closed to visitors for a few weeks, just prior to the release of the new models.

Tours are conducted from 9 A.M. to 2 P.M. on weekdays, and free tickets are distributed on a first-come basis. A word of warning though, the summer months are extremely busy, so arrive early to avoid disappointment. This is one York County tour you don't want to miss!

TIMING

S pring and fall are the best seasons to drive this route, as the scenery is magnificent. The fragrant dogwoods put on a good show in the spring, and the fall colors are simply stunning. Try to avoid spring break though, as it's especially crowded in Williamsburg at that time. This is not a winter trip, as some of the attractions are closed, and you'll definitely run into snow.

GREAT EATS

P lan a lunch or dinner stop at the historic Roosevelt Tavern (717-854-7725, www.roosevelttavern.com), while you're in York. Housed in an 1836 building, this casual dining eatery serves up the standard soup, salad and sandwich pub fare; as well as entrees such as wild Scottish salmon. The dinner menu features a number of fresh seafood entrees, including some jumbo lump crab cakes that are second to none. And don't miss the three-course Sunday brunch, which includes breakfast and lunch favorites, such as eggs and smoked turkey benedict and Asian marinated tenderloin tips. Access is good too, with plenty of accessible parking, a level entry and plenty of room to navigate inside. The service, food and atmosphere at this restaurant make it a winning choice.

DON'T MISS IT

M ake sure and stop at the Chesapeake and Ohio Canal National Historic Park 301-767-3714, (www.nps.gov/choh) in Potomac, Maryland, to learn a little bit about life on the C&O Canal and take a ride on the historic *Charles F. Mercer* canal boat. There's level access to the visitors center and accessible family restrooms nearby. The canal boat—which is pulled along the tow path by a mule and captained by a costumed park ranger—features level boarding, incline lift access to all decks and an accessible restroom. It's a great opportunity to get a real feel for 1870s canal life.

Canal boat being towed by a mule at Chesapeake and Ohio Canal National Historic Park.

And for a look at another historic era, plan a stop at the Woodrow Wilson Presidential Museum (540-885-0897, www.woodrowwilson.org) in Staunton, Virginia. The admission office is only accessible by steps, but wheelchair-users can buy their tickets at the accessible Smith Administration Building, located on Coalter Street. There's accessible parking in front of the building and behind the museum, and level access to the museum itself. Inside the museum, there's good access to all areas, except the WWI trench; however, a video of that exhibit is available. Don't miss the president's 1919 Pierce Arrow or his magnificent roll-top desk.

LINGER ON IN THE GATEWAY

Save a few days to explore Baltimore before or after your road trip. From the modern Inner Harbor to the historic attractions that dot the city, there's certainly plenty to do. And although it's no surprise that the newer attractions are accessible, the good news is, access modifications have also been added to the historic sites; so now everyone can enjoy all that Charm City has to offer.

- Get a bird's eye view of Baltimore from the 27th-floor Top of the World Observation Level (410-837-8439, www.viewbaltimore.org). The accessible entrance to the World Trade Center is located on Pratt Street, with elevator access to the top, and wheelchair-access to most of the observation areas.

- Spend the day at the National Aquarium (410-576-3800, www.aqua. org) on the Inner Harbor. There's good access throughout the facility, with an access guide available at the front desk. Disabled patrons can skip the line and purchase same-day tickets at the members entrance. The aquarium also opens up early on the first weekend of the month, to allow wheelchair-users and slow walkers a more leisurely visit.

- Take a tour of the USS *Constellation* (410-539-1797, www.historicships. org), the last of the Navy's all-sail warships. Constructed in 1854, the ship features elevator access to the main deck and stair lift access down to the gun deck.

- Take a lunch break at Harbor Place (www.harborplace.com), which features a great view of the Inner Harbor and houses over 20 casual dining restaurants. There's level access to the entrance, with elevator access to the upper floors, and barrier-free access to the eateries.

- Drive on over to Fort McHenry (410-962-4290, www.nps.gov/fomc) and see where the Star-Spangled Banner was written. Accessible parking is located near the entrance, and the paths around the fort and most of the buildings are wheelchair-accessible.

- Take a tour of the Star-Spangled Banner Flag House (410-837-1793, www.flaghouse.org), which is just a short roll from the aquarium. The historic house—which was where the flag that flew over Fort McHenry was made—contains period furnishings and features a ramped entrance and an adapted first-floor tour for wheelers and slow walkers.

- Roll on over to Fell's Point on the wheelchair-accessible waterfront promenade, then enjoy a little spirit chasing on the Original Fell's Point Ghost

Walk. Presented by Baltimore Ghost Tours (410-522-7400, www. baltimoreghosttours.com), this hour-long tour travels along an accessible route and features an entertaining look at some of the better known hauntings in the area.

FLY-DRIVE OPTION

To make this a fly-drive vacation, fly to Baltimore Washington International Airport (800-435-9254, www.bwiairport.com), then rent an accessible van at Wheelers Van Rentals (800-825-1440, www.wheelersvanrentals.com), Accessible Rental Vans (800-651-3556, www.arvl.com), AA Vans (800-880-8267, www.aavans.com) or Wheelchair Getaways (301-669-2238, www. wheelchairgetaways.com).

ALTERNATE ENTRY POINTS

- From Philadelphia, take Interstate 95 south to Baltimore.
- From Pittsburgh, take Interstate 79 south, then follow Interstate 70 east, connect to Interstate 76 East, and take Highway 30 east to York.
- From Raleigh, take Highway 64 east to Interstate 95 North, and connect to Interstate 64 in Richmond.

VARIATION ON A THEME

The Alexandria, Potomac and Manassas portion of this itinerary makes a nice five-night getaway from Washington DC; while York can easily be done as a three-day side trip from Philadelphia. If you'd like a longer trip, then take the Blue Ride Parkway south from Interstate 64 in Virginia, and connect to the Appalachia Sampler route.

- IF YOU GO
  - Alexandria Convention & Visitors Bureau, (703) 746-3301, www.visitalexandriava.com
  - Williamsburg Convention & Visitors Bureau, (888) 882-4156, www.visitwilliamsburg.com
  - Prince William County—Manassas Convention & Visitors Bureau, (703) 396-7130, www.visitpwc.com
  - York County Convention & Visitors Bureau, (888) 858-9675, www.yorkpa.org

Index

INDEX

Index

Index

INDEX